16

D0279033

Association of Teacher Educators

Research on Professional Development Schools

**Teacher Education
Yearbook VII**

EDITORS

David M. Byrd
D. John McIntyre

CORWIN PRESS, INC.
A Sage Publications Company
Thousand Oaks, California

For information address:

Corwin Press, Inc.
A Sage Publications Company
2455 Teller Road
Thousand Oaks, California 91320
E-mail: order@corwinpress.com

SAGE Publications Ltd.
6 Bonhill Street
London EC2A 4PU
United Kingdom

SAGE Publications India Pvt. Ltd.
M-32 Market
Greater Kailash I
New Delhi 110 048 India

LB
2838
.R3

CARDIFF UNIVERSITY
– 8 FEB 2000
PRIFYSGOL CAERDYDD

Printed in the United States of America

Library of Congress Cataloging-in-Publication Data

ISSN: 1078-2265
ISBN: 0-8039-6829-9 (Cloth)
ISBN: 0-8039-6830-2 (Paper)

This book is printed on acid-free paper.

99 00 01 02 03 04 05 10 9 8 7 6 5 4 3 2 1

Corwin Editorial Assistant:	Julia Parnell
Production Editor:	Denise Santoyo
Editorial Assistant:	Patricia Zeman
Typesetter:	Lynn Miyata
Cover Designer:	Tracy E. Miller
Indexer:	Rick Hurd

Contents

Teacher Education Yearbook

Volume 7 *Founded in 1991*

Editors

David M. Byrd, *University of Rhode Island*

D. John McIntyre, *Southern Illinois University at Carbondale*

Editorial Advisory Board

Introduction: Professional Development Schools

Promise and Practice

David M. Byrd

D. John McIntyre

David M. Byrd is Professor at the University of Rhode Island and has a long-term research interest in the preparation of beginning teachers and teacher professional development. He is a graduate of the doctoral program in teacher education at Syracuse University. Prior to coming to the University of Rhode Island, he was Associate Professor at Southern Illinois University at Carbondale. He has authored or coauthored over 30 articles, books, and chapters, including the textbook *Methods for Effective Teaching* (Allyn & Bacon, 1994, 1999) and chapters in the *Handbook of Research on Teacher Education* (Macmillan, 1996) and the *Handbook of Research on Supervision* (Macmillan, 1998).

D. John McIntyre is Associate Dean for Teacher Education and Professor at Southern Illinois University at Carbondale. He is past president of the Association of Teacher Educators and has received ATE's award for Distinguished Research in Teacher Education. He has nearly 100 publications in the area of teacher education. He is a graduate of Otterbein College, Ohio State University, and Syracuse University.

The purpose of the Association of Teacher Educators Yearbook series is to provide educators with current research studies on emerging topics that are likely to shape future directions in teacher education and, through analysis of these studies, provide guidelines for the improvement of preservice and in-service teacher education. The central core of this book is the rich descriptions of research on partnerships and professional development schools provided by researchers attempting to increase our understanding of how to improve the educational programs for teachers. A strength of this book is the use of respondents to introduce and set the stage for the reports of research. The challenge for the respondents is not simply to critique the research papers but to provide an overview and framework for the reader and then to synthesize, interpret, and apply the results in a context useful to both college- and school-based teacher educators.

The current issue under study in this yearbook is professional development schools (PDSs)—a movement to improve the education of preservice and in-service teachers through school-based collaborative partnerships. Although collaboratives in this movement have most often been referred to as *professional development schools* (Holmes Group, 1986, 1990), as the concept emerged terms such as *clinical schools* (Carnegie Forum on Education and the Economy, 1986) or *professional-practice schools* (Levine, 1988) were sometimes used. The common goal for PDSs is to improve the education of teachers by forming centers of collaboration between higher education and public schools that serve as models for inquiry and best practice. PDSs are sometimes compared in function to teaching hospitals in medical education. Thus, the promise of PDSs is to move beyond the limited interaction of colleges and universities with schools for the purpose of finding placement sites for preservice students to forming true partnerships with efforts to jointly improve the education environment for children, beginning teachers, practicing teachers, and college and university faculty.

This is not to say, however, that collaboration and partnerships are new to teacher education. The need for beginning teachers to have experiences during their early preparation has historically led to partnerships between college and university teacher education programs and school districts. Professional development activities for in-service teachers have also provided the opportunity for collaborative efforts between higher education institutions and school districts. Collaboration does not occur without problems, however, and perhaps all too often these inherent challenges are unacknowledged. One unanticipated outcome of the PDS movement may be a better understanding of obstacles and an incentive to collaboration in both schools and higher education institutions.

Stallings and Kowalski (1990), in a review of PDSs, found that since 1988 a number of PDSs have been formed. They were able to find only three that had made attempts to evaluate the effects of partnership, however. They suggest that without needed research on the effects of this concept, "Teacher-preparation and certification policies are being made by state legislatures on the basis of passionately held philosophical beliefs and guesses" (p. 262). Since 1990, research on PDSs has increased significantly.

Frankes, Valli, and Cooper (1998) recently reviewed research in PDSs using four primary goals proposed by the Holmes Group (1990) for PDSs and compared the extent to which these goals have been achieved. The four goals used in this analysis were teacher as researcher, teacher as decision maker, teacher as teacher educator, and teacher as political activist.

It appears that the implementation of a PDS does encourage research-related efforts. Frankes et al. (1998) provide numerous examples of teachers involving themselves in research-related activities, for example, action research projects, research sharing, and study to improve school practice (Snyder, 1994; Lemlech, Hertzog-Foliart, & Hackl, 1994; Berry & Catoe, 1994; Jett-Simpson, Pugach, & Whipp, 1992). Studies undertaken in PDSs tend to be small in scale, however, and do not often involve the entire school community. Moreover, a survey of teachers in PDSs has shown that of all the skills viewed as important for teachers research was viewed as the least important (Moore & Hopkins, 1993).

In reviewing the second major goal, teacher as decision maker, the primary finding involves a movement toward teacher empowerment and the development of new roles and democratic structures in PDSs (Francis, 1992; Whitford, 1994). For example, teachers typically take leadership in a number of activities related to PDSs: leading meetings, interviewing student teachers, reviewing budgets, delivering college courses, and motivating other teachers (Miller & Silvernail, 1994; Romerdahl, 1991).

The third primary goal for PDSs is for teachers to work more directly and collaboratively with colleges and universities as teacher educators and full partners in planning, teaching, and supervision. Including teachers as full partners would enable greater program articulation and this would lead to improved schools and improved programs for teacher preparation. The notion of full partnership is a complex one, however, and the majority of studies in this area report on the enhancement of mentoring for student teachers and the increased frequency of college and university faculty teaching in the schools and teachers teaching college courses (Berry & Catoe, 1994; Boles & Troen, 1994; Grossman, 1994; Stallings, 1991; Gehrke, Young, & Sagmiller, 1991).

Perhaps the greatest discontinuity between current practice and need exists in the last goal for PDSs—teacher as political activist. PDSs, as proposed by the Holmes Group (1990), are to bring greater social justice and equality to schools. Frankes et al. (1998) report there is little published evidence of the achievement of this goal beyond the creation of a number of PDSs in urban areas. It should be noted, however, that these PDSs were often created with the purpose of urban teacher preparation, school improvement, and equity enhancement.

Although there is not a large research base on PDSs, Frankes et al. (1998) conclude that PDSs show great promise, yet face many challenges. To succeed, they must overcome demands of increased workload, difficulties in attempting to empower teachers in traditionally hierarchical schools, and challenges of productively involving university faculty in the life of schools.

In this yearbook, a variety of partnerships and PDSs are investigated from a number of perspectives and we gain understanding of many issues that are central to our understanding of benefits and obstacles to partnerships and PDSs. The research questions investigated by our authors are of primary importance to teacher educators. These questions include the following: Do interns in PDSs believe they teach differently? Do observations support this perception? Do test scores for both beginning teachers and students increase in collaborative settings? Do college and university faculty shy away from working in professional development or partnership settings due to perceptions the role is filled with complex and messy challenges and is not rewarded as well as faculty work? Is the commitment of university faculty the major obstacle to partnership development? Must participants be assertive and seek power for partnerships to work effectively and what does an assertive role in a partnership encompass? Does initial teacher skepticism about the value of research and whether researchers understand classrooms impact collaboration and, if so, can it be overcome? Is it important for teachers to have an understanding of the PDS concept prior to program implementation and, if so, what do they need to know? How does the nature of decision making change in leadership teams with the introduction of new administrators or staff? How does involvement in a PDS influence the leadership capacity of beginning teachers? Do PDSs succeed through commitment of individuals rather than organizational commitment? Does peer support lead to greater confidence in risk taking on the part of teachers to meet the needs of at-risk students in high-stakes environments where the administration sends a strong message that the bottom line is test scores? How important are trust and ownership to the success of PDSs? Does a disciplined reflective process in a supportive community lead to changes in teaching practice that have benefits for children? Can PDSs change the culture of schools and teacher education programs and thereby improve the quality of education in the United States?

Two points that become clear through reading these studies are that research raises as well as answers questions and that the implementation of important research findings in educational programs is both imperative and difficult. The chapter authors have provided substantial information that should not only inform but also ease the movement toward creation of successful PDSs. We think you will find the particulars of how these research projects answered important questions and the recommendations made for practice both absorbing and informative.

References

Berry, B., & Catoe, S. (1994). Creating professional development schools: Policy and practice in South Carolina's PDS initiative. In L. Darling-Hammond (Ed.), *Professional development schools: Schools for developing a profession* (pp. 176-202). New York: Teachers College Press.

Boles, K., & Troen, V. (1994, April). *Teacher leadership in a professional development school.* Paper prepared for the annual American Educational Research Association Conference, New Orleans.

Carnegie Forum on Education and the Economy. (1986) *A nation prepared: Teachers for the 21st Century.* New York: Author. (ED 268 120)

Francis, R. W. (1992, October). *Issues in establishing rural professional development schools.* Paper presented at the annual Rural and Small Schools Conference, Manhattan, KS.

Frankes, L., Valli, L., & Cooper, D. (1998). Continuous learning for all adults in the professional development school: A review of the research. In D. J. McIntyre

& D. M. Byrd (Eds.), *Strategies for career-long teacher education* (pp. 69-83). Thousand Oaks, CA: Corwin.

Gehrke, N., Young, D., & Sagmiller, K. (1991, April). *Critical analysis of the creation of a new culture: A professional development center for teachers.* Paper presented at the annual meeting of the American Educational Research Association, Chicago.

Grossman, P. L. (1994). In pursuit of a dual agenda: Creating a middle level professional development school. In L. Darling-Hammond (Ed.), *Professional development schools: Schools for developing a profession* (pp. 50-73). New York: Teachers College Press.

Holmes Group. (1986) *Tomorrow's teachers: A report of the Holmes Group.* East Lansing, MI: Author.

Holmes Group. (1990). *Tomorrow's schools.* East Lansing, MI: Author.

Jett-Simpson, M., Pugach, M. C., & Whipp, J. (1992, April). *Portrait of an urban professional development school.* Paper presented at the annual meeting of the American Educational Research Association, San Francisco.

Lemlech, J. K., Hertzog-Foliart, H., & Hackl, A. (1994). The Los Angeles professional practice school: A study of mutual impact. In L. Darling-Hammond (Ed.), *Professional development schools: Schools for developing a profession* (pp. 156-175). New York: Teachers College Press.

Levine, M. (1988, November) *Professional practice schools: Building a model.* Washington, DC: Center for Restructuring, American Federation of Teachers. (SP031702)

Miller, L., & Silvernail, D. (1994). Wells Junior High School: Evolution of a professional development school. In L. Darling-Hammond (Ed.), *Professional development schools: Schools for developing a profession* (pp. 28-49). New York: Teachers College Press.

Moore, K., & Hopkins, S. (1993). Professional development schools: Partnerships in teacher preparation. *Contemporary Education, 64*(4), 219-222.

Romerdahl, N. S. (1991, April). *Shared leadership in a professional development center.* Paper presented at the annual meeting of the American Educational Research Association, Chicago. (ERIC Document Reproduction Service No. 337 420)

Snyder, J. (1994). Perils and potentials: A tale of professional development schools. In L. Darling-Hammond (Ed.), *Professional development schools: Schools for developing a profession* (pp. 98-125). New York: Teachers College Press.

Stallings, J. (1991, April). *Connecting preservice teacher education and inservice professional development: A professional development school.* Paper presented at the annual meeting of the American Educational Research Association, Chicago.

Stallings, J., & Kowalski, T. (1990). Research of professional development schools. In R. Houston, M. Haberman, & J. Sikula (Eds.), *Handbook of research on teacher education* (pp. 251-266). New York: Macmillan.

Whitford, B.L. (1994). Permission, persistence, and resistance: Linking high school restructuring with teacher education reform. In L. Darling-Hammond (Ed.), *Professional development schools: Schools for developing a profession* (pp. 74-97). New York: Teachers College Press.

COLLABORATION: BUILDING BRIDGES TO TRANSFORM INSTITUTIONAL CULTURES: OVERVIEW AND FRAMEWORK

Linda Valli

Linda Valli is Associate Professor in the Department of Curriculum and Instruction at the University of Maryland, College Park, where she teaches courses in action research and research on teaching. Her research interests are in the connections among learning to teach, professional development, school reform, and teacher education reform.

The process of educational change is often described by converting the well-known slogan "Ready, aim, fire" to "Ready, fire, aim." At a recent address to a group of PreK-12 and higher education faculty, Michael Fullan (1998) made a further modification as a way of contrasting the culture of

1

schools and the culture of universities. School-based educators, he said, tend to "fire, fire, fire" whereas university faculty rarely get beyond "ready, ready, ready." The comment evoked knowing laughter, but whether that laughter was self-directed, other directed, or both was hard to tell.

The point here is that differences in the cultures of schools and universities are so obvious that two simple words—"ready" and "fire"—evoke immediate recognition. We laugh at each other and occasionally ourselves. We even try to work with one another across institutional cultures. School-university partnerships have, in fact, become so widespread that a vast body of literature now exists (see Lieberman, 1990; Sirotnik & Goodlad, 1988, for two examples) and theories of interinstitutional collaboration are used to explain and inform the efforts (Teitle, 1991). Educators across the PreK-12 spectrum seem to realize that (a) schools benefit from the resources, perspectives, and know-how of universities; (b) universities need partner schools to prepare teachers well; and (c) social—especially urban—problems are so seemingly intractable that all public institutions have the responsibility to work together to effect positive social change. Goodlad (1990) captures the sense of this imperative well in his phrase "simultaneous renewal."

Collaboration as Cultural Bridge

For the most part, however, educators who work toward and study these partnerships act as though schools and universities have "naturally" distinct cultures. The differences are so deeply embedded in our everyday practices, and so encoded in our consciousness of what schools and universities are, that although attempts are made to work across these cultures, few serious attempts are made to transform them. Professional development schools (PDSs) are one example of such a transformative agenda, but as the authors of Chapter 2 indicate, institutional cultures are so strong that those who attempt to bridge them often end up having to develop "bicultural" personas.

We might ask why a transformative agenda is important. Why not just work across institutions on mutual problems in ways that minimize the need for either institution to significantly change? There are several answers to that question, but the one I would offer here is embodied in Fullan's (1998) caricatured, but honest, portrayal of schools and universities. Neither institution is a healthy culture. Due to historical, economic, social, and bureaucratic factors, schools are places where teachers have neither the time nor the expectation to engage in continuous learning (Cuban, 1993; Sarason, 1971; Waller, 1932). As Linda Darling-Hammond (1997) explains, the scientific management ideas that guided the development of urban school bureaucracies "separated the role of supervisor from that of worker, creating layers of people whose job it was to plan the work of others. . . . Workers were not supposed to think, just do" (p. 5). The feminization of teaching, supported by prevailing notions of what constituted women's work, both justified and intensified that split (Apple, 1988).

Similarly, the disparaging reference to universities as "ivory towers" derives from the contested role of higher education in democratic societies (Clark, 1989; Clifford & Guthrie, 1988; Harkavy, 1998). In schools, demands for action are too pressing; in universities, they are too weak. The historical trajectories of the two institutions parallel the split between theory and practice, reflection and action. Praxis, the notion that knowledge should be used for purposeful action and that theory and practice are not separate but tightly interwoven human activities, has been lost in both institutions (Beyer, Feinberg, Pagano, & Whitson, 1989; Schon, 1983).

Overview of the Chapters

A collective reading of the three chapters in this division of the yearbook gives a sense of the issues involved in collaborative work and the various ways in which individuals work across institutions to build cultural bridges. As we know from the work of anthropologists, once bridges are built and cultures meet one another, they experience immediate change. Interaction with another culture is, in itself, a transformative experience. That does not mean, however, that the bridges will endure; that the changes will be to everyone's liking; or that more unified, healthy, compatible cultures will emerge. So we need to ask, what is the nature of the cultural bridges built in these three collaboratives? What are signs that cultures are changing? Who is doing the cultural work necessary to sustain the collaboratives? And is change being asked of one institution but not the other?

The Houston collaborative described in Chapter 1 by Houston, Hollis, Clay, Ligons, and Roff involves four universities, three school districts, and two school agencies. The collaborative has been together for 5 years and is guided by 12 agreed-on characteristics, including learner-centered teaching, authentic assessment, cultural diversity, and technology. Believing that careful evaluation is part of a successful collaborative, the researchers have collected data on perceptions, behaviors, and student achievement. Some of the primary findings are that approximately half the interns believe they teach differently because of the collaborative, observations confirm differences in teaching, and standardized test scores indicate higher achievement for both beginning teachers and students in comparison to those who did not participate in the collaborative.

The Michigan collaborative described in Chapter 2 by Simmons, Konecki, Crowell, and Gates-Duffield involves 20 PDSs and at least 4 universities. Rather than focusing on the effects of collaboration, teacher behaviors, and student achievement, these authors look at the effects on teacher educators. Using a narrative, critical-incident methodology, they study the role-related "theories-of-action" that emerged from their experiences as university-based PDS coordinators. They capture these theories-of-action in three metaphors: dream keepers, weavers, and shape-shifters. As Kliebard (1992) reminds us, since the time of Aristotle metaphors have been powerful analytic tools in the fields of philosophy, linguistics, literary criticism, philosophy, anthropology, and political science. Rather than being merely ornamental, metaphoric language is "the fundamental way by which we move from the immediate and sensory into the remote and abstract, the realm of theory" (p. 206). The authors of Chapter 2 advance theories and understandings of teacher educators' work through their reflective practice.

The California collaborative described in Chapter 3 by Zhixin Su evolved from a long-standing partnership between a large public research university and a multicultural school district. The author describes participant perspectives on the development of the partnership, the goal of which was to "restructure preservice and beginning teacher education as a rigorous, high-status, field-based activity that takes place in reforming urban schools." Despite hard work, good will, administrative commitment, and sound program goals, key participants still expressed some confusion; a sense of being excluded; distrust; and, in some cases, lack of interest. These findings, however, were not used as excuses to dissolve the partnership but as ways to strengthen the collaborative work.

References

Apple, M. (1988). *Teachers and texts: A political economy of class and gender relations in education*. New York & London: Routledge.

Beyer, L., Feinberg, W., Pagano, J., & Whitson, J. (1989). *Preparing teachers as professionals: The role of educational studies and other liberal disciplines*. New York: Teachers College Press.

Clark, B. R. (1989). The academic life: Small worlds, different worlds. *Educational Researcher, 18*(5), 4-8.

Clifford, G., & Guthrie, J. (1988). *Ed school: A brief for professional education*. Chicago: University of Chicago Press.

Cuban, L. (1993). *How teachers taught: Constancy and change in American classrooms 1880-1990* (2nd ed.). New York: Teachers College Press.

Darling-Hammond, L. (1997). Reforming the teaching profession: A conversation with Linda Darling-Hammond. *The Harvard Education Letter, 13*(3), 4-5.

Fullan, M. (1998, April). *What's worth fighting for?* Vernon Anderson Lecture, University of Maryland, College Park.

Goodlad, J. (1990). *Teachers for our nation's schools*. San Francisco: Jossey-Bass.

Harkavy, I. (1998, January). *School-community-university partnerships: Their value in linking community building and education reform*. Paper presented to the Conference on Connecting Community Building and Education Reform: Effective School, Community, University Partnerships, Joint Forum of the U.S. Department of Education and the U.S. Department of Housing and Urban Development, Washington, DC.

Kliebard, H. (1992). *Forging the American curriculum*. New York & London: Routledge.

Lieberman, A. (Ed.). (1990). *Schools as collaborative cultures: Creating the future now*. New York: Falmer.

Sarason, S. (1971). *The culture of the school and the problem of change*. Boston: Allyn & Bacon.

Schon, D. (1983). *The reflective practitioner: How professionals think in action*. New York: Basic Books.

Sirotnik, K., & Goodlad J. (Eds.). (1988). *School-university partnerships in action: Concepts, cases and concerns*. New York: Teachers College Press.

Teitle, L. (1991). *Getting started: Issues in initiating new models for school and university collaborations*. Paper presented at the 15th Annual Eastern Educational Research Association Conference, Boston.

Waller, W. (1932). *The sociology of teaching*. New York: Russell & Russell.

1 Effects of Collaboration on Urban Teacher Education Programs and Professional Development Schools

W. Robert Houston

L. Y. Hollis

Diane Clay

Claudette M. Ligons

Linda Roff

W. Robert Houston is Professor, Moores University Scholar, Executive Director of The Institute for Urban Education, University of Houston, and Director of the consortium that developed the teacher education program described in this chapter. He has served as Editor of the *Handbook of Research on Teacher Education*, (1st edition), President of ATE, and Chair of the Commission on Teacher Educator Standards and in 1997 was honored as ATE's first Distinguished Teacher Educator.

L. Y. (Mickey) Hollis is Professor of Mathematics Education and Director of the teacher education program at the University of Houston. He currently is coauthoring a grades 3 to 5 mathematics series. His research interests include studying teacher induction into the profession.

Diane Clay is Assistant Professor of Reading and Language Arts and Director of the Center for Professional Development and Technology at the University of Saint Thomas in Houston. Her areas of particular interest are emergent literacy and teaching reading with children's literature.

Claudette M. Ligons is Professor and Chair of the Department of Curriculum and Instruction, College of Education, Texas Southern University. Her specializations include multicultural education, competency-based education, and curriculum and instruction. Her current research focuses on teacher preparation for urban schools and the effect on the academic achievement of university students who mentor PreK-12 students.

Linda Roff is Professor in the College of Education and Behavioral Sciences and Director of the Center for Professional Development and Technology at Houston Baptist University. Her current teaching and research interests include generic teaching strategies, multicultural education, math education, classroom management, and teacher preparation (including university-school partnerships and collaboration).

ABSTRACT

An urban consortium of four universities, three school districts, and two intermediate school agencies designed and implemented a teacher education program specifically for prospective urban teachers. The program, located in professional development schools (PDSs), was based on 12 characteristics, involved telecommunications, and was implemented for all prospective teachers in the universities. Research found that, as a result of the teacher education program, 43% of PDS teachers believed they now taught differently, observations of prospective teachers found that they taught differently and made higher achievement scores on the state certification test than a comparison group, and the achievement of PreK-12 students on the state-mandated achievement test increased after their schools became PDSs.

Perspective

The burgeoning enrollment of students in urban schools represents a valuable yet largely untapped intellectual resource in the United States. The high concentration of lower-income and ethnic minority students, a climate of low expectations, teacher and student mobility, and increasing dropout rates create major challenges in urban schools.

Meeting these challenges in Houston, the nation's fourth largest city, is especially important since Houston area schools educate one fifth of the school-age population of Texas, including 30% of all African Americans, 40% of all Asian Americans, and 16% of all Hispanic Americans in the state.

Traditional teacher preparation programs have not been designed to produce teachers who are effective in the culturally diverse and economically challenging environments that characterize Houston's urban schools. Successful research-based approaches that include multidimensional approaches that grow out of a variety of cultural and pedagogical perspectives have been needed. These challenges led in 1992 to the organization of the Houston Consortium five years ago to design a systemic program for improving learning in Houston.

Improving learning in Houston is a challenging mission. Making it a reality has required the commitment and knowledge of a wide range of educators. The design and implementation of the program has involved an extensive developmental process in which more than 1,000 educators have (a) explored research on adult learning and urban education, (b) developed relationships and created an organizational framework and a telecommunications system to share ideas and insights that enable genuine collaboration, (c) identified proficiency benchmarks for prospective teachers who are preparing to teach in urban schools, (d) developed a model of teacher preparation that includes designed differences to accommodate varying needs and contexts while simultaneously facilitating the professional development of in-service teachers and producing increased learning of PreK-12 students, (e) tested programs and procedures with pilot groups of teachers, and (f) institutionalized the program with increased numbers of prospective teachers and schools.

Six major objectives have guided the consortium's work. The design and implementation of the program is represented in the first four process objectives. The last two objectives focus on outcomes of the program, that is, change in the achievement of prospective teachers and PreK-12 students.

Objectives

1. To create a consortium of diverse institutions to demonstrate the efficacy of shared governance and collaborative program development

2. To design and implement a teacher preparation program based primarily in urban professional development schools (PDSs)

3. To provide professional development experiences for the faculties of both PDSs and universities that respond to their expressed needs

4. To integrate the effective use of technology for communication, management, and instruction

5. To increase the knowledge and performance of preservice teachers

6. To increase student learning in urban PDSs

Conceptual and Research Framework

The private sector (i.e., business leaders) and the political sector of society tend to expect succinct, hard-data analyses of the results of any enterprise. Sales, profits, and quarterly reports ("bottom lines") are part of their environment. Thus, they press educators to provide similar data on their results. They want to know how many students passed and how well they did on standardized achievement tests, how well students did in utilizing the basic skills of communication and mathematics, and retention rates for students. From teacher education, they call for the outcomes of programs—how many students were certified to teach, how long they remained in the profession, how well they did on standardized tests, and how well they performed as beginning teachers. They also press educators to tell them what impact their graduates have had on the children and youth they teach.

Educators, on the other hand, have been reluctant to provide such data even as the demands of noneducators have become more and more insistent. Educators point out the complex factors that affect PreK-12 student achievement, including ethnicity, home environment, classroom size, and resources. Teacher educators add to that list the fact that their students teach in many different schools and school districts and that they have almost no control over the more immediate influences on PreK-12 student achievement; thus, they argue, they should not be held accountable for the consequences of their programs.

The objectives of teacher education programs can be classified in four domains: *cognitive objectives* (what the teacher knows about the content being taught and the processes for teaching it), *performance objectives* (how well the teacher demonstrates these objectives in the classroom), *affective objectives* (attitudes and dispositions of teachers), and *consequence objectives* (the results of a teacher's actions; assessment is not directly of the teacher but examines the effects of teachers' cognition and performance on their students). The business community and politicians are calling on educators to provide data related to the latter type of objectives.

The current research attempts to respond to the needs expressed by others for studies of the consequences of teacher education programs (Interstate New Teacher Assessment and Support Consortium [INTASC], 1992; National Association of State Directors of Teacher Education and Certification [ASDTEC], 1993). Such an approach examines not the *processes* of teacher education but the *products* of teacher education programs. The review of similar studies is slim indeed. For the past quarter century, researchers have attempted to link teacher performance with student achievement gains (Gliessman, Pugh, Dowden, & Hutchins, 1988). Over 20 years ago, Rosenshine (1976) identified relationships between process variables (i.e., teacher behaviors) and product variables (i.e., student achievement). He found that clarity, enthusiasm, task orientation, variability, and opportunities for students to learn concepts on achievement tests appeared to be related to student achievement. Medley (1977) identified 613 findings from 14 studies that met stringent criteria for inclusion in his review of teacher education programs. Teachers who produce maximum achievement gains also are more likely to improve student self-concept. Powell (1978) concluded that effective behaviors of teachers depend on what is to be learned, that is, effective practices in reading differ from those for mathematics. Effectiveness is not a general concept but one that is specifically related to content areas; thus, art teachers use instructional strategies that differ from history teachers or science teachers and should be judged accordingly.

Other studies have related teacher training to teacher processes. Due to the inherent problems of linking processes (i.e., training programs) with outcomes, most studies have focused on in-service projects in which the participants are captive, treatments are short, and outcome variables more easily obtained (e.g., Anderson, Evertson, & Brophy, 1979, in first-grade reading groups; Good & Grouws, 1981, for secondary mathematics class-rooms).

A meta-analysis of instructional teaching skills was conducted by Gliessman et al. (1988). They identified three general categories of vari-ables (method of training, characteristics of trainees, and characteristics of the training setting) from an analysis of 26 studies. They found a strong difference between trained and untrained teachers, thus linking teacher education to specific instructional strategies. Joyce and Showers (1995) concluded after reviewing over 200 studies that preparation needs to be extensive and combined with in-class coaching to make a difference in the ways teachers function in classrooms.

Programmatic research that combined the two sets of research studies listed above—teacher processes and student achievement, and teacher training variables and teacher processes—was conducted in studies re-lated to the Teacher Corps program. Teacher Corps was funded by the U.S. Department of Education in 1965 and refunded for over 15 years to improve the quality of teachers for schools in low-income urban and rural areas. Thousands of interns learned to teach while studying in professional education programs in integrated programs. Teacher Corps spawned and supported the development of a number of innovations, including an emphasis on teaching the disadvantaged (both low income and learning disabled), recruitment of ethnic minority persons, competency-based teacher education, parental involvement, multicultural education, field-based teacher education, and the use of portal schools or PDSs where teachers could gradually be inducted into classrooms. Teacher Corps graduates "were found to be superior in . . . developing ethnically relevant curricula, using community resources in teaching and initiating contact with parents, bringing about changes in a child's self-concept" (National Advisory Council of Education Professions Development, 1975, p. 15).

Design of the Treatment Effect

Programs were implemented to achieve each of the six objectives in the demonstration program. Strategies actualized for each objective are described in this section and a description of research studies and conclu-sions for each objective are included in the following section of this chapter.

Objective 1: To create a consortium of diverse institutions to demonstrate the efficacy of shared governance and collaborative program development

The program was developed by a collaborative composed of nine
diverse institutions (four universities, three school districts, and two intermediate educational agencies). Of the four universities involved, two are
small private liberal arts institutions (Houston Baptist University [HBU]
and University of Saint Thomas). Two are large public universities (Texas
Southern University and the University of Houston); one of these focuses
largely on teaching and the other is research oriented. The three school
districts include Houston, the fifth largest in the nation; Spring Branch, a
mid-urban district that was formerly all White but is now predominately
minority; and Alief, a mid-urban district that has the most balanced ethnic
composition in the area with approximately equal numbers of African
Americans, Asian Americans, Hispanic Americans, and Whites. Together,
these districts educate over 250,000 students. The seven-county Region IV
Education Service Center (ESC IV) and the Harris County Department of
Education (HCDE) provided specialized professional development and
assessment.

Objective 2: To design and implement a teacher education program
based primarily in urban PDSs

Characteristics of Program

During 1991-1992, more than 200 persons in the consortium considered the nature of an effective urban teacher education program. There was
considerable unanimity among the more than 11 groups that explored and
agreed on 11 essential characteristics. The Consortium Policy Council
(composed of representatives from each collaborating entity who guide
the work of the consortium) reviewed these characteristics carefully, made
minor modifications, and adopted them on April 23, 1992. These characteristics continue to guide program development:

- School Based, Learner Centered
- Cooperative Learning

- Active Learning
- Authentic Assessment
- Strong Liberal Studies Background
- Identification With Cultural Diversity
- Broad Range of Teaching Practices
- Rich in the Use of Technology
- Flexibility
- Reflective, Investigative
- Outcomes Focused

Three of these characteristics are illustrated in the following paragraphs: school based and learner centered, active learning, and authentic assessment. They will be used to illustrate the processes used in the program.

Characteristic: School Based, Learner Centered. PDSs are a major key to the success of this program since they serve as the primary context for program delivery. Preservice teachers spend significant periods of time working in these schools and much of their instruction is delivered through activities that are conducted in these schools. The 16 PDSs were selected because they had large numbers of students who were at risk of failure, mirrored the urban population, and had faculties who were committed to improving the education of their students and of prospective teachers. Table 1.1 provides a profile of these schools.

Nearly 14,000 students attend these 16 PDSs. Their ethnic composition ranges from virtually 100% Hispanic American or African American to ethnically balanced. No PDS had more than 45.1% White students, and 7 of the 16 had fewer than 10% White students. Prospective teachers work in multiple diverse PDS settings, thus learning to teach urban students from several cultural groups.

An important component of the program is the way the PDSs are staffed. Each PDS has two persons, one an employee of the university and the other an employee of the school district, who complement each other and other staff in the school-based program.

- Each PDS assigns a .25 full-time equivalent (FTE) professional to act as liaison for the program; work directly with prospective teachers; present in-service programs for consortium members; and function

TABLE 1.1 Composition of PDSs

PDS	Enrollment	African American	Hispanic American	White	Asian American/ Other	Economically Disadvantaged	LEP	Mobility
Cage ES	790	2.0%	95.0%	2.0%	1.0%	91.0%	60.1%	24.0%
Lantrip ES	890	3.4%	89.6%	5.2%	1.8%	82.5%	53.4%	19.7%
Hamilton MS	1,167	18.2%	71.3%	8.8%	1.7%	67.8%	18.8%	19.8%
Sherwood ES	406	10.9%	47.0%	39.3%	2.8%	60.7%	30.2%	29.4%
Westwood ES	550	12.5%	34.6%	43.2%	9.6%	57.5%	25.2%	25.3%
Chancellor ES	1,065	20.8%	23.8%	19.3%	36.0%	33.3%	34.6%	20.4%
Holub MS	1,301	22.8%	15.1%	35.2%	26.9%	20.5%	9.6%	20.0%
Kennedy ES	896	18.4%	23.7%	37.4%	20.5%	23.5%	27.8%	20.3%
Woodview ES	650	9.5%	61.3%	25.9%	3.3%	75.4%	37.2%	23.5%
Martin ES	910	19.7%	24.2%	28.9%	27.1%	35.3%	29.3%	21.8%
Valley Oaks ES	591	3.9%	49.3%	45.1%	1.8%	56.3%	36.1%	25.3%
Milam ES	455	11.0%	86.0%	3.0%	0.0%	95.0%	66.0%	32.0%
Sneed ES	1,048	18.7%	61.5%	11.5%	8.3%	56.4%	52.6%	30.2%
Jack Yates HS	1,774	97.0%	2.0%	0.0%	1.0%	27.0%	1.0%	27.0%
Lockhart ES	602	94.0%	1.0%	3.0%	2.0%	72.0%	1.0%	16.0%
Thomas MS	873	91.1%	6.1%	2.4%	0.5%	53.8%	3.1%	31.9%

as a key member of the team that designs, implements, and evaluates the teacher education program.

- A university faculty member is assigned quarter time in each PDS as part of his or her regular workload to ensure adequate coordination between the school and the university. Like the school coordinators, these faculty members act as liaisons; work directly with prospective teachers; present in-service education programs; often teach classes for prospective teachers in PDSs; and are part of the team that designs, implements, and evaluates the teacher education program.

- Faculty from the universities teach classes in the PDSs to prospective teachers and assist in staff development experiences in their areas of expertise. Teachers in PDSs also teach some of the individual sessions of classes for prospective teachers and act as mentors and cooperating teachers (whom we refer to as "school-based teacher educators"—SBTEs). When prospective teachers tutor individual PreK-12 students they are supervised by either a university faculty member or an SBTE.

In addition, a communication network among sites in the consortium has been established using a Serial Line Internet Protocol (SLIP) connection, a recent improvement in telecommunications that is easily used. Teachers and administrators in the PDSs, university faculty, and preservice teachers have access to the Houston Consortium telecommunications server so that regular communications can be maintained.

Characteristic: Active Learning. Schools are the setting for much of our teacher preparation program. School-based experiences have been developed in conjunction with PreK-12 teachers to facilitate the integration and application of knowledge. For example, prospective teachers study ways to teach mathematics or reading and then tutor students using these methods. They are expected to demonstrate that they can diagnose a student's achievement level, tutor the student in targeted areas, and change the student's achievement level and attitude toward school. Use of reflective journals is another example of this integration. Prospective teachers are expected to maintain a reflective journal, and several preservice teachers have introduced journals to PreK-12 students.

The range of activities in the program and the number of hours in a PDS are considerably greater than in traditional programs. Depending on the level (e.g., elementary or secondary setting), students spend an average of 660 hours in schools (range 500 to 840 hours).

The program is built around *blocks of experiences* rather than independent courses. The course numbers vary among the four universities to accommodate individual credit systems (HBU is on the quarter system, the others on the semester system) and university requirements.

Characteristic: Authentic Assessment. Authentic assessment systems provide the complementary evaluation to field-based programs in teacher education. Some of the authentic assessments used include portfolios, interviews, peer review, videotaping, observations, mentor or school-based teacher review, conferences, and reflective journals.

The major instrument in this process is portfolio assessment. At three benchmarks in their preparation programs, prospective teachers are expected to demonstrate their competence to proceed to the next phase. They do this through documents, assessments, and videotapes included in their portfolios and reviewed by the Portfolio Review Team. The team is composed of university faculty and PDS teachers. The benchmark points are

> *Benchmark 1.* Admission to Teacher Education (demonstration of experiences and background related to qualifications for entering a teacher education program)
>
> *Benchmark 2.* Completion of Initial Preparation Program (demonstration of requisite skills by candidates to qualify for full-time student teaching and internship)
>
> *Benchmark 3.* Completion of Teacher Preparation Program (demonstration of skills indicative of readiness for the first job as a teacher and recommendation for certification)

Authentic assessments for each of these three benchmarks are illustrated in Table 1.2.

During their preparation program, preservice teachers collect ideas, lesson plans, and other artifacts that will be helpful when they assume full responsibility for teaching students. These *teaching artifacts* are organized in ways that are meaningful to each person and are kept separate from the professional portfolio.

TABLE 1.2 Benchmarks, Portfolios, and Teaching Artifacts

Benchmarks	*Authentic Assessment*
BENCHMARK 1: **ADMISSION** **TO TEACHER** **EDUCATION**	**Portfolio:** a. Resume b. Degree Plan . c. Transcript of credits d. Description of experiences with children e. Demonstrated technology proficiency f. Professional education goals g. Philosophy of education h. Snapshots of classroom life i. Description of Houston area, people, students, schools, including strengths and needs **Initial file of Teaching Artifacts**
BENCHMARK 2: **COMPLETION** **OF INITIAL** **PREPARATION** **PROGRAM**	**Portfolio:** a. Revised resume b. Degree Plan and updated transcript of credits c. Description of experiences with children— updated with illustrations of quality of experiences d. Disk of increased technology proficiency e. Professional education goals—updated f. Philosophy of education—updated g. Snapshots of classroom life—updated h. Expanded and refined description of Houston— including strengths and needs, with specific personal experiences and data and case studies i. Evidence of successful teaching - Sample learning goals and objectives - Sample lesson plans - Sample evaluation tools - Samples of student work with teacher feedback - Videotape of lesson with plans

(continues)

TABLE 1.2 Continued

Benchmarks	Authentic Assessment
	j. Reflective journal
	k. Record of community involvement
	l. Mentor teacher, peer, and self-evaluations
	Expanded file of Teaching Artifacts
BENCHMARK 3: **COMPLETION OF TEACHER PREPARATION PROGRAM**	**Portfolio:** a. Professional resume with current transcript b. Revised educational philosophy c. Professional placement file d. Case studies of students of diverse cultures e. Videotaped lessons, plans, and evaluations f. Record of community involvement
	File of Organized Teaching Artifacts

Results and Conclusions

Objective 1.[1] Effectiveness of Consortium

The efficacy of the consortium was assessed through a survey conducted by the Region IV Education Service Center each spring. A sample of consortium members were queried about four topics: *technology, collaboration, restructuring,* and *professional development.* Questions on this survey also provide information on Objectives 2, 3, and 4.

The 1995 survey was completed and returned by 74 persons, including classroom teachers in PDSs involved with the program, classroom teachers in PDSs who were *not* directly involved in the program, policy council members, university faculty, PDS principals, and preservice teachers.

The results showed that

- Participants unanimously indicated the worth of the consortium, that it had strengthened the teacher preparation programs in Houston, and that it should be continued.

- Nearly three fourths of respondents (74.2%) had *participated in professional development activities* offered by the consortium.
- Forty-three percent (42.9%) of teachers in PDSs indicated that they had *changed how they teach* based on information or skills acquired through participation in the consortium.
- Seventy-eight percent (78.6%) believed that *behaviors of preservice teachers changed* as a result of actions of the consortium.
- Ninety-two percent (92.9%) *engaged in cross-organizational interactions* with other consortium members.
- Seventy-one percent (71.4%) believed *the consortium addresses the needs of urban educators.*

Objective 2. Program Effectiveness

The assessment of program effectiveness was examined through external annual evaluations, internal evaluations, and product engineering studies. In addition, members of the consortium interviewed university students, PDS teachers and administrators, and university faculty and staff to elicit their perceptions of the operation and effects of the program. The 11 program characteristics describe the major changes made in the programs; however, within each characteristic, university, and program component, other modifications were (and continue to be) made in the program. The results have been used to make changes in scheduling experiences, content, and delivery of the various components. Four components-illustrative changes resulting from interview studies this year include

1. Intern feedback caused seminar time change.
2. Site feedback resulted in modifications in portfolio content.
3. Professor feedback resulted in a change in computer deployment.
4. Overall input caused modifications of dates when interns first go to schools.

Objective 3. Professional Development

Crucial to the effectiveness of the preparation program was an extensive professional development effort for both PDS and university faculty (see Table 1.3). Data from the internal evaluation studies indicated that

TABLE 1.3 Extensiveness of Professional Development, 1994-1995

Indicator	Extensiveness
Workshops being conducted through the consortium	130.0
Teachers participating	1,259.0
University faculty participating	93.0
Average number of participants per workshop	15.5

nearly three fourths of respondents had engaged in consortium professional development and that such activities had affected the ways in which they teach.

To make the extensiveness of staff development more explicit, the rosters of workshop attendance were analyzed. Table 1.4 summarizes 1994-1995 staff development activities.

The professional staffs of PDSs could determine which of the developmental experiences would be most suitable for them. Sometimes an entire school would attend a workshop (which might be held on their campus), and at other times the composition of participants would come from a half-dozen different schools.

Instructors for these staff development experiences included teachers, administrators, university faculty, community representatives, intermediate school agency staff, and prospective teachers. University professors are no longer the *principal* source of such experiences. PDSs and universities draw on the particular skills of everyone—for example, preservice teachers who have already completed a course in instructional technology serve as classroom technology assistants.

Although in-service sometimes tends to focus on universal needs and generic teaching skills and strategies, programs in the consortium have addressed primarily the specific identified needs of individual campuses and teachers. Needs assessments have been conducted each year, and collaborative groups of PDS and university faculty have analyzed test scores and Campus Improvement Plans to identify specific staff development needs.

Objective 4. Analysis of Technology Use

All PDSs and universities in the consortium have greatly strengthened their technology over the past 6 years, primarily from state allocations for

TABLE 1.4 Professional Development Experiences

Diversity: Children With Special Needs, Multicultural Education: Strategies That Free All Learners to Fly, Cultural Diversity, Strategies for Supporting the Success of Urban Learners, Strategies for Working With Youth With Limited Language Skills, Making the School Culture Friendly, Developing Cross-cultural Literacy Skills, Principles of Multicultural Education, Capitalizing on Culture, Building Teachers' Interactional and Intercultural Skills, At Risk Student Conference, Education in a Multicultural Society, Improving Interpersonal and Intercultural Skills, Integrating Diverse Language Learners Into the Academic Mainstream

Technology: Software Preview, Use of New Technologies, Computers in the Classroom, ClarisWorks Introduction, TENET Quickstart, Software Preview: English Language Arts K-5, Preview: Math and Science K-5, Multimedia in the Classroom, Learning Styles and Technology, Exploring the Internet, Student Projects in Telecommunication, Creation of Transparencies and Slide Shows, KIDPIX, Electronic Gradebook, Scanners, Video Cameras, Quicktakes, Developing Your Own Worldwide Web Home page, Netscape

Mentoring: Peer Coaching, Mentor Teacher Training, Mentoring/ Supervising, Portfolio Assessment, Use of Portfolios, Portfolios, Assessment: Portfolios, Resources, and Approaches, Behavior Management, Self Esteem: The Power of Affirmation, Behavior Management for Difficult Students

Best Teaching Practices: Multiple Intelligences, Use of Math Manipulatives, Enhancing Mathematics With Children's Literature, Reflective Inquiry, Educational Reform and the Teaching of Thinking, Creative Teaching Techniques, Creative Training Techniques, Cultural Connections in Math, Process Skills in Science Instruction, Using Diagnostic Instruments in Math

this purpose. The consortium contributed by offering a systematic staff development program combined with individual consultation. Technology was one of the four major foci of professional development, and because the programs were extensive, PDSs increased their innovative use of technology. According to findings of the external evaluator and feedback from the internal study by Region IV, some of these innovations included telecommunications with students across the country; multimedia training materials in reading and mathematics, simulations in geography and other social studies, video productions by students, and electronic gradebooks for teachers.

One study of the effectiveness of various telecommunication systems investigated two primary levels of Internet connectivity to determine whether access to graphical-user-interface (GUI) tools increased the level of use and improved attitudes toward telecommunications. In the study, the treatment group received training in the use of GUI tools over a SLIP connection. The comparison group received similar training but had access only to ASCII-based text systems over standard modems and telephone lines. The GUI group used e-mail more often than the ASCII group and also had more positive attitudes toward telecommunication. Based on this study as well as information available from other sources, the Houston Consortium adapted GUI technology in its e-mail system.

Objective 5. Increased Knowledge by Prospective Teachers

Objective 5 pressed us not only to assess program processes but also to determine the extent to which the program changed the knowledge and performance of graduates. Two studies were conducted; the first examined graduates' instructional strategies through classroom observations and the second assessed the extent of prospective teachers' knowledge base by examining their scores on a state-mandated test at the end of their program.

Instructional Strategies of Prospective Teachers. A study conducted in spring 1995 compared student teachers who had completed pre-student teaching experiences through field-based preparation with student teachers prepared in the traditional manner from the same university. The pool consisted of 320 students. From this pool, two groups of 40 student teachers were randomly selected. About 30% were male and 70% female.

These student teachers were observed and five students from each of their classes were randomly selected and interviewed. Some observations, however, were not complete (observed fewer than 5 sweeps during an observation period) and became unusable. Consequently, 72 student teachers out of a sample size of 80 and 360 students were included in the sample. Thirty-eight (38) student teachers with their 214 students were in the Houston Consortium (HC) group and 34 student teachers with their 146 students were in the non-HC group. They taught classes that ranged from prekindergarten through the 12th grade.

Results—Teacher Classroom Behavior. Student teachers in the total group generally spent over 75% of their time in instruction and 15% in classroom management. They placed students in whole class settings over 50% of the time. Their classroom instruction focused mostly on the content of a task (45% of time), followed, in descending order, by communicating the task's procedures (33%), responding to student signals (27%), discussing students' work plans or progress (20%), praising student performance (16%), and checking student's work (15%). They seldom spent time showing personal regard for students (3%) or determining the difficulty of the task (4%). Their most frequent interaction was explaining (33%), followed by questioning (21%), commenting (15%), and cueing or prompting (12%).

The results revealed significant differences in teacher classroom behaviors between HC and non-HC teacher groups. HC student teachers interacted more often with students than non-HC teachers. HC teachers spent significantly more time than non-HC teachers in (a) responding to student signals, (b) checking students' work, (c) encouraging self-management, (d) praising student behavior, (e) praising student performance, and (f) correcting student performance.

Results—Student Classroom Behavior. Students were observed spending 55% of their time interacting or doing independent work. They spent over 30% of the time interacting with teachers and about 15% of the time interacting with other students. The most frequently observed type of activity was watching or listening (35% of time), followed by working on written assignments (18%), talking (12%), and working with manipulative materials or equipment (9%). The predominant classroom setting was whole class (65%), followed by individual (19%) and small group (15%). Students were on task over 80% of the time, distracted about 13% of the time, and disruptive about 3% of the time.

Students in non-HC classes were more frequently off task. Students in HC classes were more frequently placed in small groups and less frequently placed in whole group activities than were students in non-HC classes.

A greater proportion of students in the HC program passed the ExCET tests than their peers in traditional programs (see Table 1.5). This difference

TABLE 1.5 Passing Rates for HC and Traditional Prospective Teachers on ExCET Test for 1994-1995

ExCET Test	HC Program			Control Group—Houston Universities		
	Number Tested	Number Passed	Percent Passing	Number Tested	Number Passed	Percent Passing
Professional Development— Elementary	49	45	**92**	315	237	**75**
Professional Development— Secondary	1	1	**100**	172	128	**74**
Elementary Comprehensive Exam	44	44	**100**	213	181	**85**
Early Childhood— Elementary	12	11	**92**	81	47	**58**

ranged from 15 to 34 percentage points for each of the basic tests. The same pattern held for secondary subject matter tests, but these numbers were too small to treat statistically.

This difference between the two preparation programs might be attributed to the increased realism of a school-based program or to the smaller number of candidates. Because the program numbers are growing rapidly, a far greater number of HC graduates were tested during spring and fall 1996, providing an opportunity for extended analysis. We believe that HC graduates will continue to outperform traditional graduates because of the application-oriented nature of the ExCET. Additional school-based experiences in the HC program provide a sound foundation for the simulations and problem situations found in many questions on the test.

Objective 6. Improved Standardized Test Scores of PreK-12 Students

The sixth and last objective of the Houston Consortium is to not only affect the quality of the preparation program for teachers but also to

TABLE 1.6 Synthesis of Changes in Achievement of PDSs

Subject Tested	No. PDSs With Achievement Up	No. PDSs With Achievement Down
Reading	14	2
Mathematics	16	0
Writing	10	6
TOTALS	40	8

strengthen the educational programs in each of the 16 PDSs. Texas schools are required to administer a standardized criterion-referenced test each year, the Texas Assessment of Academic Skills (TAAS). Objective 6 was assessed through analysis of changes in achievement of PDS students on the TAAS. This provides hard data related to the potential impact being made by preservice teachers and university faculty in the schools, staff development activities, and increased tutoring of individual students by prospective teachers through this program.

A study of TAAS scores was conducted to determine if the program had any effect on PDS students. The study compared achievement for mathematics, reading, and writing over a 3-year period, comparing 1992-1993 scores with those for 1994-1995. The 1992-1993 tests were administered before schools became PDSs; the 1994-1995 tests were administered after preservice teachers were assigned to them. The number of PDSs that increased achievement and the number that decreased achievement in each subject area are synthesized in Table 1.6.

When achievement in 1992-1993 is compared with achievement in 1994-1995, 40 areas increased and 8 decreased. Of those that decreased, six of the eight were in writing. Interestingly, during those 2 years, preservice teachers taught math and reading to small groups and individual students as part of their preparation, but not writing.

Conclusions.

1. Significant positive changes in student achievement occurred. These changes were greater in the first year that a school became a PDS than in the second year when achievement gains tended to stabilize but continued to be greater than scores in the school prior to becoming a PDS.

2. A causal relationship between being a PDS and increased student achievement would be misleading, however. We cannot conclude that these positive changes can be attributed to a school becoming a PDS. PDS initiatives that include aligning curriculum with test objectives, for example, may have had a greater impact on the scores.

3. Several factors related to being a PDS may have had some effect on achievement gains.

- A larger number of adults were involved in instruction with the addition of preinterns and interns in PDSs. The student-adult ratio was thus lowered, providing greater access by each student to adult mentoring, support, tutoring, and instruction.
- Teachers had opportunities to engage in professional development related to teaching in urban schools and in the use of technology.
- School leaders were engaged in a network in which personnel from schools, intermediate educational agencies, and universities had opportunities to solve problems and share ideas.
- Being part of a new movement, selection after competitive applications to be PDSs, and the Hawthorne effect of change all were factors that may have influenced achievement.

Implications

We believe other institutions can adapt or adopt this program, even though this is a complex, comprehensive, and systemic approach to preparing teachers.

1. Traditional teacher education programs typically involve collaboration between two institutions, such as a school and a university. The Houston Consortium has demonstrated a much more complex set of relationships as nine institutions have learned to work together. Can others accomplish this same level of collaboration? We believe the answer is yes. The fact that this collaboration has been successful with such a diverse group of institutions and with people who previously had only limited interaction indicates that it could work in many different contexts.

Although it is not simple, collaboration strengthens the bonding among professionals—schoolteachers with university faculty, regional centers with schools, communities with universities. Collaboration requires no additional funds; it does require time and commitment to be effective.

2. External funding is not critical to program implementation. Although a grant provided partial support for the systemic redesign of this program during a 3-year period, the institutions involved have continued without external funding. Universities draw on tuition and their regular state or private funding to support the program.

3. School-based programs require more resources than those based in universities, but they bring additional benefits to both schools and universities that more than compensate for additional costs (i.e., they result in greater cost-benefit ratios). We have found through third-party and objective studies that prospective teachers score higher on state-mandated examinations and that they are greatly sought after by schools upon program completion. These prospective teachers are more confident—and competent—than those in programs that are primarily university based.

Schools have found that the benefits gained from being a PDS far outweigh any additional challenges. Every principal of the 16 PDSs believes his or her school is far better off because of the broadened staff development, the additional adults in the school, and the enthusiasm and professionalism engendered by the school being a PDS. Scores on standardized tests of students in PDSs have increased.

4. This program demonstrates not only the efficacy of focusing teacher education on a specific population but the effectiveness of such an approach. We chose to focus on a critical concern in our area—effective teachers for urban schools. Other teacher education institutions could emulate or modify our methods and utilize the structure, content, and processes to focus on needs in their areas—rural teachers, suburban teachers, teachers of immigrant children, or early childhood teachers—and perhaps, by not being all things to all people, become more effective.

Those who choose to continue preparing teachers for all of the nation's schools can adapt important aspects of this program, particularly its processes for involving representative groups of educators in program development, locating large parts of the program in PDSs, involving prospective teachers early in tutoring and school analysis projects, and relying on assessment to guide program change.

Note

1. See the Objectives section of this chapter for full definitions.

References

Anderson, L. M., Evertson, C. M., & Brophy, J. E. (1979). An experimental study of effective teaching in first-grade reading groups. *Elementary School Journal, 79*(4), 193-223.

Gliessman, D., Pugh, R., Dowden, D., & Hutchins, T. (1988). Variables influencing the acquisition of a generic teaching skill. *Review of Educational Research, 58*(1), 25-46.

Good, T., & Grouws, D. (1981). *Experimental research in secondary mathematics classrooms: Working with teachers* (Final Report). Columbia: University of Missouri. (ERIC Document Reproduction Service No. 219 261)

Interstate New Teacher Assessment and Support Consortium. (1992, September 1). *Model standards for beginning teacher licensing and development: A resource for state dialogue.* Washington, DC: Council of Chief State School Officers.

Joyce, B. R., & Showers, B. (1995). *Student achievement through staff development* (2nd ed.). White Plains, NY: Longman.

Medley, D. M. (1977). *Teacher competence and teacher effectiveness: A review of process-product research.* Washington, DC: American Association of Colleges for Teacher Education. (ERIC Document Reproduction Service No. ED 143 629)

National Advisory Council of Education Professions Development. (1975). *Teacher Corps: Past or prologue.* Washington, DC: U.S. Office of Education.

National Association of State Directors of Teacher Education and Certification. (1993). *Outcome-based standards and portfolio assessment: Outcome-based teacher education standards for elementary, middle and high school levels* (2nd ed.). Dubuque, IA: Kendall/Hunt.

Powell, M. (1978). Research on teaching. *Educational Forum, 43,* 27-37.

Rosenshine, B. (1976). Classroom instruction. In N. L. Gage (Ed.), *The psychology of teaching methods* (77th yearbook of the National Society for the Study of Education, Part 1, pp. 335-371). Chicago: University of Chicago Press.

2 Dream Keepers, Weavers, and Shape-Shifters

Emerging Roles of PDS University Coordinators in Educational Reform

Joanne M. Simmons

Loretta R. Konecki

Ronald A. Crowell

Pamela Gates-Duffield

Joanne M. Simmons is Associate Professor of Teacher Education at Michigan State University. Since 1992, she has been the PDS University co-coordinator at two urban sites. Her teaching, writing, and consulting work focuses on reflective decision-making, action research, learning-to-teach, standards-based curriculum development and evaluation, and collaborative leadership in educational restructuring.

Loretta P. Konecki is Professor of Advanced Studies in Education at Grand Valley State University in Grand Rapids, Michigan. She is PDS University co-coordinator at two urban schools. Her teaching expertise and leadership activities are in curriculum development, science education, school reform, professional education, and early childhood education.

Ronald A. Crowell is Associate Professor at Western Michigan University in Kalamazoo and University Coordinator at a suburban elementary PDS. His work has focused on collaboration in field experiences, school reform, and the learner-centered classroom. He teaches courses in psychology, classroom management, and organizational systems for teachers and administrators.

Pamela Gates-Duffield is Associate Professor in the Department of English Language and Literature at Central Michigan University. She was involved in creating four linked PDSs, which she now coordinates—a high school, middle school, and two elementary schools. Her publications and teaching are in literacy and children's literature.

ABSTRACT

This chapter reports on grounded theory investigation of implicit theories-of-action, reflective decision-making, and subsequent actions of four teacher education professor coordinators working in seven diverse urban/small city/suburban PDS sites. It extends earlier investigations of teachers' reflective decision-making and provides a qualitative view of collaborative change efforts intended to impact both PreK-12 education and teacher preparation programs.

Three metaphors emerge from content analysis of the critical incident journal data produced by these PDS professors about their varied coordinator activities: dream keepers, weavers, and shape-shifters. In addition, other findings are reported that reveal how PDS coordinator work is vision driven in a complex, multidimensional manner and requires professors to skillfully operate in a wide range of complex roles and to use knowledge, skills, beliefs, and dispositions that are at variance with those used in other university campus-based work.

As increasing numbers of teacher education professors engage in PreK-12 and teacher education collaborative reform through professional development school (PDS) partnerships, many historically separate people and organizations are becoming committed to working together to achieve simultaneous renewal.

A common response of those engaged in this school/university/ community reform work or researching, however, is that these projects are complex, paradigm challenging, time consuming, and obstacle ridden and that change is often frustratingly gradual. At the same time, there is anecdotal evidence that many educators are strongly motivated and find genuine satisfaction in seeing the impacts of their commitments to improve learning for *all* students in schools and universities.

The early PDS literature identifies such complexity in collaborative reform. Generally, what has been published so far can be characterized as visionary, descriptive, and meta-analytic and has focused on providing the rationale and elements for an idealized vision of needed reforms, telling site-specific stories or analyzing reform issues and change strategies across project sites (e.g., Ashton, 1992a, 1992b; Darling-Hammond, 1994; Holmes Group, 1990; Levine, 1992; Levine & Trachtman, 1997). These documents also indicate the difficulty in researching what occurs and evaluating the impacts of PDS collaborative reform work from different perspectives.

The vision of engaging in long-term, collaborative reform involving diverse stakeholders requires that reform participants become able to interact effectively in complex situations involving human and institutional differences at many levels, such as prior experiences, values, vision, assumptions, power, communication habits, knowledge bases, skills, and reward structures. In the case of our research, little is known yet about the implicit perceptions, theories-of-action interpretations, and everyday decision making and actions taken by those who are professor collaborators in the complex, ill-defined reform setting of a PDS. Questions of beliefs, assumptions, knowledge base, interpretations, feelings, and judgments that underlie everyday implicit decision making and are expressed through visible actions arise. For our focus, an important question is how a new type of teacher education professor persona is being constructed by those who are engaged in this nontraditional PDS coordinator role. Furthermore, how does this PDS work enhance and/or conflict with the expectations, culture, and work activities of the traditional university setting? Finally, what are the implications for the type of knowledge base, skills, beliefs, and dispositions that would be needed for professors to do collaborative reform work effectively?

To understand better the dynamics of collaborative reform, we have been using critical incident journaling since 1995 to investigate our own implicit theories-of-action, decision making, and actions as four teacher education PDS professor coordinators at seven diverse Michigan PDS sites. Our role as "professor coordinator" is a facilitative, coordinating, and participatory role rather than a power- or authority-based position. We represent our university in project activities at the site and represent the school site back at our universities. In addition, we coordinate involvement of other university faculty and preservice teachers in sites, participate in a range of leadership and classroom reform subprojects in the PDS, and function as staff members in ordinary ways at both the school and university.

Through our work, we have been investigating the implicit thinking and visible actions of ourselves as PDS professor coordinators in a qualitative, grounded theory manner. Based on our data, three metaphors have emerged to characterize this work and our multiple roles in PDS collaborative reform: dream keepers, weavers, and shape-shifters.

Our critical incident journaling research seeks to explore our own reflective decision-making that undergirds the intense collaborative reform activities that we and others have undertaken in seven specific PDS sites. Also, we are pushing the boundaries since little is actually known about how specific individuals perceive and negotiate the conflicting issues found in collaborative reform on a day-by-day basis. Critical incident journaling methodology seems uniquely suited to investigating what happens as professor coordinators attempt to become bicultural personas working effectively to reform both PreK-12 and university worlds.

Research Questions and Methodology

This study builds on an earlier research framework and methodology developed by Georgia Sparks-Langer, Joanne Simmons, Marvin Pesch, and Amy Colton to explore classroom teachers' reflective thinking (see, e.g., Sparks-Langer, Simmons, Pesch, Colton, & Starko, 1990). Through these 1987-1990 studies of the construct "teacher reflection," a seven-level framework for Reflective Pedagogical Thinking (RPT) was developed to describe and compare how preservice versus experienced teachers interpreted critical incidents of effective and ineffective teaching they had experienced.

The RPT framework identifies seven levels ranging from simple to more complex perceived variables: (a) teaching/learning process (CAUSES),

(b) intended learner outcomes (EFFECTS), and (c) CONTEXT variables. Thus, these theories-of-action interpretations are teachers' own individually constructed hunches, predictions, or implicit hypotheses in the form of CAUSE-EFFECT-IN-CONTEXT explanations of the critical incidents. This theories-of-action view of human cognition originates in the work of Dewey, Kolb, and Argyris, and it has been used by many people involved in teacher thinking and reflection and action research (see, e.g., Ross, Cornett, & McCutcheon, 1992).

Since 1995, our PDS professor coordinator research team has been exploring what critical incident journal entries can reveal about our theories-of-action, decision making, and actions as we engage in PDS collaborative reform work. In this study, 40 semistructured journal entries by us about our PDS work have been content analyzed to investigate these questions:

1. What are the other role groups with which we need to interact effectively?
2. How is the vision of the six Holmes Group (1990) PDS principles embedded in this work?
3. What are our own implicit CAUSE-EFFECT-IN-CONTEXT theories-of-action interpretations about doing this work effectively?
4. What broad themes or metaphors for doing this work effectively can be found in these critical incidents and theories-of-action?

In another study, we have extended our data and used content analysis to identify the professional and personal knowledge base, skills, beliefs, and dispositions that are revealed in 80 critical incident journal entries about our work as PDS professor coordinators (Simmons, Konecki, Crowell, Gates-Duffield, & Hobson, 1998).

Data Sources and Analysis

We have written about 40 critical incidents in our work in seven different PDS sites since their creation in 1991-1992. Two of us have written about critical incidents about our work as co-coordinators at an urban, largely African American high school PDS and a nearby multiracial elementary PDS. One has written critical incidents about her work in coordinating four PDSs—a high school, a middle school, and two elementary schools—in a district located in a university town that serves both town children and Native American children from the adjacent reservation. Finally, an elementary PDS serving the suburban population of a small city is the focus of the fourth set. We are all employed at different universities; three of us began this work as tenured faculty and one of us successfully earned tenure and promotion recently.

In our research, we have described the concept of a "critical incident" in this manner: an incident that reveals how you "walk the talk" of your values and style in this setting; a persistent and lingering event in your head/heart; a "defining" event that shapes the project and your role in it; an emotionally strong or intellectually engaging experience; a puzzling experience; an important incident in the history of the project.

We generated data by writing semistructured journal entries about critical incidents found in our own PDS work. For each journal entry, we wrote about five aspects: demographics, description, interpretation, context generalization, and question raising. These questions were adapted from the earlier research on classroom teachers' Reflective Pedagogical Thinking (RPT).

Our decision to use a semiguided structure for writing each critical incident allowed us to analyze the data for our underlying CAUSE-EFFECT-IN-CONTEXT hunches or interpretations. This three-part variable structure forms the basic grammar or logic of people's theories-of-action interpretations of complex, interactive situations. Without these implicit interpretations of events, our subsequent actions would be random and not intentionally directed toward certain desired outcomes in a particular context. We found that this open-ended journaling format allowed us to write about any experience that we believed contained a significant example of our decision making and actions taken in doing our PDS coordinator work.

Some of what we wrote were retrospective, historical journal entries, but nearly half were journal entries about current activities. The retrospective entries cover events that occurred as our PDS projects matured across 6 to 7 years from orientation to implementation to operational stages. The time to create each journal entry ranged from 25 minutes to 2 hours, with the typical length ranging from two to three single-spaced pages. Each of our critical incidents carries a descriptive title, such as, "Merging Two Cultures—Who Am I?" and is assigned an identification code.

Conventional content analysis procedures were used to code the critical incident data. Each incident was coded for (a) participant roles, (b) the Holmes Group (1990) PDS principles related to that incident, and (c) the theory(s)-of-action interpretations underlying the decision making and actions described in the incident. (This coding sheet is available from the authors.)

The critical incident journal entries were analyzed by three coders: (a) EXTERNAL—an external coder who is familiar with PDS vision and implementation analyzed all the journal entries in a random manner across all four professors and seven sites; (b) COLLEAGUE—we rotated each professor's critical incidents as a set to another research team member to be coded; and (c) SELF—we each coded our own critical incidents as a set. The reason for this three-way analysis in our early study was to determine interrater reliability and to provide a comparison between our own perceptions of the data and what other readers found.

The coded sheets were sent to one team member who summarized the data from the three analyses into data tables and calculated an interrater reliability level of .86 for the theories-of-action analysis. The interrater reliability for identifying other participants (.54) and PDS principles (.48) was not acceptable in this early study. Discrepancies were due to some coders having a tendency to be more inclusive in identifying numerous participants and principles because they saw them as frequently integrated in practice, whereas other analysts coded only the participants and principles that dominated the content of the incidents (see Simmons, Crowell, Konecki, & Gates-Duffield, 1996). Finally, the team used content analysis to categorize the critical incidents into the three metaphor categories reported here: dream keepers, weavers, and shape-shifters.

Findings

Other Participants

A preliminary way of analyzing the critical incidents involves the role of people featured in the stories. This was to provide a more accurate picture of the collaborative scope of PDS work. We think of this work as systemic, or involving systems thinking in numerous dimensions, one of which is communication among the wide range of persons with whom we work.

In fact, the data revealed the unexpectedly wide range of individuals we work with as PDS professor coordinators—for example, PreK-12 schoolteachers, administrators, students, parents, and support staff; district administrators; university faculty, students, and administrators; funding agents; and business and community partners. The most frequent participants were PDS teachers (66%), PDS building administrators (35%), other university PDS team members (30%), district administrators (16%), PDS support staff and non-PDS university faculty (each at 14%). Such participant diversity supports the view of systems thinking, "weaving," and "bridge building" to develop common agendas with diverse populations and reveals that strong communication and problem-solving skills are important elements in this work.

Vision Driven by PDS Principles

The Holmes Group (1990) principles under which these Michigan PDSs were initiated a decade ago provide a second way of content-analyzing our critical incidents. These six principles are rank-ordered below by the frequency with which they were found in the data analysis:

- #6: Inventing a new institution (65%)
- #1: Creating a learning community (49%)
- #2: Fostering continuous learning by teachers, teacher educators, and administrators (46%)
- #5: Conducting long-term inquiry into teaching, learning, and leadership (22%)
- #3: Ensuring teaching and learning for everybody's children (12%)
- #4: Focusing teaching and learning on student understanding and application (7%)

Furthermore, we found that almost all the critical incidents contained evidence of two or more PDS principles-in-use, indicating that this work is vision driven in a complex and simultaneously multigoal manner.

The analysis also reveals that these first 40 critical incidents written about our role as PDS university coordinators had a preponderance of incidents that related to the Holmes Group (1990) PDS Principles 1, 2, and 6. We think of these as the "individual and organizational readiness PDS principles," so it is not surprising that they predominated in critical incidents written about the early years of PDS coordinator work in our sites. Because we wrote these critical incidents about our role as PDS coordinators, we also believe that they logically focus more on organizational development concerns than on teaching and learning concerns.

Theories-of-Action Interpretations of Critical Incidents

The underlying theories-of-action reveal each professor's interpretation of the CAUSE-EFFECT-IN-CONTEXT logic of complex events in the critical incidents, and the actions taken reveal how that person's beliefs, skills, and knowledge about how change occurs play out.

Data indicate that PDS professor coordinators have numerous complex, implicit theories-of-action about doing this work. Many feature theories-of-action containing rather nontraditional teacher education variables such as organizational development; administrative and teacher leadership; informal communication networks; increasing and managing community involvement in school issues; and building systemic structures that enhance organizational commitment and competency for the achievement of complex, long-term reforms. Others involve more traditional teacher education variables related to student teachers, assessment of students' learning, curriculum alignment, or classroom- and school-based inquiry. Therefore, analysis of the critical incidents makes it clear that the simultaneous reform of PreK-12 education and teacher education needs to involve increased use of what we know from research and best practice about fields such as collaborative leadership, conflict management, feminist pedagogy, family education, counseling and social work, community development, educational finance, social policy, program evaluation, marketing, and multimedia technology communications. Second, being a cross-trained generalist or having the skills and dispositions of being highly collaborative with other specialists seems to be clearly useful in today's PDS collaborative reform work.

The specific areas in which a PDS professor coordinator's theories-of-action extend or are in conflict with conventional teacher education work and university culture imply important elements of the new knowledge, skills, beliefs, and dispositions used by this emerging type of bicultural PDS professor who feels at home, is effective, and is respected in both the university and PreK-12 settings. Such a role is related to what first emerged in the earlier Teacher Center movement in the United States (e.g., Yarger, 1981). The implications of our critical incident research for identifying important components of a PDS professor coordinator's qualifications (e.g., knowledge base, skills, beliefs, and dispositions) in a grounded theory manner are explored more fully in another paper by Simmons et al. (1998). This emerging profile appears to add another layer of expectations to the traditional academic specialized or discipline-based preparation of future teacher educators.

Our data also suggest what many other people from our quarters have urged: There is an urgent need to reform the traditional evaluation and reward structures for the teacher education professorate so that PDS collaborative reform work can be more adequately and fairly recognized as worthwhile in addition to traditional credit-generating teaching and scholarly writing of university colleagues. At one of our universities, a department chair wondered aloud at a recent meeting if this PDS coordinator role wasn't more like being a junior administrator than any other role currently existing. In contrast to this view, for many PDS professors, this role is limitedly regarded as a professor's choice about where to do a service or research component in faculty load assignments. At this same university, it should be noted, there currently are some unfilled professor coordinator positions because many faculty seem to perceive (a) this role is filled with complex and messy challenges for which they have little preparation or interest, (b) this type of work isn't rewarded as well as other faculty work, or (c) both reasons.

Metaphors for Our Theories-of-Action

Qualitative analysis of the critical incident data makes it clear that collaborative reform entails complex, vision-driven work that also can be understood through reference to vivid images in the form of metaphors about common human experiences and from other professional fields and bodies of literature. The theories-of-action analysis reveals entries containing images about enduring challenges such as "building bridges," encouraging "voices," strengthening the limited action of relatively "disempowered" people, "cheerleading" to foster change "one person at a time," functioning as a "translator" and "family therapist" among historically separate groups, and struggling to maintain momentum when long-term change occurs "one inch at a time."

In an attempt to look across the 40 critical incidents as a set, we began to categorize our theories-of-action by metaphors about role and activities. The metaphors that emerged from this grounded theory analysis were dream keepers, weavers, and shape-shifters.

Dream Keepers. As dream keepers, we consistently try to focus on the principles, vision, and commitments that brought other participants and us into this collaborative reform. As Gloria Ladson-Billings (1994) says in another context, dream keepers are vigorously involved in helping other people keep a vision in sight, and this does not preclude often struggling honestly to keep a vision in front of themselves too. Thus, a dream keeper's energy, persistence, and skills in articulating, facilitating, and increasing people's understanding of shared goals, generating consensus support for the reform efforts, building trust, and guiding step-by-step actions that turn into group accomplishments are important dimensions of this role. Several of the critical incidents (30%) feature the dream keeper role for PDS university coordinators.

In our work as PDS university coordinators, the role of dream keeper focuses on the vision provided by the Holmes Group (1990) principles that guide the PDS consortium movement in Michigan. The critical incident data reveal many moments of communication to provide input and of actions intended to help maintain long-term vision. We try continually to ask ourselves and others, "How will what is being proposed or done help achieve these goals?" Sometimes that includes moments of feeling confused or discouraged about what to do or how to encourage people to do what is right and best.

This work makes us deeply aware that decision making based on a long-term vision and current status data has been relatively rare in PreK-12 schools, which have prioritized action over reflective analysis and evaluation. In the past, universities, as well, have prized individualism over cooperative progress toward a shared vision.

This PDS dream keeper role shares certain elements in common with coaches, ministers and priests, spiritual leaders, advocates, and therapists in our culture and with CEOs, organizational development specialists, and grant writers in modern organizations. On an emotional and social level, organizational development efforts attempt to build a team spirit, a climate of shared hope, vigor, and energetic commitment to that vision so that all participants can be working toward it, rather than passively ignoring or actively sabotaging it.

Weavers. The six Holmes Group (1990) PDS principles undergird current strategic planning, school improvement, outcomes-based accreditation, and teacher education initiatives at these Michigan school and university sites. The metaphor of weaver suggests how we find ourselves as PDS university coordinators consistently in the position of working with all members of the reform team—teachers; school, district, and university administrators; support staff; preservice teachers; parents; community members; university faculty—to integrate and combine these efforts without diluting the impact of different initiatives on students' learning. It means taking the ongoing "warp" of daily tasks and events in the school and university and gradually changing the color, texture, and sequence in the "woof" of people's behavior to create a new design in the "fabric" of the school and university.

Weavers try to keep things together and moving forward as a group. Strong interpersonal communication skills, facilitative leadership, trust building, conflict management, and problem solving are particularly important to weavers. In a collaborative reform project, there is no end to the people, institutions, and issues that need to be introduced, negotiated, processed, and connected in complex, multistrand ways. The task of weaving, we are finding, is never done and requires constant alertness to how each person, activity, and experience can be linked to others; it is classic systems thinking at every moment!

This metaphor implies discernment that some new connections are fostered based in interpersonal criteria, whereas other connections can result with stakeholders from very different points of view recognizing a shared professional or moral political vision such as enhanced learning for *all* children in our society. When successfully done, these connections result in people from historically separate groups making new judgments and taking joint actions about common needs. Of the 40 critical incidents, 30% illustrate the PDS university coordinator serving in the weaver role.

Thus, some weaver work occurs in small, ordinary conversations with people in classrooms, offices, hallways, and parking lots and through e-mail, simultaneous with using traditional meetings and written proposals to weave together different interests and points of view. Other weaver work involves becoming a moving, bicultural bridge between the university and PreK-12 system, resulting in a sort of hybrid or bicultural life for PDS professor coordinators who belong to two faculties; operate in two contrasting credibility/reward/recognition systems; and have two mailboxes and keys, two sets of colleagues, and a double set of workplace meetings to attend. This can mean (in almost comical "hat changing" fashion) explaining and defending multiple views or personas within hours or days of one another.

Thus, our critical incidents about this weaver role involve us coming to meet, interact, and work effectively with several types of people and issues we would rarely meet on a university campus. Our theories-of-action about this weaver role emphasize the importance of us continually being open and helping people connect to know each other better, to work successfully on little, specific aspects of reform together, to problem-solve difficult situations, and to learn lots of new things, including that there is no other way except a systems approach that will be adequate for what we must do in collaborative reform today.

Shape-Shifters. To carry out our roles as dream keepers and weavers requires that we and others work within the school, university, and community as shape-shifters (e.g., Hill, 1995) who are able to assume new roles and forms of contributing to the collaborative effort, as the situations demand. This metaphor relates to what we mean by "cross-training" in the employment world today. Leader, follower, director, facilitator, listener, speaker, researcher, information provider, challenger, protector, counselor, secretary, designer, cook, teacher, and learner have all been roles taken on by us as PDS university coordinators according to the critical incident data.

In this case, 40% of the 40 critical incidents deal predominately with this metaphor. Shape-shifters must be willing to change roles comfortably themselves and to explicitly model this behavior and address the need for others to change roles at times—for example, coaching a building principal about becoming a more collaborative leader with the staff, engaging in professional development to learn how to relate more meaningfully to today's urban learners, and so on. Although this concept of "paradigm shifts" and "emerging roles" receives much emphasis in education today (e.g., teacher leaders, site-based leadership, facilitative administrative skills), it requires a great deal of personal flexibility, self-assuredness, external encouragement, and a willingness to learn new things. These growth assumptions are frequently not found in our current school and university work settings, which can be more often characterized as stressful, conflictive, and full of power-based relationships and decision making, especially in large, bureaucratic settings.

The related notion of "stewardship" is a powerful one emerging from the PDS critical incidents themselves—the recognition and willingness to do whatever needs to be done in a collaborative arena to get the job done and to stimulate all team members to continue growing in resourcefulness, self-efficacy, and collaboration toward the vision. This metaphor means not standing on protocol or rank, not being afraid to take a risk, and not being distant and reluctant to get muddy or messy in a real-life situation that needs a collaborative response. According to the events described in the critical incidents, we often seem to be deliberately trying to demonstrate this friendliness, humbleness, willingness, and flexibility to do what is necessary to move collaborative reform forward.

Implications for Teacher Education

PDS collaborative reform work opens the door for teacher educators genuinely to face many complex, long-term educational reform and societal problems today. PDS professors report their amazement and frustration wrestling with variables such as human motivation, organizational development, systems thinking, government policy mandates, counseling, community development, family education, and leadership and school governance issues—all in addition to challenges of more "traditional" teacher education variables related to learning; social-cultural foundations; and subject area curriculum, instruction, and assessment. At the same time, many school leaders report their frustration with "ivory tower answers" to complex problems and with a shortage of well-prepared, culturally responsive new teachers to hire for today's classrooms.

Thus, our grounded theory basis for understanding these complex issues has been focused on the PDS professor coordinator role in collaborative reform. What we are learning about ourselves, our collaborative partners, and the useful characteristics of people who are involved in collaborative reform continues to unfold and provide insightful suggestions as well as raise questions. We see three areas of important impact for this study.

First, the results of this study should be useful in better understanding the constructivist "meaning-making" processes used, the perceived dilemmas and successes experienced, and the change strategies selected and implemented by teacher education professors collaborating in PDS reform. From a qualitative, grounded theory perspective, this involves investigating *how* we interpret our PDS experiences, *why* we decide to act as we do, and *what* successes, dilemmas, or impacts we may have in doing this type of bicultural work.

Although everyone agrees that there are layers upon layers of complex issues underlying "everyday life" in PDS work, little is actually known about how specific individuals perceive and negotiate these factors on a day-by-day basis. There is also the issue of knowledge usage—little is understood of how individuals determine what and how to contribute from what they know, believe, and can do in collaborative reform. Answering these questions seems important to better understand this emerging role; collaborative reform also suggests a parallel to other investigations today about how teachers and administrators engage in these same reflective processes in their work.

Second, if this type of work is different from typical professor-in-the-ivory-tower work (and this point seems clear from the Teacher Center and early PDS literature as well as our data here), this implies that somewhat different preparation, qualifications, and professional evaluation and reward structures are needed to enhance the effectiveness of this emerging bicultural teacher educator. This study also raises questions about the impact of different professional communities on reform itself.

We have come to believe with others (e.g., Hall & Hord, 1987) that seemingly "culturally innocent," external people like ourselves in this role can truly help to implement and facilitate PreK-12 school change particularly well because we are not emotionally or politically involved in the messy history and day-by-day events of a school system. In the same way, we have observed that sometimes PreK-12 school people can be more effective than we can in stimulating university teacher education reform due to the freshness of their voices and the lack of political history at the university level.

According to our data, taking on the roles of dream keepers, weavers, and shape-shifters frequently demands that PDS professor coordinators go beyond or outside the usual activities and roles undertaken by the campus professorate. Some of these role expectations and actions are not anticipated, recognized, or rewarded in the traditional school or campus world as noted in some of the critical incidents written by team members.

Collaborative PDS work raises many issues related to professors' ongoing need for a new knowledge base, skills, and beliefs related to nontraditional areas (see Simmons et al., 1998). In general, the data indicate that breadth of knowledge, skills, beliefs, and collaborative dispositions used by professor coordinators who become successful as collaborative partners goes well beyond that learned in most teacher education doctoral programs today. The critical incidents show that technical knowledge is required, but that interpersonal skills, beliefs, and dispositions are at least as critical when participating in collaborative reform.

A final area of importance involves the hope that if this methodology is suitably rigorous, it could be used to identify and compare different perspectives of the other stakeholders engaged in collaborative reform because such theories-of-action underlie their day-by-day interactions too. We believe that knowing more about the underlying perceptions and interpretations of these other participants' actions can help us improve our collaboration processes and increase the likelihood of genuine reform occurring.

Through publication of this study, we also hope that other people involved in collaborative reform will learn about and feel invited to use this promising qualitative research methodology for investigating the underlying theories-of-action found in collaborative PreK-12 and teacher education reform. We are currently establishing a "second circle" of people from other collaborative reform sites who will participate with us in further developing this exciting methodology and exploring collaborative reform in a grounded theory manner.

References

Ashton, P. T. (Ed.). (1992a). Partners in school restructuring [thematic issue]. *Journal of Teacher Education, 42*(4).

Ashton, P. T. (Ed.). (1992b). Professional development schools [thematic issue]. *Journal of Teacher Education, 43*(1).

Darling-Hammond, L. (Ed.). (1994). *Professional development schools: Schools for developing a profession.* New York: Teachers College Press.

Hall, G. E., & Hord, S. M. (1987). *Change in schools: Facilitating the process.* Albany: State University of New York Press.

Hill, U. (1995). *ShapeShifters* [CD]. Durham, NC: Ladyslipper Music.

Holmes Group. (1990). *Tomorrow's schools: Principles for the design of professional development schools.* East Lansing, MI: Author.

Ladson-Billings, G. (1994). *The dreamkeepers: Successful teachers of African American children.* San Francisco: Jossey-Bass.

Levine, M. (Ed.). (1992). *Professional practice schools: Linking teacher education and school reform.* New York: Teachers College Press.

Levine, M., & Trachtman, E. (Eds.). (1997). *Making professional development schools work.* New York: Teachers College Press.

Ross, E. W., Cornett, J. W., & McCutcheon, G. (Eds.). (1992). *Teacher personal theorizing: Connecting curriculum practice, theory, and research.* Albany: State University of New York Press.

Simmons, J. M., Crowell, R. A., Konecki, L. R., & Gates-Duffield, P. (1996, April). *Emerging methodologies for investigating collaborative partners' theories-of-action/reflective decision-making for documenting PDS educational reform.* Paper presented at the meeting of the American Educational Research Association, New York.

Simmons, J. M., Konecki, L. R., Crowell, R. A., Gates-Duffield, P., & Hobson, S. (1998, April). *The knowledge-base, skills, beliefs, and dispositions of PDS professor coordinators: Results from critical incident journaling about school-university collaborative reform.* Paper presented at the meeting of the American Educational Research Association, San Diego.

Sparks-Langer, G. M., Simmons, J. M., Pesch, M., Colton, A., & Starko, A. (1990). Reflective pedagogical thinking: How can we promote it and measure it? *Journal of Teacher Education, 41*(4), 23-32.

Yarger, G. P. (1981). A university-employed teacher educator: A week in the life of a fieldbased teacher educator. In K. R. Howey, R. Bents, & D. Corrigan (Eds.), *School-focused inservice: Descriptions and discussion* (pp. 37-54). Reston, VA: Association of Teacher Educators.

3 Creating an Equal Partnership for Urban School and Teacher Education Renewal

A California Experience

Zhixin Su

Zhixin Su is Professor of Education in the Department of Educational Leadership and Policy Studies at California State University, Northridge. She is also Director of the China Institute in the university. Her major areas of interest in teaching and research are teacher education, educational policy studies, and comparative and international education. In recent years, she has published research papers in ATE's Teacher Education Yearbook, *American Journal of Education, Oxford Review of Education, Teachers College Record, Teaching and Teacher Education, Journal of Education for Teaching, International Review of Education, Phi Delta Kappan, Journal of Research on Education and Development, Comparative Education,* and *Urban Education.*

ABSTRACT

This chapter presents multiple perspectives on the creation and development of a school-university partnership between a teacher education program in a large public university and an urban school district in California. The collaboration aims at restructuring teacher education as a rigorous, high-status, field-based activity that takes place in reforming urban education. Findings from an early evaluation study featuring intensive individual interviews of key participants of the collaboration reveal that the school people tend to hold quite different perspectives from the university people on the purposes, processes, and substances of the partnership. Although all participants believed that the partnership had achieved some remarkable successes and helped make a solid connection between urban schools and the university teacher education program, they identified the lack of commitment from the university faculty and the absence of effective communication as the major obstacles to the further development of a true and equal partnership.

In the past decade, school-university partnerships have mushroomed across the nation and have emerged as a significant social and educational experiment (Goodlad, 1993). A notable form of the movement is the partnerships termed professional development schools (PDSs), or partner schools, most often referring to the substantial involvement of one or several elementary and secondary schools in the preservice teacher education program of a college or university (see, e.g., Goodlad, 1984; Holmes Group, 1990, 1995; Clark, 1995; Zeichner, 1992; and Darling-Hammond, 1994).

Although most of the school-university partnerships tend to be one-sided efforts (i.e., they are meant to improve teaching and learning in lower-level schools but are not concerned with the restructuring of university programs), the PDSs focus on the simultaneous improvement of both school and university (Su, 1990; Goodlad, 1993). In a PDS, both school and university change the work and culture of the other, each derives important benefits from the other, and efforts are made by both to institutionalize new ways of training and educating novice and in-service teachers. This chapter presents and discusses findings from a recent research study on the multiple perspectives from different participants regarding the initial development of one such effort—the Comprehensive Urban Teacher Education Institute (CUTEI). The CUTEI was established in fall 1995 with the support of a grant from the California state Department of Education. It was a collaboration between a teacher education program in a large, research-oriented, public university and a multicultural, urban school district in California.

The major purpose of the CUTEI is to restructure preservice and beginning teacher education as a rigorous, high-status, field-based activity that takes place in reforming urban schools. Participants in the CUTEI recognize that the university alone cannot prepare educators effectively, absent close connections with urban schools. They also recognize that universities can provide important resources and scaffolding to urban schools attempting to transform the way they educate diverse groups of children. Consequently, the university and the school district formed a partnership with the overarching goal of simultaneous teacher preparation, professional development, and institutional renewal in schools in the high-minority, largely Spanish-speaking region.

The university and the school district under investigation have a long history of collaboration in education and in the academic disciplines. In the 2 years prior to the establishment of the partnership, they had been engaged in serious conversations and pilot efforts toward collaborative teacher education. In fall 1993, the Professional Development School Project launched a joint effort to implement and evaluate an alternative model of teacher education and support for new teachers. The clinical faculty in teacher education at the university and faculties of the partner schools agreed to work together to prepare a team of teacher candidates during the 1993-1994 school year. By June 1994, the group had evolved a set of principles, goals, and preliminary organizational structures to guide the continuing work together.

After the establishment of the CUTEI in fall 1995, the university and the school district collaborated in the preservice education of a team of 30 novice teachers at six schools that were engaged in an inquiry-based school reform effort. The novice teachers were learning about teaching in the context of partner schools, supervised not by the traditional "master teacher" but rather by a team of school faculty, who were supported in their professional development by the California Subject Matter Projects and a team of ladder faculty and doctoral students from the university. An important part of the novice teachers' learning to become teachers includes developing the knowledge, skills, and dispositions to create schools where low-income, minority youngsters engage with rich, meaningful content in an atmosphere of high expectations and teacher efficacy.

Methods of Inquiry

Although the university and the school district intended that their current partnership efforts become integral and permanent programs and their fledgling efforts in the past few years have yielded impressive results, they also encountered enormous difficulties in developing the collaborative, as many other partnerships across the country have. To create a solid, workable, meaningful, and long-term collaboration between the school and the university, I designed and directed an inquiry study for the CUTEI on the directions, current conditions, and future prospects of the partnership at the end of the 1995-1996 academic year, one year after the CUTEI was formally established.

For the purpose of the evaluation, interview guides were developed based on the research model created at the National Network for Educational Renewal (Puget Sound Educational Consortium, 1990) and on Lortie's (1975) and Shen's (1994) interviews with schoolteachers. They cover several areas of concern—aims and goals, commitment, benefits, leadership and organization, resources, substantive activities (social justice education and inquiry as a means for school and teacher education reform), communication, outcomes, and future directions.

A total of 57 school and university people identified as involved in the development of the collaboration in one way or the other were interviewed individually by trained researchers. The subjects included 3 university administrators, 6 clinical faculty, 1 ladder faculty, 4 doctoral students (3 of them were team leaders for novice teachers), 7 novice teachers, 4 school district administrators, 7 school administrators, and 25 schoolteachers. The results are nearly 250 single-spaced pages of transcribed interview data.

The multiple perspectives that have been constructed from the interview data represent different groups of participants in the collaborative activities—school and university leaders and administrators, schoolteachers, university faculty members, and novice teachers. Together, they illustrate a rich portrayal of the partnership as it is today and suggest significant implications not only for the future development of this partnership but also for the reform of teacher education and urban education in the larger social and educational context.

Findings and Discussion

The presentation and discussion of interview data in this section is primarily based on a summary of the major themes that have emerged from the general responses to interview questions. Comparisons and contrasts will be made among the multiple perspectives across different groups of participants in the collaboration. Whenever possible, the analysis and discussion of findings from this inquiry will be related to relevant literature on the school-university partnership development in other parts of the country.

Aims and Goals of the Collaboration

When a partnership is being formed, nothing is more important than clarifying purposes for all those involved (Su, 1990). Although the CUTEI clearly established its aims and goals in writing at the time of its inception, they were not widely shared by the participants. The stated overarching aim of the CUTEI is to restructure preservice and beginning teacher education as a rigorous, high-status, field-based activity that takes place in reforming urban schools. A chief intent of the current inquiry is to assess whether this aim and its accompanying goals are consistent with what members of the partnership believe they are and how effective the collaboration has been in achieving the aim and goals.

Findings from the interview data indicate that not all participants, including some sitting on the steering committee, are aware of the stated purposes for the collaboration. Most simply described the goals of the partnership according to their own guesses and interpretations. Some openly stated that they were very unclear about the major purposes of the partnership.

In fact, about half of the university faculty and students, schoolteachers, and novice teachers interviewed believed that there was a lack of clarity about the purposes of the partnership and although the top leadership shared some consistent views on the goals, most people working in the schools and the university only saw and could speak about different pieces of the partnership. There was no common understanding among the participants of what the goals were. As a school district administrator pointed out, the problem here was the lack of global conversation identifying the big picture. The school people were openly skeptical and critical of the partnership, especially the role played by the university, when they considered the purposes of the collaboration. They observed that although the overtly stated goal of the partnership was lofty, in reality, it was mostly a "token relationship." They expressed "real frustration" on the part of the school people.

Social Justice Education

A major goal of the collaboration is the development of social justice education in schools and the socialization of novice teachers as social justice educators. In the current inquiry, we asked all the interviewees how they define "social justice education" and "social justice educator," whether these definitions are shared among all participants in the collaboration, and how we can best translate this vision into reality.

Data from the interviews reveal a whole range of different definitions of social justice educators among different participants, although many people recognized equality, diversity, inquiry, community, and change as the major themes in their visions. The novice teachers interviewed, for example, did not feel that there was a clear definition and shared understanding about social justice education. One claimed that nobody had ever told her what social justice education was—ever. She suspected that the program deliberately wanted novice teachers to create their own definitions and she had no idea whether hers was like anyone else's. Two other novice teachers shared her claim and pointed out that none of them had the same vocabulary to define the concept, although they had a common sense of what it meant to them.

Although some novice teachers claimed that by participating in the community activities and conducting case studies they were being socialized into knowing how hard it is to be a social justice educator, others felt that they were not being socialized into the demands and expectations of being social justice educators because the school experiences they had, they observed, focused less on social justice than on lesson planning. They observed that although the novice teachers were getting the views and opinions of what social justice means from the university courses, they had not seen them delve in depth into what social justice means with their personal schools and communities.

Since the novice teachers spent much time every day in the partner schools, the schoolteachers and administrators could exert much influence on the development of their fundamental beliefs, values, and attitudes. In fact, previous research identified field experiences and mentor teachers in schools as the most important source of influence in their socialization process (Su, 1992). In this study, the school people interviewed held varied opinions with regard to the social justice education/educator issue. Some provided clear and thoughtful definitions that were close to the visions articulated by the partnership leaders and university faculty. But most of them felt that the vision for social justice education was not shared among all the school people, novice teachers, and university participants. They pointed out that the vision was shared more among the people who had been directly touched by the university but they did not see a spillover effect to teachers who had not been working with novice teachers.

Inquiry as a Means for School Reform and Teacher Education

Regardless of their different levels of understanding of social justice education, many of our interviewees agreed that the best way to socialize novice teachers to be social justice educators was through their participation in the inquiry activities in schools, which were initiated with the explicit purposes of school reform, community involvement, and teacher education improvement. In fact, the current literature on PDSs strongly advocates inquiry as both a basis and result of PDS-based reforms, although there is little evidence of educators engaged in self-reflection regarding their beliefs about equity, diversity, and social justice issues (Valli, Cooper, & Frankes, 1997).

To the credit of the partnership under the study, all the novice teachers were encouraged to participate in the total life of the school and attend all school functions—such as district meetings, faculty meetings, parent nights, back-to-school nights, and outreach community events—where inquiry was intended to be the major theme and process.

The director of the teacher education program believed that inquiry had as good a chance as anything to lead to reform and restructuring at the schools. She observed that inquiry had begun to disrupt the conventional notion that teaching was just a bunch of practices and that it offered the novice teachers firsthand experiences with schoolteachers who were asking questions and revealing their uncertainties and the complexity of their questions. Not all her colleagues from the university shared her conviction and enthusiasm, however. Three of the clinical faculty and one team leader claimed they did not know or did not have information about inquiry.

Schoolteachers' participation in inquiry also varied by individuals and by schools. The ladder faculty who had conducted research on the inquiry process in the middle school observed that the inquiry activities involved many teachers and developed a foundation of trust and a community among teachers and administrators. Still, some teachers were excluded and she felt that everyone, including students, should be involved. In another school, where a university graduate researcher did her observation, the inquiry group was "way too big" and the relationships among teachers were fractured. They voted "no confidence" for a proposal to change pupil-free days and many of them did not want to come back to the inquiry group. Still, most of the university teacher educators interviewed felt that inquiry has profoundly helped novice teachers understand student interests and concerns and stimulated their involvement in schools.

The school district administrators were very optimistic and enthusiastic about the effects of inquiry on school reform and teacher education restructuring. The school district put a lot of money into developing various inquiry activities. They believed that inquiry was the only possibility for any kind of significant systemic change because it stimulated the necessary reflection on the existing practices. For teacher education, when the master teachers examined their own practices and started to make changes in their classrooms, that impacted the novice teachers. In return, the conversations that novice teachers had with their master teachers tied in to the master teachers' reflection on their own practices. They noted, however, that inquiry had caused some discomfort among different generations of teachers and that inquiry did not trickle down to the teachers in places where they were not part of the process.

The inquiry activities also involved parents and community representatives. The district office sent out 10,000 invitations to parents and welcomed them into the schools to talk with them rather than talk at them. The district administrators observed that what was so powerful was that parents of color were open in sharing their beliefs. It was powerful for novice teachers to hear their beliefs and the poetry of their beliefs. They felt that this was one of the most successful changes in the schools and the community.

The schoolteachers were split in their observations of inquiry. Some were very positive about it and considered it "the best professional development" they had ever had, and "the best part of the partnership" because it had helped to empower teachers and parents. Some teachers observed that it would take a long time—3, 5, or 7 years—for inquiry to have a profound impact on teaching practices in schools. They saw some small, gradual, and individual changes, but not major restructuring efforts. They suggested that the inquiry group should be more practical, oriented to the everyday situations that they were living in schools. They found the existing content too philosophical.

About half of the schoolteachers and administrators interviewed were critical of the inquiry process. They felt that the inquiry meetings were frustrating and nonproductive, and they expressed feelings of "change pains" and "growing pains." The schoolteachers and administrators were also split in their observations of the effects of inquiry on novice teachers. Apparently, novice teachers were invited to participate in some inquiry meetings but not others, and most simply sat there silently as schoolteachers discussed different opinions. Some schoolteachers encouraged novice teachers to disagree with them and they were interested in novice teachers' "fresh perspectives." The novice teachers interviewed had all been involved in the inquiry activities—social justice evenings, parent surveys, and community forums. Most expressed positive feelings about these activities. It seems that when inquiry is productive all participants can learn a lot and their practices as well as their schools can change, although slowly.

Leadership and Organization

As is clearly demonstrated by the description above, the collaboration between the university and the school district under study has been more of a process than a structure or organization. There was the creation of the CUTEI with its officially stated aims and goals and a steering committee consisting of representatives from the schools and the university, who met regularly to discuss various matters concerning the partnership. The steering committee meetings stopped in spring 1996. There is no formal governing body with a designated director and staff to run everyday operations, as is the case with many formally established partnerships between one university and multiple schools across the nation (Su, 1990; Berry & Catoe, 1994; Wiseman & Nason, 1995). The university leaders and the school district administrators, together with the two liaison persons designated by each side, coordinated all the collaborative meetings and activities.

There was a lack of consensus on the purpose of the steering committee. The university people and critical friends saw it as a site for inquiry, whereas the district administrators and school people saw it as a decision-making body for the partnership. The school district administrators commented that working with the university people on the committee had shifted their paradigm and given them the tools to advocate for the partnership. They strongly believed that the school district and the university should collaborate closely in setting the directions for the partnership because both sides had really valuable information and perspectives to bring to the conversation—the theoretical perspectives from the university and the reality check from the school district.

The majority of the clinical faculty and team leaders from the university felt that they were not involved or only minimally involved in the decision-making process in developing the collaboration. They expressed the desire to have their voices heard in decision making. Most of the schoolteachers interviewed also said that they were not involved in the decision-making process for developing the partnership and some were critical of the steering committee and the university's role in it. The steering committee had not been sufficient and effective as the leadership council for the partnership. The schoolteachers felt that most of the decisions were made by the top leaders without consultation from the school people. They argued that teachers, especially mentor teachers for student teachers as well as novice teachers, should have a large voice in decision making along with the principals, school district administrators, and university people. Furthermore, they believed that the schools and university should work together on an equal basis. They perceived the current leadership for the partnership as being "set up by the university; the only thing the district decides is if there is space available and where people should go." Like schoolteachers, most of the novice teachers interviewed also felt excluded from the decision-making process in the partnership. They demanded that their voices be heard and taken into consideration in decision making.

Commitment to the Collaboration

The success of the school-university partnership depends to a great extent on the commitment of all its participants (Mehaffy, 1992, Darling-Hammond, 1994). The university administrators interviewed felt that they had made an "enormous commitment" to the partnership in terms of faculty time and resources. In reality, most of the faculty members, especially senior faculty, from the Department of Education did not participate in the partnership activities. It was not clear whether they knew that the partner schools were welcoming sites for the professors and doctoral students. But as the team leader for novice teachers in the partner schools observed, teacher education and school reform were inherently local activities and ran at odds with the broader paradigm with which research universities operate.

The university administrators interviewed believed that they were very committed to the partnership but that such commitment was not always salient or intense in the school district. The school district administrators claimed, however, that they too had "tremendous commitment, exemplified by time and resources," to the development of the collaboration—"a lot of time and effort went into it." They recognized that given the realities of too few people and too many issues, the partnership did not receive the attention it needed. For them, collaborating with a university was something very different from what they did in the past. They never collaborated with anyone, only did "a lot of internal kind of stuff." They would like to spend more time but felt "real stretched" already. In addition, the school administrators viewed the university commitment to the partnership as great and well intended but nevertheless only "another thing in addition to what they are doing." They also saw the need to work out how the school and university people could value one another and how they could reallocate the resources and have a joint agenda rather than their own individual agendas.

The schoolteachers and administrators' reaction to the questions regarding the schools' and university's commitment to the partnership was a mixed bag. Most of them believed that the schools and school district had made strong commitment and considerable efforts. They cited as examples the time spent by school district administrators on collaborative activities and support for release time for teachers to participate in inquiry. Six of them also praised the university for its commitment to inquiry and teacher development in schools. They were particularly impressed by the novice teacher involvement and the full-time presence of a clinical faculty/team leader in their school inquiry and change activities. But most of the other schoolteachers and administrators were critical of the university commitment and involvement. They felt that the "university talks the talk but doesn't always walk the walk" and that the "university hasn't made a tremendous commitment." There is a huge gap here between these observations and the views held by the university leaders and faculty and school district administrators about the university's commitment to the partnership. In fact, strong dissatisfaction over the university's role in the partnership is a consistent theme in the responses from the schoolteachers and administrators in this inquiry.

Prospects for the Future

Despite their many different views of the various aspects of collaborative relationships and activities, both the school and university people believed that the partnership had achieved some remarkable success. They felt that the partnership has given them "enormous political credibility; that we are solidly connected with each other." Most important, the partnership enabled the novice teachers to see and experience the intersection between theory and practice as well as changes in schools and in teacher education.

The participants in this inquiry offered many good suggestions for improving and developing the existing school-university partnership. They all articulated strong hopes for the future of the school-university collaboration. The general themes were very positive and great expectations were expressed. Like most other school-university partnerships across the country (see examples in Clark, 1995; Darling-Hammond & McLaughlin, 1995), the collaboration under study has been a difficult but rewarding path for most of its participants.

The university administrators would like to see the partnership move beyond the structural relationships into the more substantive reform issues—the implications of the social justice agenda for the curriculum, the classrooms, and the novice teachers. They hoped to become more comfortable with the school people, more at ease with the rocks in the road, and more forgiving of missteps. Furthermore, they wanted to try to create clinical faculty titles for members of the partnership so as to regularize the intellectual relationship between professionals in the schools and the university. They intended to encourage the faculty who are involved in the partnership to challenge themselves to stand up and say, "This is what I am doing and this is where I am doing it." All of this calls for a fundamental restructuring of the reward and promotion system and a change in the culture of the university.

The school district administrators also wanted the partnership to move beyond its present form to involve more schools and more people in the collaborative activities. Currently, the nonpartnership schools have no benefits coming out of the partnership. The school district administrators would like to become more proactive in the planning of all the components in the partnership. Most of all, they would like to develop joint research agendas and joint sharing of resources with the university.

The clinical faculty and team leaders from the university saw the future of the partnership as evolving into a PDS where schoolteachers and administrators play a significant role in planning and implementing the program. They believed that communication and working together in schools were the keys to the success of school-university partnerships. In addition, they felt that it would be important to have a chief worrier whose major role was to make sure that everyone felt acknowledged and cared about.

Schoolteachers and administrators also believed that communication was the key to improving the collaboration between the schools and the university. Right now, many teachers felt, "There are things the university does and things the school district does and then the stuff we both do." They would like to see more joint work. Improved communication can lead to clearer understanding of shared goals, greater university faculty and schoolteacher involvement, more effective exchange of support for reform, better pairing of novice teachers and mentor teachers, and an eventual blurring of the lines between the university and schools. The schoolteachers demanded that they should be treated more as intellectuals and that the collaboration with the university be institutionalized and long term.

The participants in this partnership have envisioned the creation of a center of pedagogy in the school district, with its own full-time director and secretary and its own budget. Under this center, the schools would become exemplary sites for school reform and teacher education—fertile fields for training teachers, especially for students from diverse backgrounds. In time, the center would develop enough of a critical mass so change would not be frightening or threatening, and teachers would not only react to change but think about and initiate it.

The novice teachers predicted the future of the partnership in terms of the development of the teacher education program and how it would affect the student teachers. They would like to see a more mature and more structured program where the planners know exactly what would happen at the student teaching sites. They wanted the partnership to be more inclusive—to involve more schools, more schoolteachers, more novice teachers, more community members, and more students—and to be beneficial to all involved.

It is evident that the expectations for the future of the partnership under study are extremely high and that there are great potentials for achieving those expectations. Participants from different groups have suggested different changes and the challenge to decision makers now is to select and implement those changes that will truly assist in improving the collaboration. Both the school and the university people want the partnership to move beyond its present structural relationship into the more substantive reform issues on curriculum, on the culture of the school and the university, and on creating a "third space" where the school and university people can work together in a true and equal partnership.

References

Berry, B., & Catoe, S. (1994). Creating professional development schools: Policy and practice in South Carolina's PDS initiative. In L. Darling-Hammond (Ed.), *Professional development schools: Schools for developing a profession* (pp. 176-202). New York: Teachers College Press.

Clark, R. W. (1995). Financing professional development schools. *PDS Network News, 2*(2), 1-4, 7. New York: National Center for Restructuring Education, Schools and Teaching.

Darling-Hammond, L. (Ed.). (1994). *Professional development schools: Schools for developing a profession.* New York: Teachers College Press.

Darling-Hammond, L., & McLaughlin, M. W. (1995). Policies that support professional development in an era of reform. *Phi Delta Kappan, 76*(8), 597-604.

Goodlad, J. (1984). *A place called school.* New York: McGraw-Hill.

Goodlad, J. (1993). School-university partnerships and partner schools. *Educational Policy, 7*(1), 24-39.

Holmes Group. (1990). *Tomorrow's schools: Principles for the design of professional development schools.* East Lansing, MI: Author.

Holmes Group. (1995). *Tomorrow's schools of education: A report of the Holmes Group.* East Lansing: MI: Holmes Group Inc.

Lortie, D. (1975). *School teacher.* Chicago: University of Chicago Press.

Mehaffy, G. L. (1992, February). *Issues in the creation and implementation of a professional development school.* Paper presented at the annual meeting of the American Association of Colleges for Teacher Education (AACTE), San Antonio, TX.

Puget Sound Educational Consortium. (1990). *Assessment of the Puget Sound Educational Consortium.* Seattle: Author.

Shen, J. (1994, April). *A study in contrast: Visions of preservice teacher education in the context of a professional development school.* Paper presented at the annual meeting of the American Educational Research Association (AERA), Chicago.

Su, Z. (1990). *School university partnership: Ideas and experiment (1986-1990)* (Occasional Paper No. 12). Seattle: Center for Educational Renewal, University of Washington.

Su, Z. (1992). Sources of influence in preservice teacher socialization, *Journal of Education for Teaching, 18*(3), 239-258.

Valli, L., Cooper, D., & Frankes, L. (1997). Professional development schools and equity: A critical analysis of rhetoric and research. *Review of Research in Education, 22,* 251-304.

Wiseman, D. L., & Nason, P. L. (1995). The nature of interactions in a field-based teacher education experience. *Action in Teacher Education, 17*(3), 1-12.

Zeichner, K. (1992). Rethinking the practicum in the professional development school partnership. *Journal of Teacher Education, 43*(4), 296-307.

THE TRANSFORMATIVE POTENTIAL OF COLLABORATIVE PARTNERSHIPS: REFLECTIONS

Linda Valli

These three chapters contribute to the growing body of literature on the potential and pitfalls of collaboratives (Dana, 1998). The authors discuss many important themes: shared goals, leadership, problem solving, trust, emerging roles, diversity, achievement, equity, and social justice. Although each of these themes could be used as a comparative-analytic tool, I focus primarily on collaborative partnerships as a mechanism for bridging institutions and as a lever for institutional change. I argue that these chapters add compelling evidence to the argument that universities need to recapture their historic mission of social reform and community activism. Although much work is needed to help schools become centers of inquiry and true learning communities, I focus most of my remarks on implications for universities.

Analysis of the Chapters

The Houston Consortium was established to create a better fit between the teacher education programs located in four area universities and the Houston area schools. As the authors of Chapter 1 tell us, "Traditional teacher preparation programs have not been designed to produce teachers who are effective in the culturally diverse and economically challenging environments that characterize Houston's urban schools." The consortium designed a "systemic program" to bridge this cultural divide. Over 1,000 educators helped design the program, which attended to organizational structures, programmatic issues, and outcome measures.

The existence of the consortium itself indicates a sea change in the way higher education and school systems typically relate. Scattered throughout Chapter 1 are hints of this transformation. First, the four universities, three school districts, and two educational agencies created a new interagency organization to conduct business. The consortium was not "owned" by a university, a school system, or a state department of education. It was its own entity, guided by a policy council. The organizational structure, therefore, was flat—egalitarian rather than hierarchical. No one group was structurally dominant. Second, a "critical mass" of educators are involved. Over 200 helped develop program characteristics; over 1,000 participated in program design and implementation processes; more than a dozen schools were selected as PDSs on the basis of commitment.

A third hint of the cultural transformation is the reciprocity in staffing. Each school has designated a university and school district employee who devotes one-quarter time to PDS efforts to ensure coordination, work with prospective teachers, engage in professional development activities, and evaluate the program. Fourth, technology (the Serial Line Internet Protocol) was established to facilitate communication among the PDS sites. And fifth, consortium members established mutually shared goals, which they then assessed to guide future efforts. These were all important structural decisions that helped institutionalize the consortium.

The collaborative work described in Chapter 2 is also part of a consortium (the Michigan PDS Consortium), in which the four authors have leadership roles. But this chapter highlights individual rather than institutional transformation. What happens to the people who attempt to bridge the school-university divide? Basing their analysis on "critical incident journaling research," the PDS coordinator/authors give us a glimpse of their work, their accomplishments, and their professional dilemmas.

Although the chapter does not further illuminate organizational features of the collaborative, it serves as a compelling complement to the
previous chapter. Here we see not structure, but agency: Four individuals
working hard to be dream keepers, weavers, and shape-shifters. These
authors add the missing component to Chapter 1. Consortia do not emerge
from thin air. Nor are they sustained solely by written goals, bylaws, and
evaluations. They require the daily renewed commitment of teacher educators who believe in the possibilities of and have the skills to build bridges
and transform cultures. Institutionalization will not happen—and cannot
be sustained—without individual and institutionalized commitment. We
do not know if the Houston Consortium—or all consortia—need dream
keepers, weavers, and shape-shifters. But these metaphors provide a
powerful lens for the types of roles filled by that small but growing cadre
of teacher educators whose jobs require them to spend time in two distinct
institutional worlds and to bridge the gap between them.

As dream keepers, the authors of Chapter 2 "serve a role of helping
people keep the vision." They build trust, create collaborative governance,
reallocate time for professional development, and keep the focus on student learning. As weavers, they work with other members of the reform
teams to integrate initiatives and become "moving bicultural bridges"
between universities and school systems. As shape-shifters, they "assume
new roles and forms of contributing . . . as the situations demand." These
new professional personas require a different kind of teacher educator—
one who understands organizational development, systems thinking,
finance, leadership, policy, and evaluation.

These roles, however, are a far stretch for most subject matter and
pedagogical experts. Why would anyone want to undertake these roles,
especially when reward and incentive structures are nonsupportive
(Goodlad, 1990; Valli, Cooper, & Frankes, 1997)? Unfortunately, a typical
university response is to staff PDS coordinator positions with adjunct
clinical faculty. I say unfortunately not because these individuals lack the
talent to do the work but because these roles have second-class status in
the university. Goodlad (1990) refers to these positions as "shadow faculty." He writes that few distinguished professors of education are

> found among the ranks of those who conduct teacher education
> programs: the shadow faculty of adjunct, temporary, part-time
> personnel who teach the courses required for certification but who

have little or no say about the conduct and well-being of the enterprise. It is the members of this shadow faculty who are best known
to the future teachers on the campuses of major universities. (p. 187)

Staffing PDSs with clinical faculty is a clear sign that PDS collaboratives
are viewed as marginal to university goals and culture. This marginal
relationship and resistance to change is not lost on school-based PDS
participants. Even though PDSs are supposed to focus on the simultaneous
renewal of school and university, this often occurs only at the level of
rhetoric (Valli et al., 1997).

In Chapter 3, Zhixin Su presents the candid perspectives of participants in the Comprehensive Urban Teacher Education Institute (CUTEI).
As we have seen in other PDS studies (Shen, 1994), positionality often
influences perspective. Despite a "long history of collaboration"; "enormous
goodwill"; and principles, goals, and programmatic structures such as
faculty "in residence," site-based courses, and mutually constructed case
studies, the partnership faltered. These bridges were not strong enough to
cross the cultural divide between schools and universities. Interview data
indicated that aims, purposes, and core ideas such as "social justice education" were not widely shared. The university was seen as detached from
real school issues, unwilling to engage in authentic research, and lacking
in commitment to the partnership. Inquiry activities were viewed by half
the teachers and administrators as "frustrating and nonproductive."

This is not to say that the CUTEI was necessarily a less successful
collaborative than the consortia described in the other two chapters.
Comparisons are impossible when program goals, research questions,
data sources, and authors differ. We do know, however, that the CUTEI
lacked a formal governing body and staff, that the steering committee
stopped meeting, and that many university-based clinical faculty, PreK-12
teachers, and novice teachers felt excluded from the decision making
process. But despite these stumbling blocks, participants were hopeful for
the future and talked about a structural "'third space,' where school and
university personnel can work together in a true and equal partnership"—
an idea reminiscent of the Houston and Michigan consortia.

Discussion

Few educators would say that the "fire, fire, fire" and "ready, ready,
ready" cultures described by Fullan in the introductory Overview of these

chapters are productive and healthy. But do we have any evidence from these three chapters that collaboratives can be transformative cultural levers? The evidence is stronger for schools and for individuals than it is for universities. Those who work in collaboratives—especially formal consortia—seem to develop different professional personas. And when they are functioning well, collaboratives seem to have a positive impact even on schools in such "economically challenging environments" as Houston. But because PDSs are situated in schools, not universities, the potential for cultural transformation is greater in the schools. There is no similar lever for institutional change in university culture. Only those university-based teacher educators who go out from their home institutions experience the role transformation. But that is at the individual level. Collectively, these three chapters provide little evidence of cultural change in universities. We see few signs of the involvement of a "critical mass" of tenured faculty needed to effect cultural change. Analyses of other collaborative efforts indicate the same (Valli et al., 1997).

Although many of us who work at universities, including myself, think and write about the value of reflection, it might be time to reexamine the historic role of the university. I am reminded of a collegial conversation I was part of a few years ago. I was helping to write a job description for a social foundations faculty position. A conversation arose at a search committee meeting over the wording of the announcement. The statement was something like, "The successful candidate generates rigorous and complex questions that illuminate pathways to educational reform." That one sentence led to an inquiry into the nature of the university: Is it an institution the aim of which is to generate knowledge, period? Or is it an institution where those engaged in knowledge production have a direct interest and involvement in social change? Do we merely produce knowledge for *others* to ignore, refute, transform, or use? Or do we produce knowledge for the expressed purpose of civic action and social transformation?

At a historic first joint forum of the U.S. Department of Education and the U.S. Department of Housing and Urban Development, Ira Harkavy (1998) was asked to present a scholarly paper on this very debate. As a historian and academic administrator at the University of Pennsylvania, Harkavy traced the link between community building and educational reform to John Dewey's writings on the school and society. Asking rhetorically why universities should adopt collaboration with schools and communities as a categorical imperative, Harkavy answers, "Because they will be better able to fulfill their primary mission of advancing and transmitting knowledge for a democratic society" (p. 5). What distinguished the U.S. university from the start from its European counterparts, Harkavy said, was the bold claim that the university existed, not for "the life of the mind," but for democracy itself. Cities, especially blighted urban areas, were seen as sites for both study and action.

Although this vision "failed to become the dominant model for the American university" (Harkavy, 1998, p. 15), it remains a legacy to inspire new urban partnerships. With universities lacking such an institutional mission, guiding policies, role requirements, and incentives and reward structures, I have great difficulty envisioning adequate numbers of powerful, sustainable partnerships needed to tackle the problems of urban schools and urban communities. Harkavy's summary of the history of the American university makes me question the way we traditionally, but schizophrenically, partition the mission of the university into the three disconnected arenas of teaching, research, and service. Although academics sometimes offer perfunctory arguments about the complementarity of teaching and research, Harkavy's construction urges us to seriously rethink the division we have institutionalized between research and service—a division so great that some universities have special rewards for those who actually manage to integrate their work.

Conclusion

The successes and problems described in these three chapters are powerful reminders of the need for transformed cultures if PDSs and school-university partnerships are to become more than individualized initiatives by people of goodwill. University policies, rewards, and incentives must be used to effect the normative and cultural changes needed to encourage and enable faculty to deal with real problems of urban schools and urban teachers. Without such transformed cultures, there is little basis of hope for enduring partnerships with the capacity to accomplish what none of us can do alone.

References

Dana, N. F. (1998). School-university collaboration and career-long professional development: Overview and framework. In D. J. McIntyre & D. Byrd (Eds.),

    Strategies for career-long teacher education (Teacher Education Yearbook VI, pp. 61-68). Thousand Oakes, CA: Corwin.

Goodlad, J. (1990). Better teachers for our nation's schools. *Phi Delta Kappan, 72*(3), 185-194.

Harkavy, I. (1998, January). *School-community-university partnerships: Their value in linking community building and education reform.* Paper presented to Conference on Connecting Community Building and Education Reform: Effective School, Community, University Partnerships, Joint Forum of the U.S. Department of Education and the U.S. Department of Housing and Urban Development, Washington, DC.

Shen, J. (1994, March). *A study in contrast: Visions of preservice teacher education in the context of a professional development school.* Paper presented at the Annual Meeting of the American Educational Research Association, Chicago.

Valli, L., Cooper, D., & Frankes, L. (1997). Professional development schools and equity: A critical analysis of rhetoric and research. *Review of Research in Education, 22,* 251-304.

CONTEXTS FOR PROFESSIONAL DEVELOPMENT SCHOOLS: OVERVIEW AND FRAMEWORK

Ann Larson

Sheryl Benson

Ann Larson is Assistant Professor in the Department of Secondary Education at the University of Louisville. She received her PhD in the Department of Curriculum and Instruction at the University of Illinois at Urbana-Champaign. Her current research areas and interests include preservice and in-service teacher education, technology and teacher education, social foundations of education, and English education. She has published in *Educational Foundations* and *Action in Teacher Education.* She is a former middle and high school teacher and is currently Professional Development School Liaison in the secondary MAT program with the University of Louisville and Fairdale High School in Louisville, Kentucky.

Sheryl Benson is Associate Professor and Director of Clinical Experiences at the University of Illinois at Urbana-Champaign in the Department of Curriculum and Instruction. Her current research areas and interests include supervision of preservice teachers, the role of cooperating teachers as teacher educators, and challenges preservice teachers experience in field settings. For 9 years, she has been Director of the Year-Long Project, a collaborative, elementary teacher education program that now includes three school districts. For 3 years, she has coordinated a secondary collaborative teacher education program in five school districts. She is a former elementary and middle school teacher, a past state president of the Illinois Association of Teacher Educators, and for 16 years an active member of the Association of Teacher Educators.

Overview

The chapters in this division of the yearbook address various critical issues related to professional development schools (PDS). The authors for each chapter present research from different PDS contexts. The research studies presented are situated in three distinct settings: in a West Coast urban elementary school, in a Gulf Coast large independent school district in secondary schools, and in a Midwest suburban elementary school district. In Chapter 4, Lewison and Holliday discuss the importance of communication among members in a university-school partnership and examine contexts of partnerships from the perspective of power relationships in one site. In Chapter 5, Boudah and Knight explore the application of a model of Participatory Research and Development (PR&D) as a means of integrating research and practice by linking historically separate communities of university research and teacher practice as one learning community. In Chapter 6, Redemer and Nourie examine stages of personal concerns in a developmental change process of experienced teachers and student teachers adapting to a PDS innovation. We discuss the unique contributions of each chapter in the summary following the chapters. Here, we present a brief overview that we believe may be helpful to situate the findings and implications for the chapters in a larger framework of historical and current contexts for PDSs.

Framework

Early Visions for Professional Development Schools

Historically, partnerships between PreK-12 schools and universities have been called a variety of names by different professional groups. The most recognized name that has emerged for such a partnership is *professional development school* (PDS), a phrase that originated in the work of the Holmes Group (1986) in *Tomorrow's Teachers.* In the Holmes Group proposal, a PDS

> would provide superior opportunities for teachers and administrators to influence the development of their profession, and for university faculty to increase the professional relevance of their work, through (1) mutual deliberation on problems with student learning, and their possible solutions; (2) shared teaching in the university and schools; (3) collaborative research on the problems of educational practice; and (4) cooperative supervision of prospective teachers and administrators. (p. 56)

In 1990, the Holmes Group expanded on the concept of professional development schools in *Tomorrow's Schools,* making more explicit the importance of providing professional development for novice and experienced teachers and developing research about teaching.

Early visions for professional development schools were influenced by the medical profession's teaching hospitals, in which those who are in training are placed with those providing medical service and care in authentic contexts, working alongside of and interacting with medical researchers. These roles and relationships, in a "real-world" culture, the teaching hospital became an early model for the creation of PDSs.

PDSs have been initiated and created in a variety of configurations, in various settings, and have existed for many years. In a nutshell, the attempts at successful partnerships between PreK-12 schools and colleges and departments of education include efforts that bring professionals together in a school setting to share responsibility for the preparation of new teachers, the professional development of experienced classroom teachers, the professional development of university faculty serving as teacher educators, the support of research directed at improvement of practice, and enhanced student learning.

In a seminal chapter on PDSs in the *Handbook of Research on Teacher Education*, Book (1996) describes how the Ford Foundation provided program support to create teacher education's equivalent of medicine's teaching hospitals, which, in collaboration with colleges and schools of education, would train new teachers, focus on the instruction of students, and engage teachers in improving their own practice. Like the Carnegie Forum (1986), the Ford Foundation referred to the sites in which school and university collaboration occurred as "clinical schools." Similarly, the RAND Corporation (Wise & Darling-Hammond, 1987) called for "induction schools" in which prospective teachers would fill internships. These schools were envisioned as places in which research about teaching practices would be conducted by teachers, teacher educators, and researchers in a collaborative mode. The American Federation of Teachers Task Force on Professional Practice Schools (Levine, 1992) identified what "professional practice schools" might look like. This vision included support for student learning, professional practice, professional education of teachers, and inquiry directed at the improvement of practice. The Puget Sound Educational Consortium first referred to schools in which reform of teaching and learning, teacher education, and school organization would occur as professional development centers and later as partner schools (Goodlad, 1993).

Whatever the name, the concept of these schools has remained relatively constant (Book, 1996): (a) to improve the quality of instruction for PreK-12 students, the preparation of prospective teachers, and the continuing education of professional educators; (b) to provide a research base that informs the teaching profession; and (c) to encourage the school to undergo a structural reform that allows for the collaboration between school and university faculty and supports changes in teaching and learning. Another important goal, then, of a PDS is that school- and university-based faculty serving in these contexts develop exemplary practices, demonstrate these practices, and support a culture in which exemplary practice and new knowledge gained are nurtured and sustained.

Current Visions for PDSs and Educational Reform

Attention to the importance of PDS partnerships in simultaneously improving schools and teacher education has increased (Levine & Trachtman,

1997; Darling-Hammond, 1994). The second printing of *Standards, Procedures and Policies for the Accreditation of Professional Education Units* by the National Council for Accreditation of Teacher Education (NCATE, 1997b) defines a PDS as a specially designed school in which school and higher education faculty collaborate to (a) provide student teaching and internship experiences, and (b) support and enable the professional development of teachers in the school and higher education faculty. Faculty also have joint responsibility for the provision of high-quality instruction to the school's primary clientele—students (p. 75). Definitions of PDSs vary, but a consensus definition appears to have emerged in the last 2 years:

> collaborations between schools and colleges or universities (and sometimes community agencies) focusing on high quality education for diverse students, the preparation of preservice educators and other school-based personnel including administrators, nurses, social workers; continued professional development of experienced educators and related personnel at school and college; and continuous inquiry into improving practice. These activities are guided by reciprocity and parity and by commitments to shared beliefs about teaching and learning and issues of equity. (Teitel, 1998)

Frankes, Valli, and Cooper (1998) conducted and presented a comprehensive review of the literature on PDSs. In it, they describe the many challenges and obstacles PDSs face. They identify these as intensification of work demands, difficulties in leveling traditional hierarchical relationships, and involvement of small numbers of school and university faculties. They contend that these present critical challenges to the creation of a "truly new institution. Although it shows great promise, the PDS will be difficult to sustain unless these challenges are addressed" (p. 80).

It appears to us that there is some emerging, much needed, and hopeful response to these challenges. One significant response is taking shape in the form of standards that include critical attributes to guide the development of PDSs. We believe that challenges and obstacles typically experienced in some PDSs may be minimized or overcome if quality attainment—a level articulated in one set of standards—is achieved. One potential for these standards is that they may be viewed as tangible and implementable because they are based on sound theory and research *and* on models of PDSs that "work." As quality attainment is sought and eventually realized, Whitford's (1994) points about the relationship of reform and professional development schools support this quest: "As school and university educators attempt fundamental change, the prevailing pattern of rules, roles, and relationships inside each organization is . . . challenged. If such changes are institutionalized beyond the current experimental stages, the cultures of both will be altered to include more perspectives" (p. 93).

One of the key educational reforms that has evolved over approximately 15 years is a focus on sets of standards that have helped to focus the agenda of teacher education and teaching practice on what teachers need to know and be able to do. These sets of standards have contributed to the development of new ways to assess teacher knowledge and practice, specifically through performance assessment (Diez, 1998). The importance and role of standards designed and disseminated by three governing bodies for teacher education are particularly helpful in thinking about the connections of these standards to the current structures, roles, and relationships of the work in PDSs. These organizations are the National Council for Accreditation of Teacher Education (NCATE), the Interstate New Teacher Assessment and Support Consortium (INTASC), and the National Board for Professional Teaching Standards (NBPTS).

In the 1980s, NCATE undertook a redesign of the "knowledge base" of teaching with the goal of supporting the recognition of teaching as a profession. NCATE has more recently used the term *conceptual framework* to recognize the integration of knowledge and practice in the design of well-planned programs to develop and assess individual teacher education candidates. In *Changing the Practice of Teacher Education: Standards and Assessment as a Lever for Change* (1998), Diez describes how NCATE currently focuses on ensuring that teacher preparation institutions have the structure and process in place to promote and ensure the development of individual candidates, how states have become increasingly interested in performance-based licensure, and how NCATE expectations have been increasingly clear in the expectation that teacher preparation programs assess candidates using alternative forms of assessment and multiple methods across the program. Performance-based assessment of preservice teachers teaching in authentic classroom settings is one example of an alternative form of assessment.

Formed in the 1980s following Lee Shulman's work for NBPTS, INTASC is now a consortium of more than 30 states. INTASC took on the task of developing board-compatible standards for initial licensure in 1990, publishing draft standards in 1992 and continuing to move forward with a testing/assessment framework that can be adopted by states for basic skills testing, as well as assessment of content and pedagogical knowledge to determine readiness for teaching and to evaluate teaching practice during an induction or internship year (Diez, 1998).

NBPTS grew out of a proposal in *A Nation Prepared: Teachers for the 21st Century* (Carnegie Forum on Education and the Economy, 1986), again to support the professionalization of teaching. Diez (1998) describes five propositions for a vision of teaching that the board developed into standards—for subject areas and the developmental levels of learners—in relationship to 36 certificate areas.

What Matters Most: Teaching for America's Future (National Commission on Teaching and America's Future, 1996) uses the metaphor of a "three-legged stool of teacher quality" to describe accreditation, licensing, and certification. These three areas—in addition to the teacher education policy of states, expectations for teachers in content area associations, and standards and assessment—have emerged as potentially powerful reform initiatives. Diez (1998) reminds us that the success of teacher education reform depends on conceptual principles and frameworks to guide reform, attention to local conditions and cultures, and ongoing reflection to learn from the process even as it is taking place (p. 1). Current and well-grounded visions of teacher education reform include a PDS model that is guided by principles rather than procedural or structural detail and adapted through experience and ongoing reflection and dialogue about that experience. Additionally, a PDS model has implications for educational reform that extend beyond a typically defined context of teacher education. NCATE is currently developing a set of standards that describe expectations for the educational reform and professionalization of teacher education that occur in a PDS model. This model reflects best practices by teachers; new conceptualizations of rules, roles, and relationships; and applications of a more ecological approach to PDS vision, as distinct from some of the more technical, structural, and detail-oriented ones that can cause university and school relationships to encounter friction or, worse, to separate or divorce (Teitel, 1998).

Standards for PDSs

The NCATE (1997a) Professional Development Schools Standards Project includes a set of standards for identifying and supporting high-quality PDSs. This project reflects a current educational trend that uses sets of standards to focus the agenda of teacher education and teaching practice on what teachers need to know and be able to do. As reflected in these standards, PDSs include a vision of teaching as professional practice that is learning centered, knowledge based, collegial, and inquiry oriented. The NCATE Professional Development Schools Standards call for theory and practice and content and pedagogy to be symbiotic and kaleidoscopic. Through collaboration of schools and universities, "new roles and relationships for university and school faculty members" help create a "hybrid institution much like the teaching hospital" (NCATE, 1997a). The PDS standards project (see http://www.ncate.org/projects/pds/draftsta.txt) was created to ensure that PDSs "have the kind of leverage they are intended to have and to assist in their creation by providing necessary guidelines which reinforce principles and commitments" (NCATE, 1997a). Research on successful or high-quality models of PDSs informs us that these principles and commitments are essential.

Three important features of the PDS standards have implications for reflecting on this set of chapters. The standards recognize three levels of developmental stages in organizing, implementing, and sustaining high-quality PDSs: prethreshold, threshold, and quality attainment. We now briefly describe each of these stages. In our overall summary following the three chapters, we refer to and interpret relationships of the levels of developmental stages for PDSs as these connect to the research, findings, and implications of the chapter authors.

In the *prethreshold stage*, individuals build relationships, mutual values, and understandings, and early collaboration between school and university teachers takes shape. In the *threshold stage*, conditions are established in which there is an agreement that commits the school, school district, union or professional association, and the university to the basic mission of the PDS; a commitment by the partners to the critical attributes of a PDS; a positive working relationship and a basis of trust between partners; the achievement of quality standards by partner institutions as evidenced by regional, state, national, or other reviews; and an institutional commitment of resources to the PDS from the school and the university. In the prethreshold and threshold stages, the standards document does not articulate a set of standards per se but describes characteristics of PDSs that reflect these stages (NCATE, 1997a).

In the third and highest stage, *quality attainment*, a defined set of standards is articulated. Critical attributes that include subsets of critical indicators are described. The quality standards in Stage 3 represent five essential and critical attributes:

1. *Learning Community.* The PDS is a learning-centered community, characterized by norms and practices that support adult and children's learning.

2. *Collaboration.* The PDS is characterized by joint work between and among school and university faculty directed at implementing the mission. Responsibility for learning is shared; research is jointly defined and implemented; all participants share expertise in the interests of children's and adults' learning.

3. *Accountability and Quality Assurance.* The PDS is accountable to the public and to the profession for upholding professional standards for teaching and learning and for preparing new teachers in accordance with these standards.

4. *Organization, Roles, and Structures.* The PDS uses processes and allocates resources and time to systematize the continuous improvement of learning to teach, teaching, learning, and organizational life.

5. *Equity.* The PDS is characterized by norms and practices that support equity and learning by all students and adults. (NCATE, 1997a)

We view these five essential and critical attributes as reflective of the complex interactions of individuals in contexts of PDSs. We suggest that these layers of contexts affect teacher thinking, teacher practice, and the ways in which practice is constructed in PDS settings. The three chapters that follow reflect some of these contexts: a climate for risk taking, participation in and connections among professional communities, administrative support, and new definitions of professional roles and relationships.

Summary

As you read the following three chapters, we believe it may be helpful to keep in mind the various definitions and histories of professional development schools as a framework and begin to identify stages of professional schools development as described in the studies. At the conclusion of the chapters, we identify some common threads that contribute to current understandings of PDSs and connect these to knowledge of how high-quality PDSs contribute to overall educational reform.

References

Book, C. (1996). Professional development schools. In J. Sikula, T. Buttery, & E. Guyton (Eds.), *Handbook of research on teacher education* (pp. 194-210). New York: Macmillan.

Carnegie Forum on Education and the Economy. (1986, May). *A nation prepared: Teachers for the 21st century.* New York: Author.

Darling-Hammond, L. (Ed.). (1994). *Professional development schools: Schools for developing a profession.* New York: Teachers College Press.

Diez, M. (Ed.). 1998. *Changing the practice of teacher education: Standards and assessment as a lever for change.* Washington, DC: AACTE Publications.

Frankes, L., Valli, L., & Cooper, D. (1998). Continuous learning for all adults in the professional development school: A review of the research. In J. McIntyre & D. Byrd (Eds.), *Strategies for career-long teacher education* (Teacher Education Yearbook VI, pp. 69-83). Thousand Oaks, CA: Corwin.

Goodlad, J. (1993). School-university partnerships and partner schools. In P. G. Altbach, H. G. Petrie, M. J. Shujaa, & L. Weis (Eds.), *Educational policy: Volume 7, Number 1. Professional development schools* (pp. 24-39). Newbury Park, CA: Corwin.

Holmes Group. (1986). *Tomorrow's teachers.* East Lansing, MI: Author.

Holmes Group. (1990). *Tomorrow's schools.* East Lansing, MI: Author.

Levine, M. (1992). A conceptual framework for professional practice schools. In M. Levin (Ed.), *Professional practice schools: Linking teacher education and school reform* (pp. 8-24). New York: Teachers College Press.

Levine, M., & Trachtman, R. (Eds.). 1997. *Making professional development schools work: Politics, practices, and policy.* New York: Teachers College Press.

National Commission on Teaching and America's Future. (1996). *What matters most: Teaching for America's future.* New York: Author.

National Council for Accreditation of Teacher Education. (1997a). *NCATE professional development schools standards project.* http://www.ncate.org/projects/pds/draftsta.txt

National Council for Accreditation of Teacher Education. (1997b). *Standards, procedures, and policies for the accreditation of professional education units* (2nd printing). Washington, DC: Author.

Teitel, L. (1998). Separations, divorces, and open marriages in professional development school partnerships. *Journal of Teacher Education, 49*(2), 85-96.

Whitford, B. (1994). Permission, persistence, and resistance: Linking high school restructuring with teacher education reform. In L. Darling-Hammond (Ed.), *Professional development schools: Schools for developing a profession* (pp. 74-97). New York: Teachers College Press.

Wise, A., & Darling-Hammond, L. (1987). *Licensing teachers: Design for a teaching profession.* Santa Monica, CA: RAND Corporation.

◫

4   Investigating a School-University Partnership Through the Lenses of Relationship, Self-Determination, Reciprocal Influence, and Expanding Power

Mitzi Lewison

with Sue Holliday

Mitzi Lewison is Assistant Professor of Language Education at Indiana University. Her research interests include school-university partnerships, alternative models of professional development, and encouraging reflection among in-service and preservice teachers. She has recent articles in the *Teacher Education Quarterly* and the *Professional Educator*.

Sue Holliday is Principal in an urban school district in Southern California. Her professional and research interests center around power relationships in school and district settings. She also is exploring strategies for building trust and cohesiveness among a growing teaching staff. Her recent publications include an article in the *Teacher Education Quarterly*.

ABSTRACT

Although school-university partnerships hold the promise of producing significant, mutually beneficial results for both

PreK-12 schools and institutions of higher learning, these collaborative efforts have been characterized by a continuing record of tensions and detrimental outcomes. This investigation builds on prior research conducted over a 6-year period that described the conditions that enabled a 1-year action research study to evolve into a sustainable partnership. In this chapter, the authors (a) explore traditional conceptions of power that are manifest in school-university partnerships; (b) theorize power relationships using a *power-with* orientation; (c) synthesize a framework for analyzing power-with relationships in partnerships; and (d) through this new framework, ascertain which strategies, patterns of interaction, and organizational structures led to the partnership being sustainable over time. Results document the potential of using four power-with lenses in planning, implementing, and analyzing school-university partnerships.

School-university partnerships hold the promise of producing significant, mutually beneficial results for both PreK-12 schools and institutions of higher learning. There have been instances of individual success stories (Lewison & Holliday, 1997; Sandholtz & Merseth, 1992; Starlings & Dybdahl, 1994; Zetlin, Harris, MacLeod, & Watkins, 1992) and one study that examined a number of Association of Teacher Educators' award-winning collaborative programs from 1977 to 1989 (Smith, 1992). But despite the promise, most school-university collaborative efforts have been characterized by a continuing record of tensions, detrimental outcomes, and culture clash (Bracey, 1990; Henderson & Hawthorne, 1995; Laine, Schultz, & Smith, 1994; Little, 1993; Petrie, 1995; Stallings, Wiseman, & Knight, 1995; Sykes, 1990). Through research conducted over the past 6 years, we have come to believe that investigating issues of power and control from multiple perspectives is a way to understand more fully the fine-grain dynamics of school-university partnerships.

Our present work builds on an earlier investigation in which we explored the conditions that enabled a 1-year action research study to evolve into a school-university partnership that lasted for 5 years (Lewison & Holliday, 1997). The partnership grew out of a study conducted during the 1991-1992 school year to investigate a nontraditional model of professional development designed to encourage elementary language arts teachers to adopt a more reflective approach to writing instruction by attending voluntary study group sessions, reading theory-based articles, and keeping professional journals (Lewison, 1994, 1995).

In this study, we (a) explore traditional conceptions of power and how they are often manifest in school-university partnerships; (b) theorize power relationships in partnerships using a *power-with* orientation; (c) synthesize a framework for analyzing power-with relationships in partnerships; and (d) through this new framework, ascertain which strategies, patterns of interaction, and organizational structures led to the partnership being sustainable over time.

Conceptual Framework

School-University Partnerships

Tradition of Problems. The saga of school-university partnerships and collaborations is, at best, a shaky one, in which the position of the university traditionally is privileged in relation to schools (Laine et al., 1994; Little, 1993) and there are "long-standing asymmetries in status, power, and resources" (Little, 1993, p. 9). Bracey (1990, p. 65) notes, "Most people in [PreK-12] school buildings perceive the work of universities as irrelevant" and not useful in their daily professional lives. Researchers traditionally viewed schools as "sources of data" or as "tools to carry out the universities' agenda" (p. 65). This history has prompted calls challenging us to find ways to create "status-equalizing access" so that schools can regularly be involved in interchanges with the scholarly community and gain new knowledge without the establishment of typical top-down relationships (Sykes, 1990).

Instances of Successful Partnerships. A few studies have identified factors that have the potential to lead to successful school-university partnerships. These factors include building trust among members, common goals or focus on a single issue, sharing responsibility, sharing or equalizing power, changing partnership goals, strong commitment to collaboration, ongoing communication among members, and rethinking traditional roles (Lewison

& Holliday, 1997; Smith, 1992; Starlings & Dybdahl, 1994; Zetlin et al., 1992). But despite this recent research that documents key elements for success, one still finds an overriding theme of culture clash permeating much of the literature on school-university collaborative efforts, especially those describing professional development schools (PDSs) (Henderson & Hawthorne, 1995; Petrie, 1995; Stallings et al., 1995).

Customary Roles and Traditions of Power

To understand the difficulties of creating mutually beneficial partnerships, it is useful to examine the customary roles and traditions of power among the various constituent groups of these collaborative efforts.

Teachers. The customary role of teachers has been one of disempowerment, with teachers perceived as "transmitters of knowledge and curriculum" that has been dictated from above (Aronowitz & Giroux, 1993; Barnes, 1975; Lester & Mayher, 1987; Zeichner & Liston, 1987). Aronowitz and Giroux (1993) describe how "many so-called reform efforts still reduce teachers to high-level clerks or specialized technicians" (p. 34). Kreisberg (1992) characterizes teachers as existing in a place of "paradox" in the schools. "Although they are central figures of authority and control in the classroom, in the larger hierarchy of the educational bureaucracy they are remarkably isolated and often strikingly powerless" (p. 9). Labaree (1995), like Kreisberg, notes that teachers "enjoy instructional autonomy, but this is accidental rather than intentional" (p.100) and that teachers' autonomy lacks public legitimacy. Labaree found that many teachers enter into partnerships with universities with the hope of finding allies that can help them deflect administrative control over curriculum and classroom instruction.

Principals. Over the past 20 years, there has been movement away from viewing principals as supervisors or administrators to viewing them as "instructional leaders." As an instructional leader, a principal is expected to know the best forms of instruction and lead his or her teachers to implement these best practices with students (Poplin, 1992). Even though the model of principal-as-instructional-leader may be viewed as a step forward, authority in this model still generates from the top down. The principal decides on best practices and finds ways to have teachers implement these practices in classrooms. Labaree (1995) notes that many principals join into partnerships with universities in an attempt to control teachers and lessen the classroom autonomy that teachers enjoy. But he also points out that from another perspective, principals often feel they are being controlled by superintendents, school boards, or a vocal community. So principals also look to universities as a way to help deflect control from above or from outside of the school.

University Researchers. The power that researchers hold in collaborative efforts with schools generates from two sources: from the researchers' self-perception of their roles, status, and power and from how they are perceived by school personnel. Researchers' power can be amplified when there is an expectation for them to come into schools to help teachers deflect administrative control, to help principals deflect higher administrative or public control, or to help administrators implement district-level reforms. In these situations, researchers are perceived as having inherently more power and expert knowledge than school staffs, district personnel, or the community. Rowan (1984; see Labaree, 1995, p. 97) notes that these powerful outsider perceptions can elevate a university researcher to the role of "shaman," who is expected, in some magical way, to fix troublesome situations or implement reforms in schools.

The Tradition—Power-Over Relationships. The types of relationships illustrated above are described by Kreisberg (1992) as *power-over* relationships. They have the following characteristics: (a) domination or coercion—controlling or imposing one's will or desire on another person or group (Fairclough, 1989; Kreisberg, 1992; (b) power viewed as a quantity—hoarding resources (power, information, property, etc.) perceived as scarce (Bloome, Sheridan, & Street, 1997; Kreisberg, 1992); (c) top-down hierarchies—maintaining organization hierarchies that are traditionally male dominated (Kreisberg, 1992); (d) competition—creating competition and conflict between individuals or groups (Kreisberg, 1992); (e) barriers—creating barriers to communication and human empathy (Kreisberg, 1992); (f) isolation—keeping people who have less power isolated (Kreisberg, 1992); and (g) consent—projecting existing power relationships as legitimate and routine so that those with less power go along with the existing relationships (Fairclough, 1989). In this power-over framework, power is always viewed as negative. To combat the negative influences of power, *resistance* is seen as the traditional way to challenge domination, coercion, and consent.

Reconceptualizing Power Relationships. In his book *Transforming Power— Domination, Empowerment, and Education,* Kreisberg (1992) makes a compelling case for exploring alternate, more collaborative and transforming conceptions of power—*power-with* relationships. Kreisberg's understanding of power-with relationships is grounded in feminist theory. He suggests that for power-with theories to emerge, "We must reexamine our taken-for-granted assumptions about how we should think about and analyze power" (p. 61). He challenges us to "rethink our categories, our frameworks, our underlying assumptions, and ultimately our grand analysis of how power functions" (p. 61). In synthesizing Kreisberg's work, we have developed a framework that consists of four critical dimensions of power-with relationships, how one moves toward these dimensions, and illustrations of each (see Table 4.1).

If individuals, and the groups to which they belong, are moving toward realizing these four dimensions of power-with relationships, there is great potential for creating empowering, synergistic communities in which individuals and social systems mutually create each other. In this scenario, power becomes transformative rather than oppressive, with the potential of transforming inequitable situations into ones that are beneficial for all involved.

Method

Background—School Context

The school-university partnership that is the focus of this study took place at Pine Hill School (fictitious name), an urban elementary school (Grades K-5) in a middle-class neighborhood in Southern California. The school has a population of 700 students with 25% of the school's students speaking a language in addition to, or instead of, English, and 16% demonstrating limited English proficiency. Most of Pine Hill's 25 faculty members have been at the school for their entire teaching careers. The traditions of Forrest School District (fictitious name) kept power and control out of the hands of teachers, and to some extent, principals in the district.[1]

TABLE 4.1 Four Dimensions of a Power-With Framework

Power-With Dimensions	Ways of Moving Toward Power-With	Illustration
Connection, Ongoing Relationships	Moving away from isolation and autonomy toward building relationships that are ongoing and collaborative	Creating opportunities for people who rarely meet or meet only in specific power-bound roles to dialogue regularly in new roles that have the potential for more equal status.
Self-Determination Within a Social Context	Moving away from coercion toward having individual choice and control within the context of a social group	Although people are committed to others in their social settings, they still have an individual voice. Group members are allowed the space to satisfy individual desires without imposing on each other.
Reciprocal Influence	Moving away from hierarchical structures where power emanates from the top toward mutual assertiveness and reciprocity	Instead of decisions being made by relying on authority, they are made through dialogue and debate, where influence and group goals take the place of coercion. Hierarchies and power structures begin to flatten out as each member influences the others.
Expanding Power	Moving away from viewing power as a commodity that is scarce and must be hoarded toward a perception of power as expandable and renewable	Power and decision making are distributed and shared by group members and this "exercise of power elicits further expressions of power from others" (Welch, 1992, p. xi).

SOURCE: Synthesized from Kreisberg (1992).

Participants and Partnership Activities

Participants—Year 1. The participants who volunteered for the original action research study during the 1991-1992 school year were 13 of the 25 faculty members at Pine Hill, the principal, and the researcher. The participating teachers had a wide range of classroom experience. Five of the 13 teachers were "novices," first- or second-year teachers, who taught in Grades K, 1 (2 teachers), 4, and 5. Two were at mid-levels of experience, with 7 and 11 years respectively, who taught in Grades 1 and 5. They were designated "experienced" teachers. Six were "veterans," who had taught from 18 to 33 years and taught in Grades K, 1, 2, 3, 3-4, and special education (K-5). All participants were women.

Goals of Year 1 Participants. In prestudy interviews, teachers articulated two primary reasons for volunteering to be part of the project: (a) increasing collegial contact—sharing ideas with colleagues, working more collaboratively, getting closer to other staff members—and (b) a desire for professional growth—wanting to learn, to be a better teacher, to get new ideas. The principal, who was just beginning her third year at a new school in a new district, felt the project held the possibility of initiating a cultural change at the school by encouraging teachers to reflect on and question their practice, support each other when trying new strategies, and establish a more collegial environment at the school. The researcher was interested in studying reflective practice and professional development in school settings. She wanted to find out if three strategies that had been shown to encourage preservice teachers to become more reflective— participating in discussions or study group meetings, reading and responding to theory-based literature, and keeping professional journals—would be effective with in-service teachers and if in-service teachers, as a result of reflection, would actually make changes in their language arts programs (Lewison, 1994, 1995).

Activities—Year 1. For the first year, 13 teachers, the principal, and the researcher were engaged in three major activities. The first was a study group, which met monthly between January and June 1992 for 60- to 90-minute sessions. The teachers agreed on an overall topic for the meetings— teaching writing. Different aspects of this topic were examined at each meeting, and at the end of each session topics for the next session were negotiated. The second activity was reading theory-based articles. Prior to each study group meeting, the researcher sent the teachers and principal three to seven short, research- or theory-based articles about the particular aspect of teaching writing that the teachers negotiated for the upcoming meeting. The third activity was keeping professional journals. Each month the researcher responded to the teachers' journal entries in dialogue form. The principal and researcher dialogued at least once a week through fax journals starting 6 months before the onset of the partnership and continuing throughout the first year. The principal copied and distributed her journal entries to the teachers each week (Lewison, 1997).

Participants and Activities—Years 2 Through 5. Although the formal university-school partnership dissolved after the first year, it evolved naturally into a new, less formal collaboration over the subsequent 4 years, with all 25 teachers participating at one time or another. During these years, the researcher made visits to the school to meet both formally and informally with study group members, to participate in new study group sessions with different topics and some new members, and to meet with the principal. The principal continued publishing her weekly journal for the staff. The teachers and principal initiated new organizational structures at the school (i.e., grade-level planning groups and cross-grade-level groups to analyze student writings) that enabled the teachers in the original study group to share the knowledge they gained about teaching writing with the rest of the staff. The principal and researcher continued to have informal phone and face-to-face conversations. The participants during this 4-year period varied, depending on the particular activity. (For more details on the activities during Years 2 through 5, see Lewison & Holliday, 1998).

Method of Inquiry

The initial action research study used an inquiry model that can be placed on a continuum between the *traditional qualitative* and *critical narrative* research models. The goal of the traditional qualitative model is to understand teaching and school life in the setting in which it occurs (Bogdan & Biklen, 1982; Clark, 1979; Zumwalt, 1982), with the researcher being the authority who is in control of most aspects of the study (research

questions, data sources, methodologies, data analysis, and written reports). The critical narrative research model seeks to interpret human
experience by focusing on the narratives of teachers and researchers and
to promote caring, connectedness, community, and a just society (Connelly
& Clandinin, 1990). In this model, the researcher collaborates with practitioners on most aspects of the study. Because the range of possible data
sources for these two forms of interpretive inquiry are identical, the
distinctive characteristic of "level of collaboration of informants" is the
most sensitive criterion to use when placing a particular study on the
continuum. This study was closer to the *traditional qualitative* model in the
researcher's level of collaboration with classroom teachers and closer to
the *critical narrative* model with respect to the level of collaboration with
the school principal.

Data Sources

A variety of data sources were used to help understand the multiple
dimensions and power relationships that led to the transformation of the
Pine Hill study into a sustainable school-university partnership. The
sources for the first-year study included pre- and poststudy teacher ques-
tionnaires, pre- and poststudy audiotaped teacher interviews, audiotaped
study group sessions, and journal entries of all members of the partnership. Sources for Years 2 through 5 included audiotaped principal interview, group interview with teachers, journal entries of principal and
researcher, field notes, and school records.

Data Analysis

The data were initially analyzed qualitatively, using inductive, data-
driven methods. A modification of Glaser and Strauss's (1967) Constant
Comparative Method and a variation of a method developed by Holmes
(1989) that employs the concepts of "domains" and "subcategories" as a
way to sort, categorize, label, and organize qualitative data were used.
Data were coded in a line-by-line fashion and conceptually related items
were grouped in domains. The domains were altered (either kept,
dropped, combined with other domains, or transformed in some way) into
subcategories—more consequential patterns and categories. After data
were grouped into subcategories, they were analyzed by the researcher

and principal to identify and understand the significant themes, patterns, and outcomes. Data were then reanalyzed through the lens of the four power-with dimensions—connection/ongoing relationships, self-determination within a social context, reciprocal influence, and expanding power (see Table 4.1).

Findings

By analyzing data from the perspective of understanding power as a transformative, nonfixed, and expanding resource, we identified 13 strategies, patterns of interaction, or organizational structures that, in part, explain the sustainability of the Pine Hill partnership.[2]

We found four strategies that moved members of the partnership away from isolation and autonomy and toward collaboration and trust. The strategies, which supported *connection/ongoing relationships* among the partners were (a) early communication between the researcher and principal, (b) researcher meetings with individual teachers, (c) principal making her journal public, and (d) creating a space for social interaction. Table 4.2 illustrates how each of these strategies was implemented at Pine Hill School.

Two strategies moved members of the partnership away from domination and coercion toward exercising choice, control, and self-direction. These strategies, which supported *self-determination within a social context*, allowed partnership members to satisfy individual desires without imposing on each other. The strategies were (a) voluntary nature of the initial study and ensuing partnership; and (b) building structures for choice, control, and multiple ways of participation. See Table 4.2 for descriptions of these strategies. It should be noted that since half of the staff agreed to participate in the initial study, this probably created a critical mass that had the potential to "overcome resistance and create a momentum that erodes the inertia typical in many schools" (Short, Greer, & Michael, 1991, p. 137).

We identified four strategies or interaction patterns that moved members of the partnership away from relying on hierarchical structures toward mutual assertiveness and reciprocity. In a sense, each member of the group influenced other members of the group. This also meant individuals needed be open to the influence of the group. The first interaction pattern

TABLE 4.2 Strategies, Interaction Patterns, and Organizational Structures That Foster Power-With Relationships

Power-With Dimension	Instances of Moving Toward Power-With	Specific Strategies, Interaction Patterns, Organizational Structures
Connection, Ongoing Relationships	Early communication between the researcher and principal	Informal conversations, sharing and discussing articles, weekly dialogue, fax journal entries about the possibility of collaboration for 6 months prior to the initial study commencing
	Researcher meetings with individual teachers	1-hour interviews at beginning of study including a great deal of informal conversation about topics of mutual interest
	Principal making her journal public	Weekly publication and distribution of parts of principal's journal to all teachers
	Creating a public space for social interaction	Monthly study group meetings provided a forum for teachers talk informally about curriculum and novices began interacting with veteran teachers
Self-Determination Within a Social Context	Voluntary nature of the initial study and ensuing partnership	Participation was voluntary—no coercion
	Building structures for choice, control, and multiple ways of participation	Teachers could participate in study group sessions, read articles, and/or keep professional journals—the option was always open to change the activities they participated in

Reciprocal Influence	Members accommodating other members	Conscious role change by researcher and principal, teachers accommodated the researcher
	Weekly communication	Principal and researcher, principal and new decision-making group of 5 teachers (grade-level representatives), principal's published journal
	Ongoing public talk about teaching and learning	Study groups (Years 1, 3, 4), grade-level planning groups (Years 2-5), cross-grade-level groups examined student writing (Years 4 & 5)
	Researcher continuing interaction with individual teachers	Dialogue journal writing, researcher starts new inquiry based on teacher concerns with problems of keeping journals (see Lewison, 1997)
Expanding Power	Teacher-principal decision-making group	Meets Tuesday mornings before school, makes day-to-day decisions, gives all teachers a say through grade-level representatives (Years 2-5)
	Teachers hire new teachers	Teachers interview and hire new teachers; they take responsibility for new teachers' socialization into the school
	Grade-level teacher meetings during the school day	Teachers have control over meetings; they usually share, plan, and initiate teacher-developed curriculum

that supported *reciprocal influence* among the partners was the way in which members of the partnership accommodated other members. For the teachers to assume more power, the university partner and the principal had to reconceptualize their customary leadership roles in professional development activities. When the study group sessions did not take the reflective tone the researcher had anticipated (the members were extremely polite and didn't challenge each other's ideas) she decided not to push to initiate more critical discourse in the sessions and to honor her commitment to having teachers control study group sessions. The principal discovered it was difficult to give up some of her special privileges of authority. She consciously decided to take a passive role in the study group because she was afraid teachers might place too much value on her contributions.

The teachers also made accommodations. Journal writing was the least valued of the three activities of the partnership in the first year. The teachers knew they could stop writing at any time, and some did—but many teachers continued. They seemed to want to help the university partner out with her research agenda.

In addition to members accommodating other members, three other interaction patterns that supported reciprocal influence among partners were (a) weekly communication, (b) ongoing public talk about teaching and learning, and (c) researcher continuing interaction with individual teachers (see Table 4.2).

Kreisberg (1992) defines reciprocal influence as mutual assertiveness and reciprocity. As a group, we had trouble moving toward this stance. We were certainly able to "hold back" or "accommodate" other members, but had much difficulty moving toward assertiveness. Although this did occur fairly regularly between the principal and researcher, it took a couple of years for it to occur between the principal and a few of the teachers. Some of this had to do with what we perceived as the fragile nature of the partnership in the first year because it was so different from anything that had occurred before at Pine Hill. Also, all members were female and had been teachers in elementary settings where assertiveness was often perceived as being a troublemaker.

Finally, we identified three organizational structures that moved the Pine Hill group away from viewing power as something that is scarce and must be hoarded toward a perception of power as expandable, renewable, and something to be shared. The organizational structures that supported *expanding power* were (a) teacher-principal decision-making group, (b) teachers hiring new teachers, and (c) grade-level teacher meetings during the school day (see Table 4.2). The principal was able to release teachers for 3 days during the school year through School Improvement funding from the state of California.

Implications

By analyzing the Pine Hill school-university partnership through the lens of a power-with framework, we were able to gain a deeper understanding of the intricacies and nuances of the dynamics that supported a 1-year action research study in its evolution toward a sustainable partnership that lasted for 5 years. We now believe that if there is a continuing effort between university and school personnel to move toward (a) connection/ongoing relationships, (b) self-determination within a social context, (c) reciprocal influence, and (d) expanding power, the potential of creating mutually beneficial partnerships greatly increases. It is important for all members, especially the principal, who traditionally possesses the most power at a school site, to rethink customary roles and relationships. By recognizing the transformative potential of a power-with orientation, we create the possibility of moving beyond the traditions of isolation, distrust, and coercion that permeate many school-university partnerships.

At the same time, it is also extremely important for those of us who study these partnerships to pay attention to the more traditional types of power relationships: (a) power-over—situations where there is coercion or domination that restricts freedom, (b) consent—where power is unexamined so that existing power relationships are seen as legitimate, and (c) resistance—where those with seemingly less power challenge the domination imposed by those in power (Lewison & Holliday, 1998). Examining how power relationships are played out from these more traditional conceptions of power can provide important insights for understanding why some partnerships fail or are not working as initially envisioned and it gives partnership members the option of making conscious decisions that will enable them to move toward more fruitful, empowering relationships.

This study has raised many questions, a number of which center on the difficulty the Pine Hill partnership members had in moving toward "mutual assertiveness." What do mutually assertive partnership interactions look like in elementary school settings? How do these inter-actions occur? What are the inter- and intrapersonal dynamics that facili-tate these interactions? How do issues of gender, authority, and culture affect members in adopting an assertive stance?

As we investigate new school-university partnerships, it is important to remember the myriad of difficulties that creating power-with partner-ships entail. It is inevitable that all members will be faced with the ongoing challenge of being confronted by our long-held, socially constructed roles of domination, compliance, or resistance. Since the power-over model is so pervasive, we believe that changing these roles will be a continuing struggle. Bracey (1990) uses the term *dysfunctional* to describe the typical relationships that develop in school-university partnerships when there are continuing problems around issues of power and control. We believe that using a power-with framework as an additional lens for under-standing the power dynamics between schools and universities has the potential of providing ways for university faculty to begin fostering part-nerships that move away from dysfunction toward transformation.

Notes

1. For more details on how curriculum was mandated from the district office, the isolation of teachers, and the privileges of seniority, see Lewison and Holliday (1998).

2. Due to space restrictions, we were unable to include detailed descriptions and analyses of the 13 strategies, patterns of interaction, and organizational structures that were instrumental in leading to the sustainability of the partner-ship. These can be found in Lewison and Holliday (1998).

References

Aronowitz, S., & Giroux, H. A. (1993). *Education still under siege.* Westport, CT: Bergin & Garvey.

Barnes, D. (1975). *From communication to curriculum.* Portsmouth, NH: Heinemann.

Bloome, D., Sheridan, D., & Street, B., (1997). *Literacy, personhood, power, and the everyday lives of "ordinary" people: Research with the Mass-Observation Project.* A version of this manuscript was originally presented at the 13th World Congress of Sociology, Bielefeld, Germany, July 18, 1994, and at the American Educational Research Association, San Francisco, April 1995.

Bogdan, R. C., & Biklen, S. K. (1982). *Qualitative research for education: An introduction to theory and methods.* Boston: Allyn & Bacon.

Bracey, G. W. (1990). Rethinking school and university roles. *Educational Leadership, 49*(8), 65-66.

Clark, C. (1979). Five faces of research on teaching. *Educational Leadership, 37*(1), 29-32.

Connelly, F. M., & Clandinin, D. J. (1990). Stories of experience and narrative inquiry. *Educational Researcher, 19*(5), 2-14.

Fairclough, N. (1989). *Language and power.* New York: Longman.

Glaser, B. G., & Strauss, A. L. (1967). *The discovery of grounded theory.* New York: Aldine.

Henderson, J. G., & Hawthorne, R. D. (1995). The dialectics of creating professional development schools: Reflections on work in progress. In H. G. Petrie (Ed.), *Professionalization, partnership, and power* (pp. 61-76). Albany: State University of New York Press.

Holmes, E. W. (1989, March). *Student to teacher: A naturalistic profile.* Paper presented at the Annual Meeting of the American Educational Research Association, San Francisco. (ERIC Document Reproduction Service No. ED 312 224)

Kreisberg, S. K. (1992). *Transforming power—Domination, empowerment, and education.* New York: State University of New York Press.

Labaree, D. F. (1995). Why do schools cooperate with university-based reforms? In H. G. Petrie (Ed.), *Professionalization, partnership, and power* (pp. 93-109). Albany: State University of New York Press.

Laine, C. H., Schultz, L. M., & Smith, M. L. (1994). Interactions among school and college teachers: Toward recognizing and remaking old patterns. In K. A. Borman & N. P. Greenman (Eds.), *Changing American education: Recapturing the past or inventing the future* (pp. 381-397). New York: State University of New York Press.

Lester, N. B., & Mayher, J. S. (1987). Critical professional inquiry. *English Education, 19*(4), 198-210.

Lewison, M. (1994). *Taking the lead from teachers: Investigating a reflective model of professional development.* Unpublished doctoral dissertation, University of Southern California.

Lewison, M. (1995). Taking the lead from teachers: Seeking a new model of staff development. In J. K. Lemlech (Ed.), *Becoming a professional leader* (76-114). New York: Scholastic.

Lewison, M. (1997). Writing became a chore like the laundry: The problems and potential of using journals to encourage a reflective approach to teaching. *The Professional Educator, 19,*(2), 13-31.

Lewison, M., & Holliday, S. (1997). Control, trust, and rethinking traditional roles: Critical elements in creating a mutually beneficial university-school-partnership. *Teacher Education Quarterly, 24*(1), 105-126.

Lewison, M., & Holliday, S. (1998). *Power-over, power-with, power-shift, and situated power: Understanding the complexities of power relationships in school-university partnerships.* Unpublished manuscript.

Little, J. W. (1993). *Teachers' professional development in a climate of educational reform.* National Center for Restructuring Education, Schools, and Teachers, Teachers College, Columbia University, New York.

Petrie, H. G. (Ed.). (1995). *Professionalization, partnership, and power.* Albany: State University of New York Press.

Poplin, M. S. (1992). The leader's new role: Looking to the growth of teachers. *Educational Leadership, 49*(5), 10-11.

Rowan, B. (1984). Shamanistic rituals in effective schools. *Issues in Education, 2,* 76-87.

Sandholtz, J. H., & Merseth, K. K. (1992). Collaborating teachers in a professional development school: Inducements and contributions. *Journal of Teacher Education, 43*(4), 308-317.

Short, P. M., Greer, J. T., & Michael, R. (1991). Restructuring schools through empowerment: Facilitating the process. *Journal of School Leadership, 1,* 127-139.

Smith, S. D. (1992). Professional partnerships and educational change: Effective collaboration over time. *Journal of Teacher Education, 43*(4), 243-256.

Stallings, J. A., Wiseman, D. L., & Knight, S. L. (1995). Professional development schools: A new generation of school-university programs. In H. G. Petrie (Ed.), *Professionalization, partnership, and power* (pp. 133-144). Albany: State University of New York Press.

Starlings, C., & Dybdahl, C. (1994). Defining common ground: A grass roots model for university-public school collaboration. *Teacher Education and Special Education, 17*(2), 106-116.

Sykes, G. (1990). Fostering teacher professionalism in schools. In R. F. Elmore & Associates (Eds.), *Restructuring schools: The next generation of educational reform* (pp. 59-96). San Francisco: Jossey-Bass.

Welch, S. (1992). Preface. In S. Kreisberg, *Transforming power—Domination, empowerment, and education* (pp. ix-xv). New York: State University of New York Press.

Zeichner, K. M., & Liston, D. P. (1987). Teaching student teachers to reflect. *Harvard Educational Review, 57*(1), 23-48.

Zetlin, A. G., Harris, K., MacLeod, E., & Watkins, A. (1992). The evolution of a university/inner-city school partnership. *Urban Education, 27*(1), 80-90.

Zumwalt, K. K. (1982). Research on teaching: Policy implications for teacher education. In A. Lieberman & W. Mc Laughlin (Eds.), *Policy making in education* (pp. 215-248), Chicago: University of Chicago Press.

5   Creating Learning Communities of
    Research and Practice

Participatory Research and Development

Daniel J. Boudah

Stephanie L. Knight

Daniel J. Boudah is Assistant Professor in the Department of Educational Psychology at Texas A&M University. He specializes in strategy
instruction, collaborative research, and learning disabilities. He is
currently the co-principal investigator of the project described and has
authored a number of journal articles, text chapters, and instructional
materials.

Stephanie L. Knight is Associate Professor in the Department of Educational Psychology at Texas A&M University. She specializes in observational measurement, collaborative research, and learning strategies. She is currently the co-principal investigator of the project
described and has authored a number of journal articles, text chapters,
and instructional materials.

ABSTRACT

Participatory research and development (PR&D) is a means
of integrating research and practice by linking the historically
separate communities of university research and teacher practice as one learning community. PR&D is designed to impact

teacher thinking and instruction and student performance as well as school and university systems and culture. The history of and rationale for PR&D, the characteristics of PR&D, a number of specific activities related to one PR&D model, some of the quantitative and qualitative results from the first year of the project in inclusive high school classes, and a number of implications are presented.

Introduction and Objectives

For educational researchers, the road of innovation development usually winds through the processes of planning, formulating research questions, developing measurement systems, gaining site access and subject consents, collecting data, analyzing and interpreting data, and publishing the findings. For classroom teachers, the path of innovation development is often simply down the hall and back with a suggested idea or activity (Kaestle, 1993). What is too often missing is not only a bridge to link research with practice but an inclusive learning community where innovations are developed, validated, and integrated to improve teacher practice, school systems and culture, and ultimately student performance (Malouf & Schiller, 1995).

There are a number of reasons why bridges linking research and practice have not existed. Researchers have often perceived teachers as untrained in research methodology, possessing negative attitudes toward research, and not utilizing existing research (e.g., Green & Kvidahl, 1989). For their part, teachers have cited the inaccessibility of teacher-friendly research reports, information overload coupled with a lack of reflection time, and the overdependency of researchers on quantifiable data (e.g., Merriam, 1986). Moreover, since teachers are rarely part of the research and development process, but often regarded only as "subjects," many teachers view educational research as simply irrelevant (e.g., Zeichner, 1995).

In this chapter, we summarize the history of and a rationale for participatory research and development (PR&D), describe the characteristics of PR&D, detail a number of methods and activities we have engaged in, highlight some findings from the first year of a project, and identify several implications that are emerging from our efforts.

Theoretical Framework

Participatory Research and Development

Participatory research and development (PR&D) in education has been known as participatory action research (Reason, 1994); collaborative research (Lee, 1993); collaborative inquiry (Sirotnik, 1988); and qualitative experimental research (Pfeiffer, Pasek, & Clark, 1993). PR&D has addressed instructional or other classroom dilemmas through university and teacher-researcher collaboration in targeting problems, collecting data, and analyzing and disseminating results.

In the past decade, interest in teacher research has increased in the United States. Teacher involvement in research, however, is not new (see Noffke, 1997). "Reflective action" was a component of Dewey's Laboratory School in the 1920s (Zeichner, 1983), and teacher research even has been traced to the Roman philosopher Comenius (McFarland, 1990). Teacher-as- researcher models have been established in other countries for some time. For example, in the 1970s in Britain, teachers and university faculty engaged in collaborative research (Stenhouse, 1971, 1975). During that period, John Elliott also initiated the Classroom Action Research Network (CARN) at the University of East Anglia and the Cambridge Institute of Education to support teacher researchers. Subsequently, CARN has facilitated numerous professional development and in-service activities throughout England (Nias, 1991). Teacher research has been adopted and adapted in other European countries as well (e.g., Letiche, Van der Wolf, & Plooj, 1991). The current emphasis on teacher research in the United States, referred to as "systematic and intentional inquiry carried out by teachers" (Cochran-Smith & Lytle, 1990, p. 3), is often embedded in other reform efforts, including site-based management and professional development schools (PDSs).

Key Characteristics of PR&D

PR&D is best characterized by a process that is educationally realistic, collegial, extensive, intensive, and comprehensive. First, PR&D should be situated in authentic problems and settings to ensure that the research process, as well as the innovations tested, are educationally realistic and useful (Fullan, 1991). All inquiry is aimed at relevant problems that teachers face. For teachers and administrators, being educationally realistic also implies providing system and time support. For university researchers, being educationally realistic means responding to the needs and priorities of school educators and contributing adequate time and resources to school-based efforts.

Second, PR&D nurtures collegial efforts among teachers and between teachers and university faculty in the process of integrating research and practice (e.g., Hunsaker & Johnston, 1992). Teachers have ownership in the process and outcomes as they pool their expertise to define classroom challenges, develop specific interventions, collect and analyze data, and provide feedback to their peers.

Third, PR&D requires that research and development activities be implemented over an extensive period of time. Changes in practices occur over time and with ongoing follow-up and collegial support by helpful and knowledgeable people (e.g., Showers, Joyce, & Bennett, 1987). Moreover, by implementing PR&D over several years, learning is recursive for all participants and the longitudinal effects of an intervention can be more readily measured.

Fourth, PR&D is facilitated by specific and intensive support from professional researchers (e.g., a university research team). Researchers can provide specific support by procuring funding for research projects, coaching teachers during intervention design and implementation, and providing training on research methods and analysis.

Finally, PR&D is comprehensive because the processes and innovations are supported by administrators and other stakeholders involved in facilitating change (e.g., Madden, Slavin, Karweit, Dolan, & Wasik, 1993). A comprehensive effort is more likely to develop synergy among participants involved in change that will sustain the change (Covey, 1989). Moreover, by engaging in fieldwork based on mutual trust, cooperation, and the benefit of all stakeholders, the validity of the research is strengthened (e.g., Goodlad & Sirotnik, 1988).

The overall design of this PR&D project employs a scaffolded systems change format to transfer responsibility for the PR&D process from university researchers to teachers and administrators by the end of the 4-year funding period. In Year 1, intensive training and coaching was provided by the university team to participating classroom teachers. In Year 2, university researchers began coaching a cadre of teachers from Year 1 to provide mentoring to a new group of participating teachers. In Year 3, a cadre of teachers from Years 1 and 2 are to provide mentoring to a new group of participating teachers with more limited assistance from the university team. In Year 4, the emphasis of the project will be on evaluation of systems and culture change, longitudinal analysis of data from the first 3 years of the project, systemic planning to shift ownership of the project to the schools, and dissemination of project outcomes to national audiences. The methods described and the results that follow are from the first year of the project.

Methods

Setting and Participants

Teachers, site-based and district administrators, and students with and without mild disabilities from two large urban high schools in the southeastern United States have participated in the project. Eleven teachers voluntarily participated in the first year of the project, six from one high school and five from the other. This group included four English teachers, three social studies/history teachers, two math teachers, one science teacher, and one special education teacher. One was male and 10 were female. Their mean number of years of teaching experience was approximately 15 years. All teachers held bachelor's degrees and one held a master's degree.

A total of 51 students with mild disabilities (MD) (e.g., learning disabilities, behavior disorders) as well as other low-achieving "at-risk" students not identified as disabled (ND) also participated in the study. Others were lost to attrition. Demographic data are summarized in Table 5.1.

Implementing PR&D

The first-year implementation of our PR&D model was divided into three phases: (a) development and implementation of interventions to improve student learning; (b) research design, data collection, analysis and interpretation associated with the intervention; and (c) dissemination of findings.

TABLE 5.1 Student Demographic Data

	MD Students		ND Students	
	Number	*Percent*	*Number*	*Percent*
Gender				
Male	16	66.66	16	59.25
Female	8	33.33	11	40.74
Ethnicity				
Caucasian	17	70.83	16	59.25
African American	2	8.33	4	14.81
Hispanic American	5	20.83	5	18.51
Asian American	0	0	2	7.40

Other Characteristics	*Mean*	*Percent*	*Mean*	*Percent*
Age	16.81		16.77	
Grade Level	9.68		10.77	
Years in Special Education	5.22		N/A	
Free/Reduced Lunch		13.62		N/A
Withdrew From School		0		27.65

TAAS Scores*	Number Passing	Percent Passing	Number Passing	Percent Passing
Reading	6	46.15	9	69.23
Math	7	46.65	15	68.18
Writing	6	46.15	4	80.00

Individualized Assessments**	Mean	SD
Reading Achievement***	89.71	14.62
Math Achievement***	88.88	10.60
Written Lang. Achievement***	86.83	9.34
Full-Scale IQ****	99.13	12.51

NOTES: *Based on the Texas Assessment of Academic Skills.
**All scores are standard scores.
***Based on the Woodcock-Johnson (Revised).
****Based on the Wechsler Intelligence Scale for Children-III.

During the first phase, teachers and university educators discussed the dimensions, processes, benefits, and constraints of PR&D. Next, teachers discussed instructional challenges and selected two areas for research: learning strategies and student motivation and initiative. Third, teachers collected data to confirm or disconfirm that particular challenges existed. Teachers selected a sample of students with and without mild disabilities from their classes and devised typical subject area tasks that required the use of learning strategies. PR&D staff provided teachers with a "think aloud" format and teachers later directed each student from their samples to "think aloud" through a content area task. For example, the English teachers asked each student to read a paragraph and "think aloud" during the process of drawing conclusions.

PR&D staff then provided teachers with a structure for analyzing the data and facilitated the next study group meeting. Teachers worked in content area subgroups (English, social studies, math and science) to analyze and compare findings. Teachers confirmed that learning strategies requiring student motivation was a worthy research focus for PR&D classroom efforts.

During the second phase of PR&D activities, teachers focused on the design, implementation, data collection, and analysis of strategy interventions. First, teachers worked in teams to design instructional units and materials for classroom implementation. At a minimum, teachers met weekly over 2 months. English teachers developed a peer tutoring, cross-age intervention to enable students to find main ideas in text and summarize what they read. Social studies teachers devised a graphic organizer for presenting content and for students to use in note taking. Math and science teachers devised a different note-taking system for students to use during teacher presentation of conceptual information.

Second, teachers participated in study groups to consider the question, "How will we know if our intervention has been successful?" During these discussions with university researchers, teachers learned about quantitative and qualitative research methods and acquired data collection and analysis skills to measure the effects of their interventions.

Third, teachers and university researchers collected classroom baseline data.

Fourth, teachers implemented instructional interventions over a period of 7 to 15 days and received feedback from teacher and university colleagues. During and after the intervention implementation period, university researchers collected observational data on the impact of the intervention on teacher instruction and student performance and created any necessary instructional or material refinements.

The final phase focused on dissemination of Year 1 findings. Teachers formally and informally discussed the processes and findings from PR&D activities with teachers in their schools and recruited additional teachers for the second year of the project. In addition, teachers teamed with university researchers to present papers at regional or national meetings of organizations including the American Educational Research Association and the Council for Exceptional Children.

Research Designs

This project included an experimental (quantitative) design and a naturalistic research design. The experimental design focused on student performance to evaluate the effects of teacher participation in the PR&D process and implementation of strategies. Student engagement rates across and between targeted students with and without disabilities were measured through repeated observation in three conditions: baseline (pre-intervention), intervention (while teachers implemented their interventions), and postintervention (after intervention was formally implemented). Statistical and descriptive data were compiled and analyzed using a multivariate analysis of variance (MANOVA) across four main dependent factors: initiation of engagement, non-strategy-related engagement, strategy-related engagement, and correctness of student engagement responses.

A naturalistic design focused on teacher and administrator attitudes and school culture change, particularly the participants' attitudes toward and satisfaction with the goals, procedures, and outcomes of PR&D.

Data Sources

Experimental Design Data

In the experimental design, target students with and without mild disabilities were observed and behaviors coded related to the four main factors of academic engagement. From February to May, observations were conducted using a variation of an event-recording instrument used by Boudah, Schumaker, and Deshler (1997). Observers were trained in the use of the instrument until they met minimum reliability standards.

For baseline data, teachers were asked to conduct "typical" lessons with their students and were observed for 3 days. During active intervention, teachers were observed at least three times while teaching or implementing their strategy interventions. Teachers were also observed for 3 days following the period of active implementation to determine the degree of generalized change in behaviors.

In addition, teachers collected pre- and posttests of specific unit material and written samples of students' assignments. Attendance records were also compiled.

Naturalistic Design Data

Data were collected that included transcripts from individual interviews and study group conversations, teacher written notes, and participant observations in classrooms. Teacher interviews were conducted during the implementation period to determine teachers' reactions to the intervention, perceptions of the research process, and reflections on what they had learned. Structured interviews were conducted with three administrators as well, using a protocol developed by the project staff.

Over the course of the project year, university project team members also recorded their perceptions, insights, and ideas with regard to the project. Notes were recorded in the minutes of staff planning and debriefing meetings, at project staff retreats, in meetings facilitated by a project consultant, and in the researchers' written logs.

All qualitative data were analyzed by an outside consultant using methods of naturalistic inquiry (Lincoln & Guba, 1985).

Results

Experimental Design Results

In comparing the differences in rates of engagement between targeted students with and without disabilities in the three experimental conditions, there were interaction effects related to voluntary engagement

[$F(2,64) = 7.474$, $p < .001$], non-strategy-related engagements [$F(2,64) = 5.235$, $p < .006$], and correctness of student engagement responses [$F(2,64) = 8.785$, $p < .000$]. Interaction effects did not exist for differences on the strategy-related engagement variable.

For all students across the three experimental conditions (main effects), there was a statistically significant difference in total number of engagements between baseline and intervention conditions, favoring the intervention condition [$F(1,64)=5.51$, $p<.022$]. There were no statistically significant differences between total engagements in baseline and postintervention conditions; thus the rate did not maintain an increase over baseline.

Voluntary (student-initiated) engagement was of particular interest, since changes favoring the intervention condition would suggest active engagement in academic learning. There was a statistically significant difference in the number of voluntary engagements between baseline and intervention conditions, favoring the intervention condition [$F(1,64) = 4.05$, $p < .048$]. There were no statistically significant differences between voluntary engagements in baseline and postintervention conditions; thus the rate did not maintain an increase over baseline.

Differences were expected in strategy-related engagements and, indeed, there were statistically significant differences favoring the intervention over baseline condition [$F(1,64)=88.63$, $p<.000$] as well as the postintervention condition over baseline [$F(1,64)=14.62$, $p<.000$]. Regarding non-strategy-related engagement, there was a statistically significant difference between baseline and intervention conditions, favoring the intervention condition [$F(1,64)=11.79$, $p<.001$]. There were no statistically significant differences between non-strategy-related engagements in baseline and postintervention conditions; thus the rate did not maintain an increase over baseline. Finally, regarding the correctness of student responses in engagements, there were no statistically significant differences between baseline and intervention or between baseline and postintervention conditions; thus the rate of correct responses did not increase over baseline.

Thus, for condition main effects, rates of different types of engagement improved in intervention, but most rates did not maintain statistically higher means in postintervention.

In comparing differences between students with and without disabilities (main effects), there were no significant differences on any of the four factors of interest. But in looking at the descriptive data (see Table 5.2), the

TABLE 5.2 Mean Number of Types of Engagement per Class Observation of MD and ND Students

| | MD Students | | | ND Students | | |
| | Experimental Condition | | | Experimental Condition | | |
Type of Engagement	Baseline	Intervention	Post	Baseline	Intervention	Post
Voluntary	3.33 (4.32)	2.27 (2.69)	1.29 (1.58)	1.55 (2.86)	2.85 (3.59)	2.17 (2.69)
Called upon	1.15 (1.50)	1.24 (1.26)	1.00 (1.28)	1.21 (2.17)	1.48 (1.72)	1.54 (2.00)
Individual attention	0.61 (0.88)	0.48 (0.82)	0.78 (1.13)	0.56 (1.27)	0.62 (1.29)	0.54 (1.19)
Strategy	0.02 (0.14)	1.20 (1.69)	0.20 (0.51)	0.03 (0.32)	2.39 (2.91)	0.46 (1.13)
Non-strategy	5.07 (4.30)	3.21 (2.77)	3.32 (3.00)	2.82 (3.40)	3.11 (3.47)	3.75 (3.49)
Knowledge recall	1.00 (1.74)	0.44 (1.24)	0.51 (0.68)	0.33 (0.83)	0.46 (0.88)	0.90 (1.63)
Raise question	1.31 (1.71)	0.68 (0.99)	1.00 (1.41)	0.69 (1.23)	0.81 (1.29)	0.85 (1.49)
Clarify	0.24 (1.01)	0.05 (0.27)	0.12 (0.40)	0.10 (0.40)	0.05 (0.24)	0.12 (0.56)
Incorrect	0.15 (0.45)	0.06 (0.24)	0.07 (0.35)	0.07 (0.34)	0.10 (0.36)	0.10 (0.32)
Partially correct	0.35 (0.87)	0.30 (0.93)	0.22 (0.42)	0.06 (0.27)	0.15 (0.54)	0.18 (0.43)
Correct	0.76 (1.44)	0.50 (1.24)	0.27 (0.50)	0.21 (0.65)	0.32 (0.81)	0.75 (1.68)

NOTE: Standard deviations appear in parentheses.

mean number of engagements for students with mild disabilities (MD) and students without disabilities (ND) was small. Students with disabilities were called on more often as well as volunteered more often in intervention. The mean numbers remained higher for both types of engagement in postintervention than in baseline. As expected, strategy-related engagement increased in intervention, but then decreased again to near baseline levels in post intervention. Non-strategy-related engagements increased slightly in intervention and again in postintervention conditions. Correct engagement responses followed a similar pattern to non-strategy-related engagements.

Another important source of target student data was the records of observed attendance during experimental conditions. While conducting classroom observations throughout the school year, project staff noticed that target students were sometimes absent, particularly in intervention and postintervention conditions. Given that students must be present to learn, we decided to compute absence ratios for all target students with and without disabilities across the three experimental conditions. There were a total of 13 student absences in 134 observations in baseline, 24 absences in 148 intervention observations, and 47 in 132 postintervention observations. That computed to absence ratios of 9.7% in baseline, 16.2% in intervention, and 35.6% in postintervention. Moreover, we discovered that approximately one third of the targeted students without disabilities either dropped out or were expelled by the end of the school year.

Naturalistic Design Results

The naturalistic data analysis revealed several important themes regarding changes in school climate and culture. Those themes were summarized in two major areas: (a) struggles with and perceptions of research, and (b) struggles with and perceptions of students in inclusive classes.

First, at the beginning of the project, teachers expressed skepticism about research and beliefs that researchers do not understand classroom dynamics and that researchers are not trusted by teachers. They also said they understood little about research procedures or how they could fit additional research responsibilities into their workload. In short, they struggled with methodological, practical, and perceptual issues. A few months into the project, however, it was apparent that teachers were rethinking their perceptions of the research process, examining what they had undertaken, and critiquing their instructional actions. In short, they began to see the link between their research and teaching and that research is not just an activity undertaken by outsiders to the classroom setting. As such, engaging in research was perceived as empowering.

Second, at the beginning of the project, it was apparent that teachers perceived that students were responsible for their failures and that students needed to adapt to the teacher's classroom expectations. In addition, most teachers believed that students with disabilities held back the class. After several months of project involvement, however, teachers realized that many low-achieving students, particularly students with disabilities, were hard workers rather than lazy. It also appeared that teachers began to accept some of the responsibility for their students' performance and realized that their actions did impact student performance. One teacher stated that it was important to understand student failure and to find preventive strategies. Some teachers also thought they paid more attention to their students with disabilities and that they were not as frustrated with them. It appears, therefore, that engaging in classroom research focused on low-achieving students and those with disabilities helped teachers become more cognizant of the needs and abilities of their students.

Implications

Participation in the project appeared to positively impact teachers; their school cultures; and, at least to some degree, targeted at-risk students. There are several implications of these results. First, teachers exhaust much of their energy orchestrating classroom learning communities but have few opportunities to be enriched through participation in the larger community of learners (i.e., other teachers) existing outside their classrooms. As a result, they have few opportunities to benefit from committing time and energy to roles and tasks that are not traditionally part of their job description. By facilitating relationships among the teachers and between the university researchers and teachers, however, a learning community of thoughtful, collegial inquiry can be created and flourish in schools. For example, principals in both high schools observed project teachers taking a much more confident and systematic approach to addressing problems raised in staff meetings, and a number of teachers from Year 1 have continued their participation in the project. In addition, district administrators are participating in meetings, finding materials and information for teacher projects, and initiating conference presentations that include teachers and project staff.

From the perspective of university researchers, two related lessons were clear: (a) personal, professional, and systemic change is developmental and takes time; and (b) the quality of participatory relationships between university and teacher researchers is critical for PR&D success.

First, change is developmental for students, for teachers, and for university educators as we move through the zone of proximal development (Gallimore & Tharp, 1990; Vygotsky, 1978). Teachers, as a group, do not all learn and change at the same rate, in the same way, or in relation to the same things. There are, however, at least a couple of specific stages that we noticed. The first stage of change included breaking down the barriers of traditional perceptions of teacher and university researcher roles and responsibilities. For example, university faculty are traditionally seen (and also may feel most comfortable) as dispensers of information. At the beginning of the project, teachers often looked to us to tell them what to do and, more figuratively and affectionately, referred to themselves as "the collaborative guinea pigs."

A second stage of change was empowering teachers to change the way they teach. Initially, even very experienced secondary teachers may not know how to adapt instruction in academically diverse classes or know much about conducting research. In response, we had first planned to conduct formal workshops to teach research methods and effective instructional approaches. We quickly learned, however, that such teacher knowledge and skills were best acquired by teachers in an informal fashion in the context of the interventions they designed. As a result, teachers did develop data-based instructional interventions appropriate for meeting the needs of academically diverse learners in inclusive classes.

A second critical lesson is that collaborative efforts such as PR&D are fueled by honest, ongoing relationships between university researchers and teachers, as well as among the teachers themselves. Such relationships are supported when university researchers are flexible and teachers have opportunities to share their expertise with each other. As university researchers, we must be willing to find a balance between imposing our agenda for changing practice and allowing teachers to guide the PR&D process. For example, it was critical that we (a) allow teachers to determine which instructional challenges to address through classroom inquiry,

(b) continually revise timelines for accomplishing tasks in light of teachers' changing classroom demands, and (c) carefully identify and spend time discussing data collection and analyses that teachers can readily learn, have time and energy to accomplish, and that will yield useful data for teachers. By doing these things, we will more readily facilitate our objective to transfer ownership of the PR&D process to schools when the project funding ends.

There are implications for student performance results as well. First, consistent with teacher perceptions, students with disabilities were given more attention, that is, engaged more in these inclusive classrooms. Still, the overall amount of academic engagement in these secondary inclusion classes was small. This is consistent with the findings of others (e.g., Boudah et al., 1997) and raises further questions regarding the likelihood of students with disabilities receiving sufficient instructional practice to be successful in secondary content classes.

The high rates of absenteeism and number of dropouts may shed additional light on teacher-collected content test scores that showed few effects of individual teacher interventions. Both high schools involved in this project have schoolwide discipline systems in which a certain number of offenses results in a detention, then an in-school suspension, then expulsion. Given that the target students were chosen because they were academically at risk, clearly just keeping them in class must be an important priority for schools to be successful with these students. In short, educators cannot expect that teacher- or researcher-designed interventions will significantly impact the performances of at-risk students if the students are not highly engaged or, worse yet, not in class.

Despite the outcomes, additional changes in teachers and students may not have been manifested or measurable in the first year of the project. Although differences in behaviors that promote student achievement were detected in teachers' classes (some increased academic engagement), few differences in other specific academic measures (i.e., unit test scores) were noted. What this has meant for the future of the project is that not only do we and the teachers need to more carefully design student performance measures, but that we also need to longitudinally measure teacher and student change, when possible, over succeeding years.

The results and lessons learned from the first year of the project have greatly informed our subsequent efforts. Together with teachers, we are continuing along this road less traveled because, similar to what Robert Frost wrote, it does seem to make a difference.

References

Boudah, D. J., Schumaker, J. B., & Deshler, D. D. (1997). Collaborative instruction: Is it an effective option for inclusion in secondary classes? *Learning Disability Quarterly, 20*(4), 281-304.

Cochran-Smith, M., & Lytle, S. (1990). Research on teaching and teacher research: The issues that divide. *Educational Researcher, 19*(2), 2-11.

Covey, S. R. (1989). *The seven habits of highly effective people.* New York: Simon & Schuster.

Fullan, M. G. (1991). *The new meaning of educational change.* (2nd ed.). New York: Teachers College Press.

Gallimore, R., & Tharp, R. (1990). Teaching mind in society: Teaching, schooling, and literate discourse. In L. Moll (Ed.), *Vygotsky and education* (pp. 175-205). New York: Cambridge University Press.

Goodlad, J. L., & Sirotnik, K. A. (1988). *School-university partnerships in action: Concepts, cases, and concerns.* New York: Teachers College Press.

Green, K. E., & Kvidahl, R. F. (1989, March). *Teachers as researchers: Training, attitudes, and performance.* Paper presented at the meeting of the American Educational Research Association, San Francisco.

Hunsaker, L., & Johnston, M. (1992). Teacher under construction: A collaborative case study of teacher change. *American Educational Research Journal, 29*(2), 350-372.

Kaestle, C. (1993). The awful reputation of educational research. *Educational Researcher, 22*(1), 23-31.

Lee, R. M. (1993). *Doing research on sensitive topics.* Newbury Park, CA: Sage.

Letiche, H., Van der Wolf, J., & Plooj, F. (1991). *The practitioners' power of choice: In staff development and inservice training.* Amsterdam: Swets & Zeitlinger.

Lincoln, Y. S., & Guba, E. G. (1985). *Naturalistic inquiry.* Beverly Hills, CA: Sage.

Madden, N. A., Slavin, R. E., Karweit, N. L., Dolan, L. J., & Wasik, B. A. (1993). Success for all: Longitudinal effects of a restructuring program for inner-city elementary schools. *American Educational Research Journal, 30*(1), 123-148.

Malouf, D. B., & Schiller, E. P. (1995). Practice and research in special education. *Exceptional Children, 61*(5), 414-424.

McFarland, K. (1990). Teacher-as-researcher timeline. In L. Patterson, J. Stansell, & S. Lee. (Eds.), *Teacher research: From promise to power.* Katonah, NY: Owen.

Merriam, S. B. (1986). *The research to practice dilemma.* Columbus, OH: National Center Publications, National Center for Research in Vocational Education. (ERIC Document Reproduction Service No. ED 278 801)

Nias, J. (1991). How practitioners are silenced, how practitioners are empowered. In H. Letiche, J. Bell, & F. Plooj (Eds.), *The practitioners' power of choice: In staff development and inservice training* (pp. 19-36). Amsterdam: Swets & Zeitlinger.

Noffke, S. E. (1997). Professional, personal, and political dimensions of action research. In M. W. Apple (Ed.), *Review of Research in Education* (Vol. 22, pp. 305-343). Washington, DC: American Educational Research Association.

Pfeiffer, L. C., Pasek, L., & Clark, C. M. (1993, August). *Recognizing the faces of trust: A step toward understanding partnerships in inquiry.* Paper presented at the International Study Association on Teacher Thinking, Gothenburg, Sweden.

Reason, P. (1994). Three approaches to participative inquiry. In N. K. Denzin & Y. S. Lincoln (Eds.), *Handbook of qualitative research* (pp. 324-339). Thousand Oaks, CA: Sage.

Showers, B., Joyce, B., & Bennett, B. (1987). Synthesis of research on staff development: Framework for future study and a state-of-the-art analysis. *Educational Leadership, 45*(3), 77-87.

Sirotnik, K. A. (1988). The meaning and conduct of inquiry in school-university partnerships. In K. A. Sirotnik & J. I. Goodlad (Eds.), *School-university partnerships in action: Concepts, cases, and concerns* (pp. 169-190). New York: Teachers College Press.

Stenhouse, L. (1971). Humanities curriculum project: The rationale. *Theory Into Practice, 10,* 154-162.

Stenhouse, L. (1975). *An introduction to curriculum research and development.* London: Heinemann.

Vygotsky, L. S. (1978). *Mind in society: The development of higher psychological processes* (M. Cole, V. John-Steiner, S. Scribner, & E. Souberman, Eds. and Trans.). Cambridge, MA: Harvard University Press.

Zeichner, K. (1983). Alternate paradigms in teacher education. *Journal of Teacher Education, 34*(3), 5-6.

Zeichner, K. (1995). Beyond the divide of teacher research and academic research. *Teachers and Teaching: Theory and Practice, 1*(2), 153-172.

6 Concerns of Professionals Involved in Implementing a Professional Development School

Judith D. Redemer

Barbara L. Nourie

Judith D. Redemer, Field Experiences Coordinator for the Department of Curriculum and Instruction, Illinois State University, and a recent doctoral graduate, continues her research in professional staff development, teacher preparation, and clinical supervision of preservice teachers.

Barbara L. Nourie, University Accreditation Officer for Teacher Education at Illinois State University, engages in research in teacher performance and teacher enthusiasm, as well as implementing Interstate New Teacher Assessment and Support Consortium (INTASC) principles in preservice programs.

ABSTRACT

The personal concerns of teachers and student teachers, referred to here as cadets, implementing a professional development school (PDS) were examined in this qualitative study. The researchers examined pertinent documents, interviewed university and public school officials, discussed the activities of teachers and cadets, attended workshops and meetings in the district, observed the working environment, and used the Concerns-Based Approach Model (CBAM) instruments and ethnographic methodologies. The researchers aggregated and profiled data. Findings from this research indicated that teachers' concerns reflected early stages of adapting to the PDS innovation. Cadet concerns related to the stresses of adapting to a new environment rather than to pedagogical matters. Recommendations from this study addressed obstacles preventing teachers from moving through the developmental change process and ways cadets can make the transition to a new setting.

Educational change is not a new phenomenon. Throughout the history of public education the demand for educational change has been evident. National concern for public education; the call for complex, comprehensive educational change; and the changing needs of society continue to confront public education with demands for reform. Educational changes are sought in school goals, practices, organization, administration, credentialing practices, curricula, and financing. A review of educational research reveals that (a) teachers in the school context are at the heart of change; (b) staff development is an essential component of effective change; (c) change is a continuous learning process; (d) change is a personal developmentally varied experience; (e) linking preservice teacher development to authentic school context merges theory with practice as well as opportunities for learning and change; (f) the professional development school (PDS), defined by the Holmes Group (1990, p. 1) as "a school for the development of novice professionals, for the continuing development of experienced professionals, and for the research and development of the teaching profession," is a relatively new change concept, which lacks structural specificity; (g) there is a paucity of research developing the concerns side of the PDS change; and (h) recognizing and attending to innovation concerns can effectuate change.

Viewing teachers as pivotal change agents, as current educational research advocates, places professional development at the center of successful change and school improvement.

Central to this study is the premise that staff development, program implementation, and individual change are best achieved when the professionals' personal concerns are addressed. The change experience examined in this study focused on the concerns of professionals involved in the initiation of a PDS. The PDS project was the first year of a 5-year pilot program developed by Illinois State University Department of Curriculum and Instruction in the College of Education (ISU) and Community Consolidated Elementary School District 21 in Wheeling, Illinois (Wheeling). CBAM (Concerns-Based Assessment Model) methodologies and instruments were selected as the method for developing a profile of professional concerns during the sixth to eighth months of PDS implementation.

Objectives

Utilizing the CBAM model, this study sought to describe the stages of cadet and teacher concerns. The research questions that served as objectives for this study were (a) What is the pattern of concerns stages expressed by the teachers involved with the PDS innovation? and (b) What is the pattern of concerns stages expressed by the cadets involved with the PDS innovation?

Theoretical Framework

This study was designed to examine the teachers' and the cadets' PDS experience of change and analyze and interpret the elements of their personal PDS concerns based on concerns theory of change. Concerns theory, which evolved from the teacher concerns research of Fuller (1969), holds that the individual is a vital consideration in change and that the individual experiences differing developmental stages of change. Concerns theory and this study are built on the following axioms: (a) teachers are important in the process of change, because change is a personal experience; (b) personal concerns relate to how an innovation is implemented; and (c) concerns information facilitates staff development strategies.

Building on Fuller's theory, research teams at the Research and Development Center for Teacher Education (R&DC) at the University of Texas developed the CBAM conceptual framework and instruments. The CBAM research team of Hall, Wallace, and Dossett (1973) identified and defined a set of characteristic concerns common to most innovation and change. Because concerns changed over time, the concerns were viewed as stages. The change in intensity of the different stages of concerns produces a pattern and that pattern is linked to the change process. The seven concerns identified and defined in the CBAM model are summarized in Appendix 6.1. According to concerns theory, as individuals move on a continuum from unawareness and nonuse of an innovation to use and then finally to sophisticated use, characteristic patterns can be identified and interpretations rendered.

Methods

Site Selection

The PDS project, guided by the ISU/Wheeling Steering Committee, represented the collaborative efforts of university faculty, ISU/Wheeling administrators, and Wheeling teachers. Because the PDS project was a "first" and staff development was a District 21 priority, the Wheeling PDS Project was selected for this study.

Population

PDS teachers and ISU cadets at the Wheeling project setting were the study population. Respondents were teachers and cadets involved in the Wheeling PDS project.

Instrumentation

CBAM diagnostic tools provided change data regarding the stages of the PDS innovation. Instruments specific to CBAM (personal dimensions) and this study are Stages of Concerns (SoC). The concerns-based approach developed by Hall and others at R&DC at the University of Texas at Austin offered a conceptual framework and tools for assessing and describing the individual change experience.

The SoC dimension describes the teachers' perceptions and feelings about the innovation as stages of concerns. The SoC describes seven kinds of concerns that individuals experience at various times in the change process. The SoC range developmentally from early "self" concerns (concerns are more "I" focused), to "task" concerns (logistical and scheduling concerns regarding the innovation), and finally to "impact" concerns (concerns with increasing the effectiveness of the innovation).

Research conducted at R&DC documented that at different points in the change process different SoC were more intense. In other words, earlier concerns must be resolved before later stage concerns emerge; in addition, an individual's concerns about an innovation develop toward the later stages with time, successful experience, and the acquisition of new knowledge and skills.

At the beginning of the change process, the typical "nonuser" has concerns that are relatively high in Stage 0 Awareness, Stage 1 Informational, and Stage 2 Personal. As the individual begins to use the program, Stage 3 Management concerns become more intense, and when the person becomes experienced and skilled with the innovation, Stage 4 Consequences, Stage 5 Collaboration, and Stage 6 Refocusing become more intense. As the intensity score (percentile score) increases in Stages 4, 5, and 6, the intensity of concerns scores decreases in Stages 0, 1, and 2.

Project staff (Hall, George, & Rutherford, 1979; Newlove & Hall, 1976) at R&DC have documented the reliability and validity of CBAM instruments. The researchers and developers of the Stages of Concerns Questionnaire (SoCQ), Hall et al. (1979), provide examples and interpretations of common concern profiles. Also, documented in the SoC manual are the CBAM validity and reliability studies of the project staff (Hall, George, & Rutherford, 1979; Newlove & Hall, 1976) at R&DC. The SoCQ was normed on a stratified sample of 646 elementary school and higher-education individuals ranging in experience with the innovation of teaming or modules.

The open-ended statement of concerns technique, a format introduced by Fuller and Case (1972) and developed by Newlove and Hall (1976), was utilized to assess written (few sentences to a paragraph) PDS concerns. Content analysis of the open-ended narratives of the teachers and cadets provided data regarding the intensity of various stages and topics of concern. The open-ended statement of concerns was utilized because previously scheduled calendar events interrupted interview scheduling and teacher availability. Wanting to maintain participant interaction and yet respect the participants' time, the researchers distributed the open-ended statement forms to the participants.

Data Source

An essential aspect of this focused ethnographic study was eliciting the views of the professionals whose behaviors, beliefs, and personal development cause change. Data collection was completed through ethnographic methodologies (documents, records, surveys, open-ended statements, interviews, and observations). The SoC was administered to teachers and cadets in January 1995. Formal and informal interviews, which served as primary data collection techniques, were conducted during February and March.

All of the teachers in District 21 were invited collectively and individually to participate in the Wheeling Professional Development School project. The ISU site supervisor asked the faculty of each school to serve on a mentoring team or as primary mentor for the PDS effort. After the initial group invitation, the site supervisor solicited PDS mentor support on an individual basis. The collective and individual PDS invitation resulted in 61 teachers agreeing to serve as primary mentor teacher (PMT) or on a PDS mentoring team. Seven PMTs assumed sole responsibility of a cadet and the remaining 54 teachers were assigned to a team (2 to 4 members). From the 54 teachers, 24 teams were established and each team had a designated PMT. The distinctions between the PMT's role and team teacher mentor were (a) the PMT assumed principal responsibility for the cadet, (b) the PMT was to be the cadet's sponsor (advocate), (c) the PMT was to supervise the student teaching phase, and (d) the PMT was to coordinate the mentoring team. The degree to which team teachers interacted with the cadets varied depending on the demands on the program as it unfolded. Although the role of the team teacher was not clearly articulated, the team concept, according to the ISU site supervisor, "offered a network of support and flexibility for teachers and cadets." The 61 teachers formed a mentoring nucleus across the 11 PDS schools in the district.

A total of 32 "typical" ISU education students volunteered for the first year ISU-Wheeling PDS project. In the fall 1994 semester, the chairman of Curriculum and Instruction, the coordinator of Student Teaching and

Supervision, the coordinator of Undergraduate Studies, and a Curriculum and Instruction faculty member (PDS Steering Committee chair) invited entry-level (Curriculum and Instruction Course 254) education students to serve as the first class to be involved in the establishment of a PDS in Wheeling, Illinois. This 5-year PDS pilot, a collaboration between Wheeling District 21 and the College of Education Department of Curriculum and Instruction, involved elementary education majors in a full school year of studying, observing, and teaching in Wheeling District 21. The pool (106 students) of interested elementary education majors was narrowed to a group of 32 students. Narrowing the field occurred when the pool of interested students along with their academic advisors examined each student's plan of study. The PDS student screening process consisted of balancing the student's education credit hours and course schedules. In the spring 1995 session the Curriculum and Instruction education advisement center notified 32 students that their plans of study were amenable to a full-year PDS placement with the Wheeling School District. In fall 1995, 32 students entered the Wheeling PDS program, but after the first semester one student did not continue the program due to an insufficient grade point average.

All of the teachers (mentor and team mentors) and cadets involved at the beginning of the second semester of the PDS pilot program were "purposefully" selected to attain a comprehensive sampling of the PDS change experience. All of the teachers and cadets involved with the PDS pilot program were invited (verbal or written) to participate in the study. The invitation described the study intent and involvement.

Results

Teacher SoC Pattern and Interpretation

The procedures for analysis of SoC data were followed as suggested by CBAM developers. The relative intensities of the different stages produce a pattern, or "profile," of an individual's concerns. To determine the group's pattern of concerns, an average raw score for each stage of concerns was computed and converted to a percentile. The results for the teachers' SoC are shown in Table 6.1.

TABLE 6.1 SoC Results: Teachers

Stage	Aware 0	Info 1	Person 2	Manage 3	Conseq 4	Collab 5	Refocus 6
M	8.91	18.32	19.70	16.64	22.66	19.26	17.21
P	77	66	72	65	43	44	52
$n = 47$							

At the beginning of the change process, the typical nonuser has concerns that are relatively high in Stage 0 Awareness, Stage 1 Informational, and Stage 2 Personal. As the individual begins to use the program, Stage 3 Management concerns become more intense, and when the person becomes experienced and skilled with the innovation, Stage 4 Consequences, Stage 5 Collaboration, and Stage 6 Refocusing become more intense. As the intensity score (percentile score) increases in Stages 4, 5, and 6, the intensity of concerns decreases in Stages 0, 1, and 2.

The teacher SoC profile indicates high scores (intense concern) in the rank order of Stage 0 Awareness, Stage 2 Personal, Stage 1 Informational, and Stage 3 Management. Percentile rank for Stage 4 Consequences, Stage 5 Collaboration, and Stage 6 Refocusing indicates concern is less at these stages. According to concerns theory the teachers' profile is that of nonuse or unawareness of an innovation. The teachers are in the early stages of change development.

Complete analysis of the teachers' stages of concerns consisted of examining the mean percentile scores for all seven stages and interpreting the meaning of the different highs and lows and their interrelationships. In summarizing where the teachers are in their stages of concerns, only high score interpretations are presented. The high scores in the early stages of Awareness, Informational, and Personal are noteworthy.

The high score pattern of teacher concerns indicates a great deal of personal concern regarding the PDS innovation. Figure 6.1 indicates a nonuse profile (high scores in Stages 0, 1, and 2). The nonuse pattern suggests that the teachers' lack of information regarding the principles, structure, and functioning of the PDS causes concern for the effectiveness and efficiency of their roles and responsibilities. The management and organizational concerns the teachers are experiencing heighten their concerns for other responsibilities.

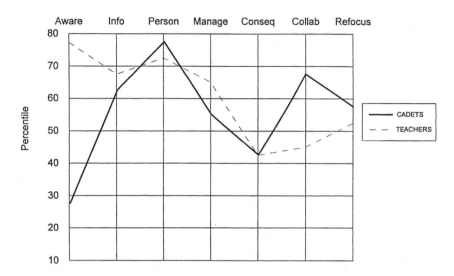

Figure 6.1: Profiles of Concerns

Cadets' SoC Pattern and Interpretation

The 31 cadets were also asked to respond to the questionnaire to ascertain stages of concerns. In spite of the lack of norms specifically for student teachers, or cadets, the items on the instrument and the scoring process was the same as was used for teachers. To determine the group's pattern of concerns, an average raw score for each stage of concerns was computed and converted to a percentile. The results for the cadets' SoC are presented in Table 6.2.

The cadet SoC profile indicates high scores (intense concern) in Stage 2 Personal, Stage 5 Collaboration, and Stage 1 Informational. Low percentile ranks are noted in Stage 0 Awareness, Stage 3 Management, Stage 4 Consequences, and Stage 6 Refocusing. The cadet profile does not demonstrate a single high score, but two high scores (Stage 2, Stage 5). According to the concerns developmental theory, one high score or peak would be anticipated. The scores adjacent to the high score at Stage 3 and Stage 4 do not suggest a developmental progression (see Figure 6.1).

The completed analysis of the cadet profile consisted of examining the percentile scores for all seven stages and interpreting the meaning of the different highs and lows and their interrelationships. Summarizing where

TABLE 6.2 SoC Results: Cadets

Stage	Aware 0	Info 1	Person 2	Manage 3	Conseq 4	Collab 5	Refocus 6
M	2	17.48	21.87	14.8	22.68	25.1	18.23
P	29	63	78	56	43	68	57
$n = 31$							

the cadets are in their stages of concerns is presented as a high score interpretation only. Examination of the cadets' SoC profile in Figure 6.1 reveals that the cadets have two stages of intense concerns. The profile does correspond with coded data. The cadets are experiencing intense personal concerns trying to orchestrate student and teacher responsibilities, maintaining cooperative working relationships with a number of supervisory people (evaluations), and establishing an exemplary model. The cadets' position in the program is that of students, even though they felt incorporated into the Wheeling District as teachers. As students, or "recipient-participants," their concerns for management were concerns questioning the feasibility of meeting deadlines: "Can I get this completed by this date?" or "If I lose my calendar, I won't know where I am supposed to be." Time became a stressful issue for students and perhaps created concern for managing the requirements of the PDS program but not the day-to-day management issues faced by teachers. University student concerns for the cadets were a higher priority than classroom teacher responsibilities. Thus, the profile does reflect cadet concerns, even though the pattern is not a single peaked profile.

Comparing the two profiles (Figure 6.1) illustrates the marked contrast in teachers' and cadets' scores on the stage of Awareness. As indicated earlier, students were totally involved in the PDS project. It was their life for one year. They had volunteered for the project; it was a chance to demonstrate their capabilities; they were part of a pilot program; and the novelty and excitement were evident in their commitment to perform. Because the cadets were neophytes, they had no experiential basis for relating to a PDS program.

The teachers on the other hand were veterans. They had been through practice teaching and many had supervised practice teachers, some for years; this program was only secondary or even peripheral to their professional work; and the rewards for being a participant were minimal. Their experience, maturity, and status provided a reasonably certain set of expectations. But as the program unfolded, management issues, role responsibility, ambiguity, and unmet needs enhanced concern for their involvement in the program.

Conclusions and Recommendations

The findings provide a description of the PDS change condition and when linked with theory provide an overall picture of the development of the PDS effort. The findings in this study and the propositions of change found in the literature formed the bases for the conclusions regarding the teachers and the PDS innovation. The comparison, the theory, and the lived experience all form the conclusions derived from the confluence of individuals and the context in which the PDS is housed.

Coded responses indicated four major categories of teacher concerns: concerns of self, program, others, and communication. The categories of self, program, and others align with the developmental stages of concerns described by Fuller (1969) and Hall et al. (1979). The progression of stages described by the researchers were concerns for self, concerns for task, and concerns for others. Communication as a coded core category of concerns is an organizational dimension that is woven into and impacts the dynamic process of concerns of self, task, and others. Concerns for program structure, channels of communication, and lines of authority heightened personal concerns. These concerns, linked with an unidentifiable PDS vision, suggest that the teachers lack an overall conceptual understanding of the PDS innovation. Teachers viewed the PDS primarily as a practice-oriented experience for the cadets rather than an ideal or vision for professional development. Teachers need to deal cognitively with the PDS innovation before they can act on it. To facilitate teacher learning, teachers need to understand the PDS and why the PDS change is an improvement.

Strengthening the teachers' understanding and vision of the PDS also strengthens communication, because a common PDS language is developed. Without a common PDS language, teachers and faculty will talk "around" each other, rather than "with" each other. Establishing a common PDS conceptualization, vision, and language are fundamental to change.

How the PDS program was to function constituted a major concern for the teachers. Teachers were not prepared to deal with the unpredictable nature of the program and conveyed the impression that they had planned on implementing a "familiar, prepackaged" student-teaching program. The PDS program focused, according to interview responses, on the practice of the "real-work world," suggesting an apprenticeship conceptualization. The responses also demonstrated a lack of program ownership. For example, statements directed to program improvement were "*They* need to fix it" as opposed to "we" need to make some changes. These responses suggest an attitude of detachment. In this case, teachers were "mentally" prepared to implement a "structured" student teaching program. When the teachers discovered that there were issues of change and uncertainty, many were not prepared to be inventive or assume the responsibility of "fixing it." Incorporating the teachers into the process brings the innovation to a personal level. The ambiguity of program design was less threatening to the cadets. The cadets appeared to have been prepared for the inventive nature of the program design.

The demands on the PDS teachers' time and energy were observable. The district has an active staff development program and encourages teachers to grow professionally. Innovations currently being developed in the district include multiage programs, middle school programs, bilingual programs, and team teaching. Balancing a number of innovations places the teachers in need of services and programs that help them to understand and cope during the change process. An important element in that change process is time—time to deal with the frustration and confusion, time to develop skills and reflect, and time to share and be with other teachers.

When the teachers' personal concerns are intense, they inhibit their ability to view the PDS innovation objectively. Apparently, as suggested by the high State 2 Personal concerns score, the teachers need to receive additional support and services if they are to maintain an open and receptive attitude toward the PDS initiative.

The variance in PDS concerns and mentoring skills illustrates the importance of helping the teachers develop in the change journey. Opportunities to foster collegiality, to learn from each other, and to discuss practice as well as to help individuals and teams develop are needed.

Even though the cadets had concerns of adaptation rather than pedagogy, both teachers' and cadets' perceptions are real and indicate the importance of staff development facilitators in helping teachers in the process of change.

In formulating PDS recommendations, the theoretical constructs of the concerns change process were compared against the "lived" phenomenon of the PDS change effort. Discrepancies between the theoretical model and diagnostic conclusions of the experience reported are the bases of these recommendations.

A major recommendation that has many implications calls for the involvement of teachers in the articulation (definition, mission, goals, design, and implementation) of the PDS. The evidence cited in the previous chapter strongly indicates that many teachers are not totally aware of what the program is or what it entails. This uncertainty, particularly when it is accompanied with more work and responsibility, is seen as a cause of frustration, anxiety, and resistance. Anxiety and discomfort are naturally associated with the introduction of something new.

The year's PDS experience should be highly valuable in articulating or refocusing the PDS effort, and input from the teachers who are currently involved should be sought. Establishing a common PDS definition, a common understanding, and a common purpose as well as role structure in the program are central to maintaining the PDS effort.

Serious consideration of the veterans' experience would also provide the advantage of capitalizing on past experiences. In addition, disseminating information on the goals and functions of the program enhances the credibility of the program and increases levels of use.

The redefinition of the PDS should strongly emphasize the professional development of all personnel, not just the cadets. Identification and commitment to the PDS will come only if the teachers experience a concrete gain from it. Professional development through the PDS effort should increase the capacity of teachers for continuous improvement and encourage collegiality.

Programmatic considerations must address the sources of stress for all participants. Therefore, some mechanism to monitor the PDS effort should be formalized. Providing time and mechanism to elicit thoughts and concerns would provide feedback in a systematic manner.

Another program consideration would be to clarify the roles and responsibilities of all participants. The ambiguity cited by teachers calls for more defined structure and clearer delineation of the specific functions in that structure.

A continuous and systematic method of information exchange for all district PDS participants should be provided. These information exchange sessions could include successful practices, problem identification, and continued focus on the totality of the program. From these sessions, a common language, intense awareness, camaraderie, and personal growth emerge.

University involvement in this aspect of the program is desirable to enhance communication between the district and the university, to maintain a focus on the theoretical dimensions of the program, and to assist in a more comprehensive development of the PDS concept. University faculty and teacher collaborative opportunities build program continuity, establish trust, strengthen parity, and cultivate professional development. Increased interaction between the university faculty and district teachers promotes the blending of theory and practice. An ombudsman should be designated to help ISU students in their transition with new roles, new locations, and new commitments.

Implications

Linda Darling-Hammond (1994) posited that "the PDS developed at the intersection of the preservice education and inservice teaching is a critical linchpin in developing teachers who can create learner- and learning-centered schools" (p. 6). The PDS represents an overarching reform strategy of educational change and it represents an innovation strategy as a site for preservice preparation and staff development. But understanding the individual level of the teacher's side of change is an important piece of that innovation as a change process. This research demonstrates that the teachers' perceptions and concerns impact the implementation of change. Monitoring personal concerns has profound implications for staff development as well as for preservice teachers.

Appendix 6.1: Stages of Concerns

0 Awareness: Little concern about or involvement with the innovation is indicated.

1 Informational: A general awareness of the innovation and interest in learning more detail about it is indicated. The person seems to be unworried about herself/himself in relation to the innovation. She/he is interested in substantive aspects of the innovation in a selfless manner such as general characteristics, effects, and requirement of ruse.

2 Personal: Individual is uncertain about the demands of the innovation, her/his inadequacy to meet those demands, and her/his role with the innovation. This includes analysis of her/his role in relation to the reward structure of the organization, decision making, and consideration of potential conflicts with existing structures or personal commitment. Financial or status implications of the program for self and colleagues may also be reflected.

3 Management: Attention is focused on the processes and tasks of using the innovation and the best use of information and resources. Issues related to efficiency, organizing, managing, scheduling, and time demands are utmost.

4 Consequences: Attention focuses on impact of the innovation on students in her/his immediate sphere of influence. The focus is on relevance of the innovation for students, evaluation of student outcomes, including performance and competencies, and changes needed to increase student outcomes

5 Collaboration: The focus is on coordination and cooperation with others regarding use of the innovation.

6 Refocusing: The focus is on exploration of more universal benefits from the innovation, including the possibility of major changes or replacement with a more powerful alternative. Individual has definite ideas about alternatives to the proposed or existing form of the innovation.

SOURCE: From *Measuring Stages of Concern About the Innovation: A Manual for Use of the SoC Questionnaire,* by G. Hall, A. George, and W. Rutherford, 1979, p. 7. Austin, Texas: Research and Development Center for Teacher Education, The University of Texas. Copyright 1979 by Southwest Educational Development Laboratory. Reprinted with permission.

References

Darling-Hammond, L. (1994). Developing professional development schools: Early lessons. In L. Darling-Hammond (Ed.), *Professional development schools: Schools for developing a profession* (pp. 1-27). New York: Teachers College Press.

Fuller, F. (1969). Concerns of teachers: A developmental conceptualization. *American Educational Research Journal, 6*(2), 207-226.

Fuller, F., & Case, C. (1972). *A manual for scoring the teacher concerns statement* (Report No. 0003). Austin: University of Texas at Austin, Research and Development Center for Teacher Education. (ERIC Document Reproduction Service No. ED 079 361)

Hall, G., George, A., & Rutherford, W. (1979). *Measuring states of concern about the innovation: A manual for use of the SoC questionnaire.* Austin: University of Texas at Austin, Research and Development Center for Teacher Education.

Hall, G., Wallace, R., & Dossett, W. (1973). *A developmental conceptualization of the adoption process within education institutions* (Report No. 3006). Austin: University of Texas at Austin, Research and Development Center for Teacher Education. (ERIC Document Reproduction Service No. ED 095 126)

Holmes Group. (1990). *Tomorrow's schools: Principles for the design of professional development schools.* East Lansing, MI: Author. (ERIC Document Reproduction Service No. ED 328 533)

Newlove, R., & Hall, G. (1976). *A manual for assessing open-ended statements of concern about an innovation.* Austin: University of Texas at Austin, Research and Development Center for Teacher Education.

CONTEXTS FOR PROFESSIONAL DEVELOPMENT SCHOOLS: REFLECTIONS

Ann Larson

Sheryl Benson

Discussion and Implications

In this summary, we discuss some common threads that emerged for us in our readings of the three chapters in this division of the yearbook. Our intent here is not to summarize or critique the chapters but to highlight the findings and connections among the findings. Finally, we refer to and interpret relationships of the levels of developmental stages for professional development schools (PDSs) (National Council for Accreditation of Teacher Education [NCATE], 1997) as these connect to the research findings and implications of the chapter authors and to school reform.

Lewison and Holliday in Chapter 4 describe and analyze the Pine Hill elementary school and university partnership through what they call "the lens of a power-with framework." An important goal for this work was for the researchers to better understand ways in which PDS collaborations or partnerships can evolve into more sustainable relationships. From their data sources, the authors were able to identify strategies, interaction patterns, and organizational structures among PDS participants that contributed to building the kind of sustainable relationship they advocate for PDS work and that was emerging in the Pine Hill partnership. Two of the strategies, interaction patterns, and organizational structures that we found particularly interesting in the data are the voluntary monthly study group meetings for veteran and novice teachers and the influence of the principal's published journal entries.

Boudah and Knight in Chapter 5 provoked us to think about the importance of nontraditional roles for teachers and university faculty as coresearchers in a collaborative school and university relationship. It appears to us the authors have combined research methodologies using the participatory research and development (PR&D) model to help structure and implement a quantitative study of academic engagement of students with and without mild disabilities in various content area classrooms of two high schools. We identify three lessons from this study that we believe have implications for PDSs: (a) there is a continued need to link historically separate communities of university research and teacher practice into a collaborative research and learning community; (b) personal, professional, and systemic change is developmental and takes time; and (c) the quality of relationships between and among university and teachers as coresearchers is critical.

Redemer and Nourie in Chapter 6 examine the patterns of concerns expressed by teachers and student teachers in an elementary school as each group adapted to a PDS innovation. The authors used the Concerns-Based Approach Model (CBAM) to analyze the data. As we anticipated, the data in this study revealed differences in the concerns expressed by experienced teachers and student teachers. We believe several of the more salient findings from this study address teacher learning and professional development. The authors state that teachers in this study viewed the PDS as primarily a practice-oriented experience for preservice teachers. The authors report a need for teachers to expand their visions of PDS by having opportunities and experiences to "deal cognitively" with the innovation. Several recommendations for how the opportunities and experiences contribute to further teachers' understandings of PDS and to support the notion of "concrete gain" include (a) consider and address sources of stresses for teachers; (b) clarify the roles and responsibilities of participants; (c) implement a continuous and systematic method of information exchange; (d) capitalize on the advantage of past experiences of teachers; and (e) strongly emphasize professional development of all PDS participants.

One common thread we identify across the three chapters is the authors' recommendations of activities, processes, and dispositions that contribute to the growth and sustainability of PDSs. Even though these studies emerge from very different contexts, they all report the value and importance of building trust among PDS participants. They also all report the importance of clarifying and redefining *rules, roles,* and *relationships* (Schlecty, Ingwerson, & Brooks, 1988) among PDS participants and they provide recommendations for how this may be accomplished in real PDS settings.

In two recent journal articles, Neubert and Binko (1998) and Mantle-Bromley (1998) report similar findings in two contexts of PDSs. Neubert and Binko (1998) describe a PDS in which there was a sheltered forum where participants raised questions, expressed concerns, and acted on these in a community of learning for teachers, preservice teachers, and students. Mantle-Bromley (1998) describes one PDS in which the school and university partnership is interpreted as a process of continual improvement in which participants plan as much for the next level as they do for their present work.

Another way to interpret the findings and implications of these chapters is to relate them to the NCATE (1997) Professional Development School Standards. It appears to us that each of the school and university partnerships described in the three chapters have elements that may be associated with the three stages of PDS development: prethreshold, threshold, and quality attainment. We have found some characteristics of all three stages across the university and school partnerships as described in these three studies. For example, we found that building trust, establishing commitment, redefining relationships, and enabling cultures that are open to change emerged from these partnerships.

We encourage the reader to consider *if* and *how* the Professional Development School Standards can inform and guide research and practice in contexts of school and university collaborations. Perhaps this will enable us to better focus on what those who participate and engage in PDSs need to know and be able to do to establish, nurture, and sustain a level of quality attainment. Will the standards facilitate this level of quality attainment for PDSs? We believe research in PDSs is needed on the characteristics and critical attributes identified in the developmental stages. Research is also needed on mechanisms and structures that will foster the growth and development of the characteristics and attributes in PDSs.

The Professional Development School Standards appear to us to be tangible and concrete guidelines that may enable school reform. Darling-Hammond (1994) writes that PDSs "allow school and university educators to engage jointly in research and rethinking of practice, thus creating an opportunity for the profession to expand its knowledge base by putting research into practice—and practice into research" (p. 1). Darling-Hammond also describes PDSs as a special context for school restructuring:

> As they [PDSs] simultaneously restructure schools and teacher education programs, they redefine teaching and learning for all members of the profession and the school community. Extending beyond the analogue of the teaching hospital that supports medical internships and clinical research, the PDS intends not only to support the learning of individual faculty members, it also aims to redesign university programs for the preparation of educators and to transform the teaching profession. (p. 1)

We believe there is potentially an important place for the Professional Development School Standards in the landscape of school reform, following the vision articulated by Darling-Hammond above. But we caution that these standards are guidelines and cannot be mandated. The unique contexts and complexities of PDSs must be carefully considered as partnerships and collaborations between schools and university are built and sustained. Consideration of the uniqueness and contextual nuances is essential if PDSs are to be lasting contributors to overall school reform.

Summary

This division of the yearbook creates new insights and poses questions about research and practice related to PDSs. The authors raise issues that remind all of us who work in PDSs of the need to better understand the complexities of blending multiple perspectives, authentic experiences, and professional goals in the development of high-quality partnerships. For us, listening to and valuing the diverse experiences of *all* PDS participants to form new learning communities is perhaps the most important lesson to be learned.

References

Darling-Hammond, L. (Ed.). (1994). *Professional development schools: Schools for developing a profession*. New York: Teachers College Press.

Mantle-Bromley, C. (1998). "A day in the life" at a professional development school. *Educational Leadership, 55*(5), 48-51.

National Council for Accreditation of Teacher Education. (1997). *NCATE professional development schools standards project*. http://www.ncate.org/projects/pds/drafsta.text

Neubert, G., & Binko, J. (1998). Professional development schools: The proof is in performance. *Educational Leadership, 55*(5), 44-46.

Schlecty, P., Ingwerson, D., & Brooks, T. (1988). Inventing professional development schools. *Educational Leadership, 46*(3), 28-31.

TAKING MEASURE OF OUR WORK:
PROFESSIONAL DEVELOPMENT
SCHOOLS AND THE
MATTER OF LEADERSHIP:
OVERVIEW AND FRAMEWORK

Gerald M. Mager

Gerald M. Mager is Professor of Teaching and Leadership Programs
in the School of Education at Syracuse University. He coordinates
graduate programs in Teaching and Curriculum and formerly in
Educational Leadership. His scholarly interests include teacher careers, induction, and mentoring; teacher preparation for inclusive
classrooms and schools; and leadership in education.

It has been only little over a decade since the Holmes Group began its work
on the reform of teaching and schooling and teacher education—work

captured in its landmark trilogy of reports. The first volume in the trilogy, *Tomorrow's Teachers* (1986), reviewed the then-current state of the teaching profession, including the issues of teacher preparation and the conditions of practice. This first volume crystallized descriptions of the obstacles to better teaching and outlined the commitments that would be needed to overcome them. Reaching a consensus on the state of affairs, as represented in this first volume, allowed the profession to consider what steps might need be taken to achieve substantial reform in policy and practice.

But when the second volume, *Tomorrow's Schools* (1990), was issued 4 years later, it called for more than reform. It called for "inventing a new institution": the professional development school (PDS). It called for a new organization, a new ethic, and a new view of learning and teaching and the systems and processes by which they are carried out. Given the level of activity and the number of PDS sites that now describe themselves as such, it is hard to recall that the timeline for this development has been so short. Much has been done in this short history.

We who would design and enact PDSs would be starting from our past experiences. Accordingly, we were cautioned that PDSs were not to re-create the laboratory schools of an earlier era of teacher preparation or to serve as new vehicles for delivery of the standard "clinical experience" in contemporary teacher preparation. They were not to become sites for the conduct of academic research as it has so long been conceptualized and carried out. Nor were PDSs to simply formalize the good but limited partnerships that existed between schools and universities.

Rather, the PDS was to serve as the medium in which we could come together to conceive and create a "new institution" with all the attendant features of mission and policy, ethic, spirit, practice, and results. *Tomorrow's Schools* used the nexus of preparation and practice as the point around which teacher educators and practicing teachers and administrators might come together in the redesign of schooling itself.

Tomorrow's Schools called for the design of PDSs around six principles. I recall them here without the elaboration that appears in the original text:

Principle 1. Teaching and learning for understanding

Principle 2. Creating a learning community

Principle 3. Teaching and learning for understanding for everybody's children

Principle 4. Continuing learning by teachers, teacher educators, and administrators

Principle 5. Thoughtful, long-term inquiry into teaching and learning

Principle 6. Inventing a new institution (Holmes Group, 1990, p. 7)

Reviewing these six principles reminds us of several important features of a PDS. Obviously, it is guided by principles, not prescriptions. Learning is at the heart of the enterprise. It is to serve all learners—children, youth, and adults—as members of the learning community. It is complex organizationally, bringing together individuals with different roles and representing different institutions. It is dynamic, changing as it is created. And, indeed, it is to be created, not "borrowed whole." The organization that emerges from the efforts of the educators and teacher educators and other stakeholders is to be the "new institution" called for in the final principle.

Woven into this new fabric is the matter of leadership. Does not such a new institution create the possibility of a new view of leadership? Does it not demand leadership in a new form? In fact, the matter of leadership for and in PDSs has emerged as a point of interest, particularly because the PDS has moved beyond traditional forms of policy and practice. But exactly where we are headed in this matter is yet unclear.

Of course, the character and practices of the many so-called PDSs that emerged have led us to raise questions among ourselves about the very nature of this new institution. By the time of the publication of *Tomorrow's Schools of Education* (Holmes Group, 1995), those who had provided the first visions of the PDS were aware that their cautions were well founded. Many so-called PDSs had been created and were being touted as genuine; yet they seemed like poor copies of the ideas that underwrote their initiation. The variances between sites were and are many. Often sites seem at odds with each other and untrue to the core principles presented in *Tomorrow's Schools*.

But it may also be the case that genuinely high-quality and real effects take time to emerge. Leadership that might galvanize the effort is still forming. Perhaps the PDS as a concept, and these PDSs, as enactments of the core principles, are yet to take their greatest strides.

Indeed, *Tomorrow's Schools* itself suggests that the PDS is ever developing, ever renewing. And the engine of that invention is inquiry. Inquiry into our own practice drives us to recreate our work. What we learn from responding to the questions that emerge from our practice becomes the basis for designing, acting, leading, and inventing.

The three studies that follow in the chapters making up this division of the yearbook exemplify exactly that: studying our own practice. Each comes to the inquiry with a different set of questions, and with a different basis for responding. Each in its own way is instructive to the educators who pursued the research; what we learn from them together has value for all who are engaged in the PDS endeavor. Though the studies are broader, a theme common to all three is the matter of leadership—clearly, a crucial component of organizational invention, and thus crucial to the PDS.

Below I introduce each study briefly. But I allow each to present itself in the chapters that follow. Then, in the summary that concludes this division of the yearbook, I sort out, from my own point of view, key issues related to each study and how they bear on the matter of leadership in PDSs.

The Measures Taken

If we were inclined to forget that the PDS is not just about the conduct of teacher preparation, the first study, presented in Chapter 7, disburdens us of that view. "Teacher's Stories of Professional Development School Restructuring: Decision Making," by Nihlen, Williams, and Sweet, brings us subtly but surely back to that realization. For not once in the description of the PDS formed at Emerson Elementary School is mention made of field experience, clinical practica, or student teaching. The description of this PDS focuses on the remaking of that school. It hearkens back specifically to that core principle of *Tomorrow's Schools.*

The second study, in contrast, focuses on preservice teacher preparation and connects the PDS effort to the development of knowledge, values, and skills that beginning teachers might need to be successful and to sustain their careers in classroom work. In Chapter 8, "Teachers as Leaders: A Question or an Expectation?" Reinhartz and Stetson provide an interesting look at two contrasting groups of novice teachers—those prepared in the context of a PDS, and those provided a more "traditional" preparation—to begin to understand whether engagement in a PDS might lead to successful teaching.

Different from the first two studies, the study presented in Chapter 9 looks across many sites to develop a perspective on the PDS that is not directly tied to any one site. "Professional Development Schools: A Comprehensive View," by Kochan, approaches the issues of the PDS as issues that need be seen more generally to be understood. It provides an opportunity to consider matters on this larger scale. This study is important in developing perspective on PDS work.

References

Holmes Group. (1986). *Tomorrow's teachers.* East Lansing, MI: Author.

Holmes Group. (1990). *Tomorrow's schools: Principles for the design of professional development schools.* East Lansing, MI: Author.

Holmes Group. (1995). *Tomorrow's schools of education.* East Lansing, MI: Author.

7 Teachers' Stories of Professional Development School Restructuring

Decision Making

Ann S. Nihlen

Melissa Williams

Amy Sweet

Ann S. Nihlen is Associate Professor in the Division of Language, Literacy, and Sociocultural Studies, College of Education, University of New Mexico. Her current research interests include work with schools and teachers in conducting practitioner research. She is also involved with a community college in studying the influences of race, class, and gender on the acquisition of math skills in developmental programs. She has coauthored a book, *Studying Your Own School: An Educator's Guide to Qualitative Practitioner Research,* and published in *Anthropology and Education Quarterly* on gender, in *Elementary School Guidance and Counseling* on nontraditional work roles, and in the United States and Latin America on practitioner research.

Melissa Williams is an elementary school teacher at the Emerson Elementary Professional Development School, Albuquerque, New Mexico. As an elementary school teacher-researcher, she is focusing her work in the area of early childhood. She has worked at Emerson Elementary School for 10 years. She has been in a leadership position in the school for years and was a member of the Leadership Team for

5 years. She is currently a member of the Kindergarten Curriculum Team and also serves on the Curriculum Committee.

Amy Sweet is an English as a second language teacher-researcher and has worked at Emerson Elementary Professional Development School, Albuquerque, New Mexico for 13 years. She was in a leadership position at the beginning of the restructuring process and served on the Leadership Team. She now serves on the Professional Development Committee, the Literacy Team, and the Fifth-Grade Curriculum Team.

ABSTRACT

This is an oral history that records the process of decision making undertaken to develop teacher leadership in a professional development elementary school. The collaborative research team consists of two elementary school teachers and one university professor who have worked together for 8 years. The school initially sought to restructure to better serve the children in classrooms and the families in the community. Through training in leadership and practice in decision making, teachers believe that they have become high-quality teachers who provide high-quality learning for students.

Elementary and secondary school restructuring is currently under way throughout the United States, with its successes as well as failures discussed by academics in various publications. Little is heard, however, from the teachers who are often the actual architects and always the implementors of the plans and changes.

The Emerson Elementary School Oral History Project in Albuquerque, New Mexico, was begun in 1990 to capture the ongoing stories of actual participants in the restructuring and development changes at Emerson Elementary School. The school has been in a process of Holmes Group restructuring as a professional development school (PDS) for the past 10 years and has made significant changes in leadership, personnel and hiring, curriculum, and scheduling. Now we are in the process of recording the process of decision making undertaken to develop teacher leadership. This serves as a record of how a group of teachers restructured a school and provides insights to them/us in planning for future development. It also serves as an important example to other teachers, schools and school districts, and the universities.

The term *professional development school* (PDS) comes from the Holmes Group, a consortium of education deans and administrators from research universities across the nation. In *Tomorrow's Teachers*, (Holmes Group, 1986), and *Tomorrow's Schools*, (Holmes Group, 1990), this group responded to the nation's dissatisfaction with the public educational system and years of calls for school reform. The Holmes Group envisions PDSs as sites where teachers, teacher educators and educational researchers work collaboratively to contribute to the knowledge base of the profession and to develop collegial relationships that encourage their respective intellectual and professional growth (Holmes Group, 1986).

In 1987, the Albuquerque Public School District, in collaboration with the University of New Mexico and the American Federation of Teachers union, encouraged the development of PDSs. The purpose was to create school climates where teachers would engage in reflective inquiry about their practice and develop new understandings about teaching and learning (Albuquerque Public Schools/American Federation of Teachers/University of New Mexico, 1987).

Schools in the Albuquerque school district applied to become PDSs and Emerson was chosen in 1988. Later that year, an in-service training helped the staff at Emerson begin to govern themselves. Group process, prioritizing issues, and concrete ways to help people make decisions were all discussed. Nevertheless, many tense moments occurred as important issues were brought up and discussed. Many staff members were not sure of the direction the school was taking or what the form of governance would look like. There was a lot of fear of the unknown as well. Disagreement was encouraged, but at times mediators were called in to help ease the process and make it more fluid and helpful.

Initially, one part-time coordinator, or facilitator, was released half-time and received a stipend to coordinate. Later, the school went to a leadership group of four teachers, and each received a small stipend. One member had responsibility for each area, such as facilitating meetings, acting as treasurer, and keeping records as historian/minute taker.

Eventually, the Leadership Team, as it came to be known, had 6 to 10 members at any one time. They met once a week in an open meeting, which lost attendance year by year. Four years ago the regularly scheduled schoolwide meetings were combined with the Leadership Team meetings. Today, people tend to come if the issues interest them, but sometimes the meetings are rather cut and dried.

Approximately 5 years ago, the staff voted to change from a traditional Title 1 model of literacy and reading to a schoolwide Title 1 Literacy and Reading Program. To meet the goals of this model they formed curriculum teams to implement collaborative work on an integrated curriculum. The teams were composed of teachers and educational assistants at each grade level, plus support staff in the bilingual, Title 1 reading, and special education programs. Three years ago, the Leadership Team suggested that it would be a good idea to have a member from that team on each curriculum team, and this was done with all six teams. This has helped the Leadership Team gain a wider participation from teachers and staff, and such issues as funding, scheduling, staffing, and so on are now regularly discussed along with curriculum issues.

An important issue from the beginning has been the issue of trust. In the beginning, teachers wondered if administrators were telling them everything they needed to know to make informed decisions. And today, the teachers still wonder if they are getting all the information they need, and if they are being included when important decisions are made.

Two different teachers talk about their conception of professional development and how it evolved in their school. The first is a young woman who is a relative newcomer to the school but already active in leadership activities. The second woman is support staff and has been at Emerson for a long time.

> It kind of came about just as giving more decisions to the whole staff, making this a group effort instead of decisions being made for us. That's the way I see it. And really empowering ourselves and believing in ourselves that we can make those decisions. That we don't have to be shut up in our room and not knowing what's going on and have everything told to us.

> For me it means a place where there's shared decision making. It's basically instead of top-down management it's bottom-up

management where representatives from all parts of the staff are involved in decision making. It also means having opportunities as a staff member to grow. It means choosing your level of partici- pation in this growth even though you would hope that everyone would take advantage of it in some way, that you do have the freedom to choose your level of involvement in that professional growth.

The above quotes are in sharp contrast to the "traditional" stereotype one teacher gives us of a teacher as a person with a clearly defined role:

And in the educational hierarchy this group makes this decision, this group makes this decision. And . . . teachers have been taught in a way or it's been modeled for us that we belong only in our classroom. Our door is closed, we've got 20 kids, this is what we do, that is what the administration does.

The Emerson oral history project is a unique venture in this school and is documenting the school's history of professional development; how it affects individuals personally and professionally; how decision making occurs; and different interpretations of these events based on personalities, jobs, and positionality. We are also documenting the lives of teachers in a low socioeconomic community with vast multicultural diversity and giv- ing teachers an opportunity to speak and be listened to, to be validated as professionals. This will give Emerson public acknowledgment for the work being done and help the university stay in touch with the reality of the school. Last, we hope this work will connect teachers to the theories behind their practice.

For the three researchers, it has given us skills of how to do research in the schools and how to do it collaboratively. We hope it will further involve teachers to see themselves as researchers-learners.

Methodology

As the Emerson teachers read articles and attended conferences about restructuring and PDSs, they often found that the ideas and information were not challenging or new. It seemed that Emerson was ahead of others in some of the processes. This realization led to the desire to document the history of Emerson as a PDS and to share that information in published articles.

The Leadership Team approached Nihlen, who was from the university, for help. She was familiar to many teachers at Emerson through her own research there, and had also assisted teachers with their research projects through classes taught on site. She was also seen as an advocate for the school at the university. Out of that came a sense of trust that she would listen to them and record accurately what they said. Nihlen heartily agreed to work with the project and suggested oral history as a way to document the process. This seemed ideal to the Leadership Team members, who wanted to capture more than just chronological information.

From the beginning, it was a collaborative project. Sweet and Williams volunteered to work with Nihlen and looked to her for information about qualitative research, oral history, and academic writing. Nihlen looked to them for information about school life and the restructuring process. There was mutual respect for the knowledge and experience each person brought to the project. Out of this respect, trust developed quickly among the researchers. Work sessions each Thursday around Nihlen's dining room table, after a day of teaching, were exciting and bound us to each other in a warm working relationship and friendship.

Sweet and Williams brought a high degree of integrity to the research. Both had served on the Leadership Team for years, Sweet in the early phases of restructuring and Williams in the current leadership. Both were highly respected at Emerson for their honesty and loyalty to the school and their principles in working with others. The teachers listened to them, sought their advice, confided in them, and knew they would honor confidences. Thus, a high level of trust of the researchers was there from the beginning. This helped during the interviews in gaining the confidence of the participants.

The study interviews teachers about their/our experiences at Emerson over the past 10 years of change. Some of the teachers have been at this school for over 13 years; their perspective includes that history as well as what the recent changes have meant to them/us and the community. Others have been there a shorter period, including teachers who sought out the school because of its growing reputation as a school where the teachers provide leadership and are genuine change agents.

A central premise of the book *Women's Words: The Feminist Practice of Oral History,* by Gluck and Patai (1991), is that oral histories are especially suited to those whose voices often go unheard, such as women and minority men. In the book, Kathryn Anderson and Dana Jack discuss the fact that:

> Oral interviews are particularly valuable for uncovering women's perspectives. Anthropologists have observed how the expression of women's unique experience as women is often muted, particularly in any situation where women's interests and experiences are at variance with those of men. A woman's discussion of her life may combine two separate, often conflicting, perspectives: one framed in concepts and values that reflect men's dominant position in the culture, and one informed by the more immediate realities of a woman's personal experience. Where experience does not "fit" dominant meanings, alternative concepts may not readily be available. (p. 11)

For the purpose of this study, the term *oral history* encompasses the ideas of (a) multiple and in-depth interviewing, (b) encouragement of participants to tell stories or narratives, and (c) an emphasis on the developmental movement or "careers" of informants through life experiences. Because we are studying the movement of teachers and their school into self-selected positions of leadership, it is vitally important that we learn to hear their, at times, muted voices describe behaviors considered atypical in the general arena of education.

The school's Leadership Team approved our research. We chose 20 teachers, the principal, and several support staff to be interviewed. We selected participants on the basis of age, years of teaching, ethnicity, and participation or nonparticipation in the school change committees and processes. Everyone asked agreed to the series of three interviews, one every year or year and a half. Each interview was tape-recorded and lasted for approximately 1 to 1½ hours. Each interviewee has been interviewed twice to date. The tapes are transcribed and then analyzed using a modified approach from Spradley (1979) and an approach of seeking and identifying themes we found in common in the transcribed interviews.

The methodology of any study tries to inform the reader about how the study was conducted, and it is the "unpacking" of this collaboration that will help you understand not only the methods but the process and therefore some of the underlying and tacit data of the study.

Our initial question was, "Talk to me about your years at Emerson." We also asked each participant, "Describe the school." If the subject had not been brought up in the earlier answer or discussion, we then asked them, "Talk about professional development at Emerson."

It was at this time that we began to meet regularly as a research group. We each read all 13 of the teacher interviews, putting aside the principal and secretary and other support staff interviews for later. Nihlen discussed with Sweet and Williams how she would begin analyzing text and we initially read and reread the interviews looking for themes and for responses to our particular questions. Then, we made notes on the interview transcripts themselves by relevant passages and discussed them with each other.

We then each made a list of what we considered the most relevant themes. At this point, it became clear that the two teachers were seeing and identifying different dominant themes from the university professor. Here is an excellent example of where positionality influences the data and the results in quite a significant manner. As teachers, they saw and read the text in certain ways, primarily through the filter of their subjectivity and concrete experiences in the school. They also discussed how they felt that knowing the other teachers as they did influenced how they read the interviews and what they got out of them. The professor, on the other hand, read them as an ethnographer who comes from the university, a friendly "other" in the school, who knew half of the teachers interviewed.

Nihlen wanted to hear how the interviewees conceived of PDS and wanted to understand the connection between professional development work and their own individual classroom. Sweet and Williams, the teachers, were fascinated by the views their colleagues had about professional development and felt frustrated about the views of how the Leadership Team had functioned over the years. They had both served on this team, and Sweet was still on it. Although we were all surprised by some of what the individual interviewees said, the salient points we identified to follow up on differed.

At this juncture, we gave precedence to the teachers and their knowledge of the environment and timeliness of issues. What was also at stake was a need to know how the interviewed teachers felt about how decisions were made. This influenced the immediate and practical future governance of the school. The everyday life of the school, both institutionally and personally for the teachers, was dependent on how all the teachers interpreted their own behaviors and experiences as individuals and as a group. Therefore, these interviews were far from a removed academic exercise we three were performing. Nor was the project a simple history of what had happened in years past. It became a living documentary of what was unfolding in the school and could influence what happened in the future. The interpretation of what was happening by the participants would help determine the future of the institution.

The final five thematic categories on which we based the analysis of the interviews were the following:

1. Personal development
2. Decision-making processes
3. Staff
4. Stress of school/community/kids
5. Multiple roles of teacher

Decision Making in the School

This section presents the emic voices of the teachers as they talk about decision making in a PDS—from issues of voice to different levels of work and participation, from work as a member of a committee or curriculum team to the school's governing Leadership Team.

The quotes reflect different aspects of the teachers as they reflect on their role in the school. The first quotes speak directly about voice. As women, the speakers weave their thoughts through their relations with others, in context between the school and their personal lives. The first teacher has been at the school for several years and is somewhat active; the second teacher has been around for a while but has never been very active.

And that's one of the reasons I like being at this school, because I think everybody does have a voice and even being a quiet person or a reserved person you can get your say in there and I feel like everybody kind of works together at the school. I think the Leadership Team and being a professional development school has really helped that.

I already know one person, who I would rather not name right now, who didn't feel like their voice was heard and is now transferring. 'Cause she didn't really feel her voice was being heard concerning the program. So, I mean I don't know what should have happened when they spoke out. I don't know about that. But I hope everybody can continue to have that good feeling that their voice is being heard. Even if it's something to do with the bilingual program. Because it has the potential to divide people. It has the potential to be politicized and split people up because they feel political about it, cultural about it, emotional about it. I hope that everybody still feels heard, sticks together, has that community feeling as a staff and doesn't end up taking sides.

Shared decision-making for the school did not come easily or quickly. There were years of endless meetings and workshops on how to make decisions and share power. Some teachers left the school rather than keep working through these issues around decision making. Following are two quotes, the first from a longtime member of the Emerson faculty, the second from a young man who was new to the Leadership Team.

I think shared decision-making is most important. I think the staff is more invested in the school because we feel like we can make policy, we can make changes. I think that's a very important difference. I think when Roy [former principal] was here that also was happening just because of who he was. So that sort of started before we actually became a professional development school. He seemed open, not maybe initially, but after he got broken in. That started to happen. Valued what staff had to say. I think our shared decision-making probably has been the most important factor change in this school.

I think we got to a point where we really got good at making decisions. And I think we even amazed ourselves at how smoothly everything flowed. Once we kind of got into the rhythm of it and we knew how to go through group process, we knew how to handle conflict.

One issue that was initially hard to accept for the most active members of the Leadership Team and committees was this idea of different levels of participation depending on what interested individual staff members. One active participant reflects on what she learned:

> That when you turn into a PDS school everyone's just not going to magically jump in and we're going to be involved and do all these wonderful things. . . . What you have to realize is everyone is going to be participating at their own level and some won't participate at all. But you can't let that stop you. You just have to keep moving. . . . And eventually what is going to happen is people who are on the outside rings are going to see something that interests them. And it will pull them in and that's how they'll get involved.

In this process, certain decisions had to be made and elected representatives had to make the decisions with the principals. For example, the district had mandated half-day school attendance on Wednesdays so that teachers could have in-services and other work in the afternoons. The teachers knew how hard it was in the community to pick up children and provide day care for them if the parents were working. They discussed their right to change this decision. Eventually, the school went to all day on Wednesdays and the final decision was made by the Leadership Team. Some staff felt they had not been listened to about their opinions on the half-day Wednesday. When these things happen, it is inevitable that some people would think that decisions were closed and that the leadership would not listen to them. An old hand on the Leadership Team reflects:

> The hard thing then is educating people to that possibility. Some people have that mind-set. "No one will listen, I can't do anything." Because of the way they were raised, where they worked before. No matter how many times you say to them, "This meeting is open, please come and let us know how you feel." They would rather say, "Oh, I can't. No one will listen to me." But I feel really strongly that it's been an open process. And at any point any teacher or staff member at this school can attend a meeting and people will listen. So if you have the energy for it. . . .

Another old hand reflects on who does the work:

> Again, if people say, "I want someone to fix this," well, no, that
> probably won't get anywhere, but if you say, "I want to fix this
> and I would like some help," that would be fine. But if you want
> someone else to fix it, no, that doesn't work. You have to be able
> to put some energy out.

Some questioned the constant meetings and said that the school was
talking too much and doing too little. A teacher who had been around for
several years says,

> I think we spend too much time talking about things and not
> applying them. And I wish we did more, you know, because being
> a professional development school to me, I think, means some-
> thing different to everybody. But to me it means you are trying to
> better your profession and therefore you should be trying to also
> benefit children. And the things that you do aren't always for you
> necessarily as a teacher, but what could you do to make your job
> easier so that your children learn easier. And so on and so on.
> Sometimes I feel like "do we talk about things so much but we
> don't ever actually do?"

Everyone felt at times that the school and faculty were trying to do too
much all at once and perhaps should slow down. A teacher who had been
at Emerson a long time and worked on a committee says,

> The staff as a whole feels that perhaps we have been a little
> fragmented this year. Lately, it's like you're working on this com-
> mittee and that committee and that committee and pretty soon
> you are like you've got three meetings on the same day after school
> and, I don't know, it's kind of like one hand didn't know what the
> other one's doing. We had too much, too much going on. So a lot
> of teachers talked about, let's step back and let's see if we can't
> focus (laughs).

The issue of gaining power as a decision maker and as a person
knowledgeable about how the school worked was a scary one for many
teachers. Teachers had begun with feeling that we/they were powerless to

effect change outside of the classroom and now teachers were regularly changing things for the entire school. One male teacher on the Leadership Team who had been at the school for several years says,

> It seems like just comparing when I first started teaching and when I first went to Emerson and now there just, oh, the way meetings are run and the way decisions are made, it just seems like people are so much more comfortable having that power. Even though I don't think we have as much power as we could. But I think we're a lot more comfortable having some leadership roles. I don't, it seems like before I got to Emerson there were people there who had all those great ideas but didn't know how to put them into motion. And now it seems like we're learning how to put them into motion.

Conclusion

The basic premise of the teacher leadership movement, according to Odell (1997), is that high-quality teachers provide high-quality learning for students in school. This is also a thesis of Darling-Hammond's work (1998). By encouraging and supporting teachers to professionalize the occupation and hearing the teachers' own sense of growth and development through the oral history project, the teachers at Emerson Elementary School developed their own self-empowerment from learning how to be decision makers. They learned that the process has to be learned and that it keeps evolving and changing.

A teacher who wants to be listened to and respected as a professional must also listen to and respect his or her colleagues. The skills learned during the restructuring process—listening, researching, presenting information, reaching consensus, resolving conflicts—were applied to the curriculum teams with student success as the common goal. The interviews speak to the working together and listening to each other that occurred as the process unfolded. They also speak about teachers being invested in the school because they can make policy as well as changes, at how smoothly things run after they learned group process and how to handle conflict. Thus, sharing curriculum and ideas flows from the trust established in the governance of the school.

Another facet of decision making we/they learned was that everyone sees an issue differently and therefore also conceptualizes the solutions differently. Teachers felt that the level of personal and professional growth they underwent as they became better decision makers also often made them better teachers in the classroom. But some were also concerned that the time constraints on being on the Leadership Team as well as a curriculum team and perhaps other committees sometimes meant skimping on lesson plans. That led to feelings of guilt and reevaluation of the decision-making work.

Touchy issues remain difficult to discuss in the interviews as well as out in the open. For example, the fact that the Leadership Team and the very nature of decision making for all the teachers changes with the introduction of new key people in administration and staff is an important reality. The level of trust they engender, their style of presenting their new ideas, how they gain power and authority, all pose threats for the status quo and need to be worked out through negotiation. When this does not happen, a tension builds that is not helpful for change and growth.

In the early years, when the staff began trying to discover what their power was, each small issue was debated by the entire staff. When people spoke against a proposal, the predominately female staff would often take it personally and feel hurt and betrayed. They had to learn how to argue and defend their ideas without taking umbrage at dissent. Many women at Emerson have learned this, and the feelings of self-empowerment and self-efficacy are very apparent in the strong leaders who have emerged at the school.

The work of Gilligan (1982) and Belenky, Clinchy, Goldberger, and Tarule (1986), speaks to the relational manner in which women approach life. Certainly, we saw that at Emerson in the manner in which women worked together and in the crises provoked by dissent. The contextual nature of the debate helped the women discuss their school and educational issues in the classroom. It also allowed them to ground themselves in that reality.

What began as a journey steered by the Holmes Group became a place of mutual respect and decision making throughout the school. Issues were handled by teachers that previously had been handled by the principal alone. Emerson Elementary School teachers made some major changes for the sake of the children and built a community for themselves.

References

Albuquerque Public Schools/American Federation of Teachers/University of New Mexico. (1987). *Report of the Professional Development School Planning Committee.* Unpublished document, Albuquerque, NM.

Belenky, M. F., Clinchy, B. M., Goldberger, N. R., & Tarule, J. M. (1986). *Women's ways of knowing: The development of self, voice, and mind.* New York: Basic Books.

Darling-Hammond, L. (1998). Policy and professionalism. In A. Lieberman (Ed.), *Building a professional culture in schools* (pp. 55-77). New York: Teachers College Press.

Gilligan, C. (1982). *In a different voice: Psychological theory and women's development.* Cambridge, MA: Harvard University Press.

Gluck, S., & Patai, D. (Eds.). (1991). *Women's words: The feminist practice of oral history.* New York: Routledge.

Holmes Group. (1986). *Tomorrow's teachers.* East Lansing, MI: Author.

Holmes Group. (1990). *Tomorrow's schools.* East Lansing, MI: Author.

Odell, S. (1997). Preparing teachers for teacher leadership. *Action in Teacher Education, 19*(3), 120-124.

Spradley, J. (1979). *The ethnographic interview.* New York: Holt, Rinehart & Winston.

◉

8 Teachers as Leaders

A Question or an Expectation?

Judy Reinhartz

Ranae Stetson

Judy Reinhartz is Professor of Education at the University of Texas at Arlington. She has been an advocate of university-public school collaborative partnerships and has served as a university field-based faculty member for the past 5 years. Her areas of expertise include science education, instructional leadership, curriculum design, and professional development.

Ranae Stetson is Assistant Professor at Texas Christian University. She was the founder and former director of the Collaborative Redesign of Education Systems in Texas Program—Center for Professional Development and Technology. Her areas of specialization include teacher education, instructional leadership, and program development.

ABSTRACT

This research identified the differences in the leadership skills and instructional effectiveness of first-year teachers trained in a professional development school (PDS) program and those trained in a traditional teacher education program. The study included 22 novice teachers and 9 elementary school principals who had hired teachers trained in both types of

157

programs. Data gathering consisted of (a) a survey completed by participating teachers regarding their perceptions of their teacher preparation program, beginning of school year skills, instructional effectiveness, classroom management, and over-all leadership skills; and (b) open-ended interviews with prin-cipals. Data derived from the principals' interviews were com-pared to the teachers' responses to determine the consistency between the teachers' self-perceptions and the principals' per-ceptions of the same categories. The findings indicate that the leadership skills and instructional effectiveness of teachers trained in a PDS exceeded those of teachers trained in a tradi-tional teacher preparation program.

It seems naive to continue thinking that the only leaders in a public school setting are those who hold positions as department chairs or team leaders or are in the hierarchies of various administrative positions. Teachers are *indeed* leaders, but as a topic of study, teachers as leaders is a fairly new addition to the teacher education literature. According to Gehrke (1991), the classroom performance of teachers who acquire leadership skills, whether they assume formal leadership positions or not, is enhanced. Although leadership skills are now expected of effective teachers, such skills have not been included or intentionally taught as part of the teacher preparation curriculum.

Lieberman, Saxl, and Miles (1988) offer guidance to teacher educators who want to formalize the development of teacher leadership behaviors. According to their study, effective teachers developed competency in a number of leadership skills, such as building rapport with others, finding and using resources, managing the leadership work, and building skills and confidence in others.

The purpose of this chapter is to describe the findings of a study conducted during spring 1997 that focused on identifying the differences in the overall leadership abilities and instructional effectiveness of first-year teachers trained in a professional development school (PDS) program and those in a traditional teacher education program (Reinhartz & Stetson, 1997). The goal of this study was to establish benchmarks for teacher preparation programs and to contribute to the literature regarding teacher leadership behaviors, with the long-term goal being the identification of teacher leadership behaviors that may enhance the likelihood that teachers will remain in the profession.

Background

In their book *Leaders,* Bennis and Nanus (1997) report that in the past 30 years over 350 definitions of leadership have emerged. To facilitate discussion of this topic as it relates to preservice teacher preparation, we agree with Knezevich's (1984) definition that leadership is a process of stimulating, developing, and working with people within an organization, focused on personnel motivation, human relationships, interpersonal communications, and organizational climate and contributing to personal growth and development.

Andrews (1987) found "a powerful relationship between leadership . . . and student outcomes" (p. 15). Leadership can be so pervasive, it affects not only how teachers perceive the work environment, but ultimately impacts student achievement. Mortimore and Sammons (1987) identified 12 factors that contribute to effectiveness as related to "purposeful leadership." Purposeful leadership happens when the instructional leader articulates a vision and creates a positive classroom environment in which all students experience success (Beach & Reinhartz, in press).

Teachers who have not developed or learned leadership behaviors may experience failure and ultimately leave the profession. According to Darling-Hammond and Cobb (1996), 50% of teachers will leave the profession in their first five years of service, with the highest attrition rate being among beginning teachers. Teachers who are effective in their classrooms and would like to exercise their growing leadership skills often have only one option—to advance to administrative roles and leave the classroom (Bartunek, 1990). In either case, teachers do not remain in the classroom as career-long educators.

Theoretical Framework

The assumption underlying this study is that teaching is a complex process in which leadership behaviors are embedded. Therefore, if the teacher preparation programs continue to exclude opportunities for developing leadership behaviors in real-world classrooms, then teacher educators may need to assume some of the responsibility for the high attrition rates in the profession.

Educators are acutely aware of the current research indicating that teacher education preparation programs need to change (Goodlad, 1994). Andrew (1997) suggests, "There is a need to benchmark best practice . . . to prevent poor teaching [and] to prepare top-flight teachers" (p. 172). Brennan and Simpson (1993) agree and state that schools will be better places for all students only if teachers are better prepared. For them, the cornerstone for preparing a teaching force is through a PDS model.

PDSs become laboratories in which there are opportunities to experiment with a variety of instructional strategies, materials, equipment, educational technology, and leadership roles. In studies conducted in 1994, Boles and Troen found that a PDS environment could nurture teacher leadership behaviors because leadership activities are a natural outgrowth of professional interests and working in team situations. Likewise, Yoder (1994) has collected over 135 articles and related anthologies that have been used by teachers to grow professionally and enhance their leadership skills and abilities.

Because PDSs have been touted to be a major solution to improve teacher preparation, it becomes critical for teacher educators to gather evidence that sheds light on the effectiveness of such programs. Andrew (1997) states, "Good teacher education programs will produce a high percentage of teachers who are successful and remain in the field" (p. 174). He defines as "good" programs with a plan that includes "sustained leadership, clear direction of improved practice, incentives for change, and ready access to help in planning and implementing change" (p. 174).

Program Description

This study involved preservice teachers who were enrolled at an urban university located in the southwestern region of the country with an enrollment of approximately 20,000 students. Because the teacher preparation program had a traditional teacher education program as well as a PDS model, it was possible to collect data from these two groups. The PDS model from which the participants in this study graduated was an intensive yearlong field-based program leading to initial elementary certification. The PDS program was collaboratively designed by teachers, principals, education professors, and business and community representatives to prepare graduates who were "job ready."

Interns (first-semester students) reported to a selected school site in either August or January with the public school faculty. Cohorts of up to 10 interns were assigned to an instructional leadership team (ILT) consisting of two to four mentor teachers and a university professor. Interns spent the majority of their week at the school site gaining knowledge about teacher decision-making, instructional strategies, classroom management and discipline strategies, and the infusion of technology as a teaching tool.

Residents (second-semester students) began teaching full-time and assumed leadership roles and responsibilities that emulated those of their mentor teachers and university professors. Much like leaders in other fields, these preservice teachers made a myriad of decisions regarding the management of resources, human relationships, and selection and sequence of events.

The students who chose the traditional teacher education program at the university had education classes taught on the university campus with field assignments associated with specific courses, culminating in a 10- to 12-week student teaching experience.

Methodology

This qualitative research study was designed to generate descriptive data that identified the differences, if any, between beginning teachers trained in the PDS model described above and those in the traditional program. As it was a qualitative study, there was no attempt to generate statistical analyses on the data collected or to statistically compare these two groups. It is hoped the descriptive results reported, which are based on the principals' and teachers' feedback, prove helpful in expecting teachers to become leaders.

Data-gathering procedures consisted of two methods: (a) a survey completed by participating teachers, and (b) open-ended interviews with principals who had hired the novice teachers. Data derived from the principals' interviews were compared to the teachers' survey responses to determine the consistency between the teachers' self-reported perceptions and the principals' perceptions of the same experiences.

Participants of the Study. A total of 22 elementary school teacher participants had completed at least one year of classroom teaching in a public school setting. All but one of the 22 participants were female. Twelve of the respondents were graduates of the PDS model and 10 were graduates of the traditional model. The average age of all participants was 30. The ethnicity of both groups was primarily Caucasian, with two African Americans in the traditional group and one Hispanic American in the PDS group. There was an equal distribution of degreed and nondegreed students in each group.

All teacher participants completed their training program during the same time frame. Also, they met the minimum entrance requirements established by the teacher education unit (2.75 or higher overall grade point average) and had passed all areas of the Texas Academic Skills Program exam (reading, writing, and math proficiencies). Participants were contacted by telephone to determine their willingness to complete the Perceptions of First Year Teachers Survey, originally designed by Stetson and Riner (1993).

The nine participating principals, from two local school districts, had 3 to 27 years of experience. All had recently hired first-year teachers from both programs. Each principal participated in an interview focused on his or her perceptions of the novice teachers' abilities in the five categories described in the Perceptions of the Principal Interview Protocol (Stetson & Stetson, 1994; Stetson & Reinhartz, 1997b, adding demographic data portion). The categories of central interest to the researchers included the principals' perceptions of their teachers' abilities in beginning of school year skills, instructional effectiveness, classroom management, and overall leadership skills and abilities. Interviews lasted 60 to 90 minutes, and each principal had a copy of the protocol.

Instruments. The Perceptions of First Year Teachers Survey (Stetson & Riner, 1993; Stetson & Reinhartz, 1997a) assessed the teachers' perceptions of their preparation, beginning of year skills, instructional effectiveness, classroom management, and overall leadership skills and abilities. Open-ended questions also provided information concerning the novice teachers' satisfaction with their programs in preparing them for successful first year of teaching. Each item in the remaining sections of the survey (i.e., Opening of School Functions; Instructional Effectiveness; Classroom Management, and Leadership Skills and Abilities) was designed to be answered using a 5-point Likert scale response format from three perspectives:

Importance: How important is knowledge or skill in this area to be an effective teacher?

Preparation: How well do you think your teacher preparation program prepared you to demonstrate skill in this area?

Need: How great is your need to obtain additional information or training in this area? (PRAXIS III, 1987)

Cronbach's alpha was the measure of reliability used to establish coefficients on this instrument. Kanouse (1996) lists alpha coefficients for internal consistency ranging from .88 on the Importance section, to .97 on the Preparedness section, and to .99 on the Need section.

The second instrument, Perceptions of the Principal Interview Protocol (Stetson & Stetson, 1994; Stetson & Reinhartz, 1997b), was designed to explore differences, if any, in overall instructional effectiveness, classroom management, and leadership ability of participants.

Findings

The following section reports data from the Perceptions of First Year Teachers Survey and comments from interviews with principals. Interviews with the principals were conducted before the data from the teachers were received, and findings are reported for each of the five categories in the survey. Group data used to test the comparisons include the mean scores of the respondents in the three categories previously discussed, Importance, Preparation, and Need.

Perceptions of Quality—Teacher Preparation Program. One of the questions the graduates were asked was, "Looking back at the beginning of the school year, do you believe that you had an advantage over other new teachers who graduated from programs different from yours?" Participants responded yes or no, and, if yes, a rationale and example(s) of some advantages were cited.

All 12 (100%) of the PDS-trained teachers responded, yes, they felt they had an advantage over other applicants. Their comments included, "[I had] less fear of teaching," "[I] settled into the routine of teaching much sooner with less stress," "My computer knowledge has put me far ahead of other teachers," "I have spent the last year fine-tuning my skills, not just trying to survive," and "I was well prepared for parent conferences, field trips, school programs, discipline problems, etc. Because I was able to participate in a full year of education training *with children,* as opposed to popping in for 10 weeks."

In contrast, only two (20%) of the traditionally trained teachers answered, yes, and they responded, "I am a mother and now a teacher," and "I had substituted while I was enrolled in [the teacher education program named]."

During the interviews, the principals were asked to comment on teachers who interviewed for a teaching position. Sample comments from the principals regarding the hiring of PDS- and traditionally trained teachers included,

- "PDS were better versed—more confident, knowledgeable, gave more global responses that required understanding the big picture in teaching. Answered questions like a veteran. Instead of saying, 'What I *would* do . . . ,' PDS students answered, 'Well, what I *did* was . . .'."
- "[PDS teachers] saw the big picture, for example, how teachers work together, utilizing technology, less timid in asking for help/assistance. They were more relaxed in the school setting."
- "[PDS] students were more fluent in their responses. They have more confidence because they have more experience to draw on; they have a better understanding of what it takes to be a teacher."
- "[PDS teachers] talk in specifics; for example, they can share how to modify a lesson because they have lived side-by-side with a teacher who did this."

Opening of School Functions. Another section of the survey sought information about the general organization of the classroom. Many of these items are consistent with those that Appleton (1995) contends are contributing factors to establishing a well-ordered classroom. Examples included the teachers' perceived ability in establishing routines early in the year, understanding the impact and implementation of school or district policies and procedures, having knowledge of available materials and resources, communicating with parents, and having a plan to handle emergency situations.

On all 10 items, the PDS participants felt the topics were more important to learn than their traditionally trained peers did because they felt better prepared and felt less need for more additional training.

These self-perceptions were supported by the principals' comments. The following quotes from principals regarding the ability to handle the Opening of School Functions include:

- "One [PDS teacher] in particular was very different. She was a consummate risk taker. The first day she had no bulletin boards— they were for the kids' ideas and products. The classroom was truly centered on teamwork and cooperation."

- "[PDS teachers] were less frustrated, their level of anxiety at a lower level; required less attention than other beginning teachers. They were confident and enthusiastic. One would think they had taught several years."

- "PDS teachers have a better sense of what needs to be done; they don't wait to be told."

- "[PDS teachers] already knew school schedules, there were fewer surprises they had to face—they knew the faculty, they don't act estranged."

- "[PDS teachers] are not isolated from the faculty; they talked to them as they had over the course of the past year."

Instructional Effectiveness. Participants were asked 21 different questions about their self-perceptions of instructional effectiveness. Sample items included planning and preparing lessons, integrating curriculum, using supplementary materials, using a variety of instructional strategies, modeling for students, making transitions, developing student confidence and esteem, addressing needs of diverse learners, using grouping techniques, and implementing a variety of assessment and evaluation methods.

The PDS-trained teachers rated themselves much higher on 18 of the 21 questions regarding effective instructional practices. The items with the greatest differences were planning for instruction (including long-range curriculum goals, daily plans, and unit planning), integrating curriculum, using a variety of teaching strategies, modeling for students, making smooth transitions, monitoring and adjusting, and using grouping techniques. The only items where differences in measures were minimal were assessing and reteaching, appropriate pacing and wait time, and using supplementary materials. The traditionally trained teachers reported a greater need for more information in those areas.

The following comments were recorded from principals and serve as a sample that reinforces the participants' perceptions of their teaching effectiveness.

- "[PDS teacher] needs less of everything. . . . She didn't struggle as a first-year teacher. You hear of differences [strategies] to use and she understood this concept and practiced using them."

- "The PDS teachers are more child driven. Planning started from student needs whereas the traditionally trained students were more curriculum driven."

- "The PDS teachers come with a lot more under their belts. When new students came into the classroom, the [PDS] teacher did not skip a beat about what to do."

- "The PDS program provides students with a more comprehensive view of planning for instruction. The university-based students don't plan as thoroughly. [PDS] people come in with planning built in."

- "The PDS teachers are professionals. They have a repertoire of strategies. They hit the ground running. They can anticipate what students need next. Non [PDS] teachers experience a period of tentativeness; they are unsure about working with parents at first."

- "[PDS teachers] come with more strategies because they tried more and failed more . . . "

- "[PDS teacher] seems to be able to work with students and knows how to assess levels of abilities. She makes good referrals—before she comes to us for referral she had assessed and knew where the student stood."

- "[PDS teachers] are better at self-analysis and consider the consequences."

- "[PDS] teachers show evidence of self-reflection. . . . They would say, 'I did _____, and it did not work. Do you have any ideas?'"
- "PDS teachers are better at self-evaluation . . . they are more honest with themselves. University-based teachers don't examine themselves."

Classroom Management. It has been well documented that both management and instruction are essential for effective student achievement in classrooms (Doyle, 1986; Freiberg, Prokosch, & Stein, 1990; Good & Brophy, 1994; Weade & Evertson, 1988).

Sample items from this category on the survey included attention-getting strategies, routines for materials distribution and collection, giving clear directions, establishing rules and routines, motivating students, preventing and redirecting off-task behaviors, using appropriate reinforcements, knowledge of patterns of student movement in the classroom, with-itness, multidimensionality, and using nonverbal communication cues.

The PDS-trained teachers rated the importance of learning about classroom management higher than those traditionally trained. Conversely, the traditionally trained teachers rated their level of preparedness lower, compared to the PDS teachers. Furthermore, need for further training in classroom management and discipline was rated lower by the PDS teachers.

On all items in the Classroom Management and Discipline category, the PDS teachers rated themselves better prepared than their counterparts did. Perhaps working with actual children over an extended period of time adds a degree of credibility to the classroom management theories that is not accomplished during a short-term experience. The findings that the development of classroom management and discipline skills are not only important but central to good preparation are consistent with the plethora of research by Veenman (1984) and cited in Murray (1996).

In the area of classroom management skills, the principals had a lot to say about both groups of teachers. The most often cited comment was similar to this one, "Yes, there is a difference. Office referrals for PDS teachers are disproportionately lower—they seem to be able to handle their difficult students. They generate their own solutions." In addition, the principals commented,

- "[PDS teacher] is very organized and not afraid to ask for help. She has a lot of self-confidence, is very aware of grouping strategies. . . . She is willing to share her ideas."

- "I did note that the referrals to the office are less for PDS teachers because they try to problem-solve."

- "The field-based teachers are more willing to let go and learn from different situations. They are not afraid to try new things—they have divided students into groups where other new teachers are more reluctant to try new grouping patterns and management techniques because more new teachers are concerned that students will get out of control."

- "It's hard for first-year teachers to keep up with everything like multidimensionality and transitions. [PDS teacher] knew how to get from A to Z within the time frames given."

- "[PDS] teachers do a better job of using their time. Their momentum and pacing are excellent."

- "There is a difference in two areas. The [PDS] teacher is better at engaging students, making transitions, keeping students on task, and monitoring students. The second area is that she is better at pacing and maximizing learning during the day."

- "She [PDS teacher] knew all the tools of helping kids, cueing systems, etc. . . . She has very 'healthy discipline' habits."

- "Redirecting and maximizing student behavior was definitely better [PDS]."

Leadership Skills and Abilities. Another section of the survey dealt with traits commonly identified as indicative of leadership skills and ability. The leadership behaviors studied included risk taking, taking the initiative, building relationships (students, peers, parents, administrators), building positive esteem in others, managing diversity and inclusion in a group, making decisions, being self-reliant, managing resources, and reflective self-evaluation.

Under the Importance category of this section, the PDS teachers rated all items more important to learn than did those traditionally trained. Items in which the mean scores of the PDS respondents were much higher included managing diversity and inclusion in a group, building relationships, and reflective self-evaluation. Under the Preparation category, PDS teachers reported that they felt they were especially well prepared in reflective self-evaluation, building relationships, managing diversity and inclusion, risk taking, and taking initiative. Conversely, the traditionally trained teachers reported feeling the least prepared in these same areas.

The mean scores under the Need category were 1.9 for PDS- and traditionally trained teachers (scale, 1 = low; 5 = high). This was the only category that had the same mean score for both groups. Apparently both PDS- and traditionally trained teachers felt the need for more training in this area.

Level of self-confidence of the PDS teachers was most often cited by principals in the category of Leadership Skills and Abilities. All but one principal cited self-confidence as one of the indicators of leadership for the PDS teachers they hired. Their comments support this assertion: "The main difference was that PDS people had more self-confidence," "[PDS teacher] wasn't that nervous. She was ready to go," "Especially the self-confidence—the field-based [PDS] teachers are more like second-year teachers," "The PDS teachers were part of several innovations this year (i.e., class participation to Kiwanis Club for funding)," "The PDS teacher seemed more accustomed to diversity. Some of my traditionally trained teachers did have a course but it depends on working with the individuals," and "[PDS teachers] worked with different students more effectively. They were more aware of their individual learning styles."

Discussion

The strength of this initial study lies in establishing a relationship between a PDS program and enhancing the leadership capacity of beginning teachers. Based on the qualitative data collected, it appears that PDS-trained teachers may have a more positive attitude about their training, which may translate into having better feelings about being better prepared. It may be making a cognitive leap to suggest that teachers who feel better prepared are more likely to be leaders and remain in teaching, but it is an area that certainly warrants further attention.

The traditionally trained teachers in this study reported they had greater needs and many did not feel prepared for their first day of class. They reported gaps in their teacher education knowledge that greatly concerned them. None of the traditionally trained teachers reported taking on leadership roles in their grade-level teams or at the campus level. The principals interviewed confirmed this information. Many of the traditionally trained teachers frequently made comments alluding to the fact that they were still learning and needed more time to get into the role of being a teacher.

PDS teachers seemed to volunteer more than most new teachers at their school and the principals openly valued and admired their emerging leadership abilities. The principals cited as evidence of teachers' leadership skills (a) taking risks in trying new strategies and using technology in their classrooms, (b) appearing not to be threatened or intimidated by students who challenged them or by their supervisor's classroom observations, and (c) working long hours and the workload seeming not to come as a surprise. The principals concluded the PDS-trained teachers seemed better at evaluating themselves and dealing with their personal weaknesses by participating in problem-solving sessions.

According to the principals, both groups of teachers were involved in school functions, but the PDS teachers distinguished themselves by assisting other teachers, finding and using a variety of resources, and implementing ways to use technology in their classrooms. They, in effect, broke the mold of the timid, quiet beginning teacher who often functions from crisis to crisis.

What may have made the PDS model described in this study successful was the level of collaboration that implemented a vision of what was possible in creating new and better schools with new and better teachers and teacher educators. PDS team members spent their time brainstorming better ways to reach children, to present information, to use technology, and to be better teachers and leaders.

Teachers may not automatically become leaders; the development of leadership skills has to be deliberately built into the teacher preparation program, nurtured, modeled, and implemented in a safe environment. As Knezevich (1984) stated, leadership is "a process of . . . working with people within an organization." (p. 60). In PDSs, preservice teachers may have more opportunities to practice leadership behaviors in their classrooms and at the campus level because there is an environment that encourages them to focus on significant issues, including decision making and the development of teacher leadership skills.

We fully realize that further research is needed to look more closely at the relationship between teacher leadership development, instructional effectiveness, and longevity in the profession. Preliminary results from this study seem to suggest that teacher leadership skills are a part of effective teaching and can be identified, but more in-depth studies are needed to determine the most efficient manner for translating these leadership skills into pedagogical applications in the teacher preparation curriculum. Teacher educators should be proactive to ensure that "purposeful leadership" skills are developed and expected of teacher education graduates. Leadership skills should not be random, unplanned acts, but intentionally embedded in a teacher preparation curriculum.

References

Andrew, M. D. (1997). What matters most for teacher educators. *Journal of Teacher Education, 48*(3), 167-176.

Andrews, R. (1987). On leadership and student achievement: A conversation with Richard Andrews. *Educational Leadership 45*(1), 9-16.

Appleton, K. (1995). Routines and the first few weeks of class. *The Clearing House, 68*(5), 293-296.

Bartunek, H. M. (1990). *The classroom teacher as teacher educator.* (ERIC Document Reproduction Service No. 335 297)

Beach, D. M., & Reinhartz, J. (in press). *Supervision: Focus on instruction* (2nd ed.). Boston: Allyn & Bacon.

Bennis, W., & Nanus, B. (1997). *Leaders: The strategies for taking charge.* New York: Harper & Row.

Boles, K., & Troen, V. (1994). *Teacher leadership in a professional development school.* (ERIC Document Reproduction Service No. ED 375 103)

Brennan, S., & Simpson, K. (1993, Summer). The professional development school: Lessons from the past, prospects for the future. *Action in Teacher Education, 15*(2), 9-17.

Darling-Hammond, L., & Cobb, V. (1996). The changing context of teacher education. In F. B. Murray, (Ed.), *The teacher educator's handbook: Building a knowledge base for the preparation of teachers* (pp. 14-62). San Francisco: Jossey-Bass.

Doyle, W. (1986). Classroom organization and management. In M. Wittrock (Ed.), *Handbook of research on teaching* (3rd ed., pp. 392-431). New York: Macmillan.

Freiberg, H. J., Prokosch, N., & Stein, (1990, April). *Turning around at-risk schools: A three-year perspective.* Paper presented at the annual meeting of the American Education Research Association, Boston.

Gehrke, N. (1991). *Developing teachers' leadership skills.* (ERIC Document Reproduction Service No. 330 691)

Good, T. L., & Brophy J. E. (1994). *Looking in classrooms* (6th ed.). New York: HarperCollins.

Goodlad, J. I. (1994). *Educational renewal: Better teachers, better schools.* San Francisco: Jossey-Bass.

Kanouse, C. A. (1996). *Characteristics of candidates completing two teacher education program models.* Unpublished doctoral dissertation, Texas A & M University—Commerce.

Knezevich, S. J. (1984). *Administration of public education* (4th ed.). New York: Harper & Row.

Lieberman, A., Saxl, E., & Miles, M. (1988). Teacher leadership: Ideology and practice. In A. Lieberman (Ed.), *Building a professional culture in schools* (pp. 148-166). New York: Teachers College Press.

Mortimore, P., & Sammons, P. (1987). New evidence on effective elementary schools. *Educational Leadership, 45*(1), 4-8.

Murray, F. B. (1996). (Ed.). *The teacher educator's handbook: Building a knowledge base for the preparation of teachers.* San Francisco: Jossey-Bass.

PRAXIS III. (1987). *Classroom performance assessments.* Princeton, NJ: Educational Testing Service.

Reinhartz, J., & Stetson, R. (1997, February). *Enhancing preservice teacher leadership behaviors: Best practices in classroom management.* Paper presented at the American Association of Colleges for Teacher Education (AACTE) Annual Conference, Phoenix, AZ.

Stetson E., & Riner, P. (1993). *Perceptions of first year teachers survey.* Unpublished document, Texas A & M University—Commerce.

Stetson, E., & Stetson, R. (1994, February). *Perceptions of principal interview protocol.* Presented at the American Association of Colleges for Teacher Education (AACTE), Chicago.

Stetson R., & Reinhartz, J. (1997a). *Perceptions of first year teachers survey.* Unpublished document, Texas Christian University, Fort Worth.

Stetson, R., & Reinhartz, J. (1997b). *Perceptions of principal interview protocol.* Unpublished document, Texas Christian University, Fort Worth.

Veenman, S. (1984, Summer). Perceived problems of beginning teachers. *Review of Educational Research, 54*(2), 143-178.

Weade, R., & Evertson, C. 1988. The construction of lessons in effective and less effective classrooms. *Teaching and Teacher Education, 4*(3), 189-213.

Yoder, N. (1994). *Teacher leadership: An annotated bibliography.* Washington, DC: Danforth Foundation, National Foundation for the Improvement of Education.

9   Professional Development Schools

A Comprehensive View

Frances K. Kochan

Frances K. Kochan is Director of the Truman Pierce Institute and Associate Professor in Educational Foundations, Leadership, and Technology, Auburn University, Alabama. Her current research interests focus on school-university collaboration and school and curriculum transformation.

ABSTRACT

This study gathered data regarding the problems encountered, the solution strategies employed to solve them, and the benefits received through professional development school (PDS) endeavors. The majority of problems dealt with human and structural issues. Those involved in these endeavors view them as having a positive impact on preparing preservice teachers, improving schools, and creating learning communities. They appear to be the result of individual commitment rather than institutional change. Thus, whether individual effort can overcome institutional inertia and whether these schools will and should continue are yet to be determined.

Professional Development Schools: Examining the Big Picture

The desire on the part of teachers and teacher educators to raise the status of teaching to that of a profession has a long history (Devaney, 1990; Holmes Group, 1986; Murray & Fallon, 1989). This desire is one of the focal points of the present educational reform movement, which calls for a transformation of teacher education and schools (Holmes Group, 1995; Stallings & Kowalski, 1990). A cornerstone of such transformation involves connecting the schooling of PreK-12 students with the education of teachers. One strategy for making these connections and enhancing the profession of teaching is through the creation of school-university partnerships (Berg & Murphy, 1992; Combs, 1988; Lanier, 1994; Zimpher, 1990). There have been numerous proposals for creating such relationships (American Association of Colleges for Teacher Education, 1994; Carnegie Forum on Education and the Economy, 1986; Glickman, 1993; Goodlad, 1990; Holmes Group, 1986, 1990; Sizer, 1992). Among the most visible is the Holmes Group proposal (1990), which suggested creating professional development schools (PDSs).

Although the National Council for Accreditation of Teacher Education (NCATE) is engaged in developing PDS standards, there are presently no commonly established criteria for designating a school as a PDS (Nystrand 1991) and these schools are diverse in structure and organization (Fullan, Galluzzo, Morris, & Watson, 1996; Hardin & Kunkel, 1994). Labaree and Pallas (1996), however, suggest that a PDS "seeks to establish a wide-ranging and long-term collaboration whose goals include promoting intensive professional development, restructured educational roles and practices, establishing sites of best practice for the preparation of future teachers, and carrying out educational research" (p. 25).

Research Objectives

Successful collaboration between schools and universities is unusual. The primary reason is that the goals, values, cultures, and governance styles of these organizations are very different, thus hindering the ability of individuals to maintain collaborative relationships (Button, Ponticell, & Johnson, 1996; Colburn, 1993; Restine, 1996). Some problems have been identified in creating PDS initiatives. Among the most common are a lack of time, funding, and personnel resources; policy constraints; and conflicts in the cultures that inhibit communication and the ability of individuals to work together effectively (Darling-Hammond, 1994; Ishler & Edens, 1994; Labaree & Pallas, 1996; Nystrand, 1991; Yinger & Hendricks, 1990). There are those who argue that such endeavors are "costly, time-consuming, and labor-intensive" and rob the institutions of resources to deal with other important parts of their mission (Labaree & Pallas, 1996, p. 27). Although claims for the benefits and importance of such initiatives are often made, there has been little research into the factors that contribute to PDS success or the benefits from such endeavors (Button et al., 1996).

Most of the research on PDSs has involved case studies. In fact, Murray (1996) suggests individual case studies are a preferred method for understanding these endeavors. There has been minimal research done to gather information across cases and settings to examine the problems encountered, solutions attempted, or benefits accrued in a wide range of institutions. This study sought to investigate the developmental aspects of PDS initiatives across sites.

Methodology

A survey was sent to participants who had attended a national conference on PDSs. The respondents were asked to anonymously identify their position and to respond to open-ended questions about the primary problems they encountered, the solutions they implemented to overcome the problems, the major frustrations they faced, and the major benefits accrued from PDS initiatives. Respondents were asked to rate their levels of success in implementing their PDS. There was also a section provided for individuals to make additional comments.

A total of 75 individuals, representing 50 institutions, submitted the completed forms, resulting in a response rate of 51%. Fifty-eight percent of the respondents were from higher education, 45% of whom were faculty and 13% administrators. Thirty-three percent of the respondents were from the PreK-12 area. Twenty-two and a half percent of them were faculty and 9.5% were administrators. The remaining 9.5 % classified themselves in the "other" category. As in any study, it is difficult to ascertain whether those who responded were more committed or involved in PDS endeavors than those who did not respond. It is likewise not possible to determine whether responses from those who did not participate would have changed the results. All that can be said is that the conclusions reached represent the compiled responses of 51% of the group surveyed. Likert-scale questions were analyzed to compute the means, standard deviation, and range for each question. A content analysis was conducted for open-ended questions by grouping responses into like categories and reclassifying until saturation occurred. A quantitative analysis was also conducted to determine the number of times each problem, frustration, or benefit was identified and the percent of total for each response in any category.

Results

Problems and Solutions

There were 101 problems identified. After examining them, I determined that they fit into the four environmental frames identified by Bolman and Deal (1991). These authors organize all organizational activities around four frames: Human, Structural, Political, and Symbolic. The frames are described more fully in the results that follow. The percent of total of the responses in each of these frames is described in Figure 9.1.

The Human Frame. The majority of problems (34%) were found in the Human Frame, which stresses the needs, motives, and actions of individuals in the organization. Problems in the Human Frame were separated into two subcategories: lack of commitment and communication. In the area of commitment, people wrote of the lack of a "critical mass" of people who both believed in and participated in the initiative. Comments such as "lack of total commitment from the university faculty," "need cooperation of all faculty in the PreK-12 school," and "it is not a priority among all our other responsibilities," were very common. There were also indications that some faculty at both sites were opposed to the idea and "vocally work against" these efforts. Respondents also noted a "lack of trust" on the part of school personnel that hindered their desire to commit themselves to these activities. Part of this mistrust seemed to be connected to the communication subcategory. Problems here involved those engaged in the endeavor as well as those who were not involved from whom support

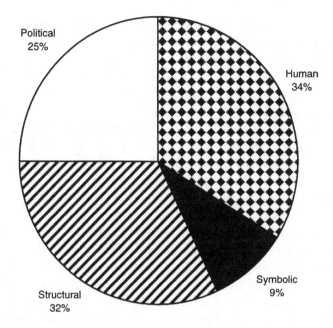

Figure 9.1: Categories of Problems Encountered in Creating a PDS by Percent of the Total for Each of the Environmental Frames

would be beneficial. Communication difficulties included such things as the "lack of a shared vision, among and between the partners" and "a need to keep everyone better informed."

Solution strategies for dealing with these problems centered on establishing personal trust. Conducting regularly scheduled meetings, creating faculty teams rather than "working alone," and engaging in a "constant struggle to communicate" were typical solution strategies to problems in this frame.

The Structural Frame. The Structural Frame deals with issues related to coordination, rules, and goals and the extent to which work gets accomplished. There were almost as many problems reported in this frame (32%) as in the Human Frame. The majority of difficulties in this frame were placed in a subcategory labeled time. Responses in this subcategory dealt with the limited time available for individuals to engage in these activities. Job responsibilities and time demands remained at the same level while new responsibilities for the PDS were being added. This "add-on" mentality has made it extremely difficult for people to find time for meetings, which has negatively impacted their efforts to coordinate tasks, roles, and responsibilities. One respondent wrote, "It is difficult to commit the necessary time to get the program going." Others agreed, writing that the biggest problem is "time on all levels and in many ways. It takes an intensive commitment of faculty time."

The structures in which these people are operating are not being reorganized to permit opportunities to develop policies or structures that could transform roles and responsibilities and enhance trust. People wrote of not being able to "find time to discuss ideas and develop strategies." This has hampered the planning process, which in turn has impeded progress. These data suggest there are few overall plans being developed that delineate rights, responsibilities, and expectations for these efforts, and this has hindered the creation and maintenance of PDSs.

The second subcategory in the Structural Frame dealt with logistics. People had difficulties in dealing with conflicting schedules, traveling long distances, and operating in inadequate facilities. Among the comments made concerning these problems were, "working out logistics of courses," "difficulty getting faculty to distant PDS," and "trouble in scheduling meetings and classes."

In trying to resolve these problems, respondents dealt with the time issue through strategies such as reduced course loads, paying for periodic teacher release time, expanding classroom time for interns, rotating job responsibilities, and conducting university classes at school locations They also handled this problem by sacrificing and simply "investing personal time" in the process. Other than holding classes on site to deal with logistic difficulties, there were few solutions offered to overcome distance and scheduling problems.

The Political Frame. The Political Frame focuses on issues of power, control, and authority. In the Political Frame, problems were reported in three subcategories: leadership, funding, and policies. The leadership issues dealt with the inability or lack of desire on the part of school leaders to engage in innovation and with a lack of leadership support at higher organizational levels. Illustrative responses included, "We work in a large urban setting. It is hard for the leadership to put PDS on a priority with everything else that has to be accomplished" and "The leader is not a person of vision." Another problem in the political realm was the lack of funding for this effort. Those with power in both organizational settings do not appear to be forthcoming with funds. Although respondents simply noted "lack of funding" as a problem and did not specify the impact associated with it, it is easy to connect this problem with those identified in the other frames. Without adequate funding, it is difficult to provide time, restructure roles and responsibilities, and provide financial and other rewards to facilitate the development and long-term operations of the PDS.

The third subcategory in the Political Frame concerned policies. The comments in this category referred to such things as "conflicts with the Master Contract," " bureaucratic rules and policies hindering efforts," and "institutional constraints." These barriers appear to block individual capacity to plan and act in ways that build community and serve educational needs.

Some individuals were able to overcome the funding problem through the acquisition of outside grant money. There were no solutions offered to deal with the lack of leadership or for coping with the policy issues that impeded PDS efforts.

The Symbolic Frame. The Symbolic Frame relates to issues of tradition, symbols, and beliefs steeped in operations, history, and culture. Problems in the Symbolic Frame fell into two subcategories: cultures and traditions. Those responses that dealt with difficulties in blending the two organizations were labeled as cultures. Those things related to specific ways of operating were classified as traditions. When writing of cultural issues, respondents noted that problems were due to "the different cultures, calendars, daily rhythms." One wrote, "Building the relationship between two constituencies who have operated independently and focused solely on their projects" is difficult. Another remarked, "The university people take so long to make decisions and don't seem to be all on the same page as the public school faculty." In the subcategory of traditions, respondents wrote of the inability of individuals to move beyond their traditional ways of functioning. One individual put it this way: "Moving university personnel into a new paradigm of teacher prep" is the biggest problem. Another wrote of difficulties in "merging training philosophy of best practice with training teachers' philosophies." A third cited "university rigidity and tradition" as a problem. Another noted, "Persons [are] reluctant or unwilling to relinquish territory."

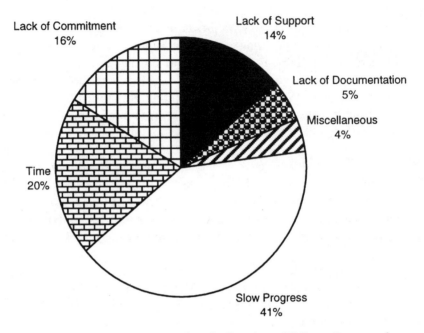

Figure 9.2: Categories of Frustrations in Creating a PDS as a Percent of Total Frustrations

Solutions in the Symbolic Frame were very similar to those in the Human Frame. Respondents sought to blend cultures through bringing people together to share ideas and learn to understand one another in a more in-depth manner. Many wrote of being "persistent" and understanding that such change "takes time."

Areas of Frustration

Addressing the issue of problems in a slightly different way with the question, "What is your greatest frustration?" elicited responses illustrating a somewhat altered perspective. There appeared to be five major categories of frustration. Four percent of the responses could not be categorized and were placed in a "Miscellaneous" category. The categories and percent of total responses are presented in Figure 9.2.

Three of the categories identified as areas of frustration were previously identified in the problems analysis. The lack of commitment on the part of a large majority of faculty and the open resistance to the effort cited in the Human Frame were identified by 16% of respondents as a primary cause of frustration. Another previously identified concern in the Political Frame, the lack of support through funding and leadership, was identified as a source of frustration by 14% of the respondents. The lack of time to do what is required and the fact that this is "labor intensive and lonely," cited as a problem in the Structural Frame, was also singled out as a cause of frustration by 20% of individuals. The lack of a systematic method for documenting the effort was listed as a source of frustration by 5% of the individuals. Interestingly, 41% of the respondents reported the greatest degree of frustration as the slow pace of change that was occurring. People wrote comments like, "It is a slow process and we can't get beyond small pockets of change." One person commented on "the slow paced integration between schools' philosophies and actual practices vis-a-vis university training philosophies. In a word, they are same—in practice they differ." Another respondent noted, "Despite 7 years at the effort, the work doesn't get any easier—that has been the biggest surprise." A comprehensive response capturing the essence of this issue was, "Change is a process, not an event. It takes time to become what it needs to be."

Perceived Levels of Success and Benefits

Using a 5-point Likert scale from no success (1) to highly successful (5), respondents were asked to rate their level of success in achieving PDS purposes. The five purposes used were those identified by the Holmes Group (1986). These purposes and responses are presented in Table 9.1. Participants were also asked to respond to the question, "What are the greatest benefits of your PDS?" There were 143 benefits listed. They were placed into six categories depicted as a percent of total in Figure 9.3. Since the benefit categories are closely related to the PDS purposes, these data are being reported together.

The response to the question regarding overall success with a mean of 3.69 and a range of 2 to 5 indicates that most respondents viewed their endeavors as successful. The most successful PDS purpose was "preparing preservice teachers," which had a mean score of 4.06 and a range of 2 to 5. This perception of success was verified in the responses to the benefits question. Forty-one percent of the respondents identified benefits in the

TABLE 9.1 Respondents' Perceived Levels of Success in Achieving PDS Purposes

Questions Asked of Survey Subjects	Mean	S.D.	Skew	S.E.	Min	Max	N
Extent to which you believe your PDS is operating successfully	3.69	.73	−.13	.28	2	5	71
Success level for preparing preservice teacher and other educators	4.06	.78	−.48	.29	2	5	70
Success level for providing opportunities for developing collaborative learning communities	3.62	.82	.00	.29	2	5	69
Success level for providing continuing education for professionals	3.25	.79	−.67	.28	1	5	71
Success level for providing an exemplary education for all PreK-12 students	3.35	.79	.15	.28	2	5	71
Success level for conducting research and inquiry	2.81	.89	−.13	.29	1	5	70

category Improved Teacher Education. There were three subcategories in this area. The first and most often listed benefit was enhanced preservice experience. Typical responses in this subcategory were, "a much more realistic experience for pre-service teachers," "preservice teachers [are] exposed to tremendous student and program diversity," and "preservice teachers have received more authentic preparation." A second subcategory of benefits was program improvement. Benefits in this subcategory involved improvements in the teacher education programs. Illustrative responses were, "helped us build a model demonstration program," and "enlivened our teacher education program." The third subcategory of benefits in improving teacher education was self-renewal. One faculty member wrote that this initiative had resulted in "personal enrichment for my own graduate teaching and research." Another commented, "Approaches to curricula have rejuvenated some professors."

Mean scores for success rates on "forming collaborative learning communities" of 3.62, with a range of 2 to 5, indicated that respondents again felt somewhat to highly successful in their ability to form a collabo-

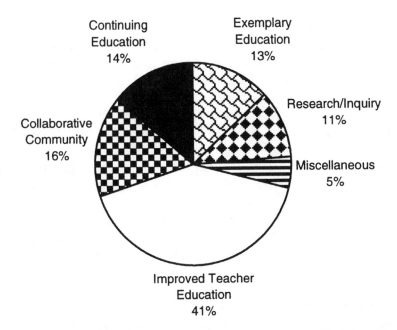

Continuing
Education
14%

Exemplary
Education
13%

Research/Inquiry
11%

Collaborative
Community
16%

Miscellaneous
5%

Improved Teacher
Education
41%

Figure 9.3: Categories of Benefits of PDS by the Percent of Total Benefits

rative learning community. This was confirmed when respondents identified benefits using the open-ended question. The category in which the second highest number of benefits was identified was Creating Collaborative Communities. Sixteen percent of the responses identified benefits related to forming these communities. Responses were organized into three subcategories. The first of these, trust, dealt with the expansion of respect and trust among university and school faculties. Participants wrote of "the mutual respect and better understanding of each others' organizations, jobs, and cultures," "changing of roles," and "reduced barriers between universities and schools." A second important benefit was in the subcategory theory and practice. There were many remarks such as "being able to bridge the gap between theory and practice" and "undergraduates are more able to relate theory to practice" that described this benefit. The third subcategory dealt with the change in roles and relationships that helped create an increase in collaborative activities and an ability to learn from one another. This was reflected in remarks such as "professional growth for all faculty," "we can learn from one another," "close collaboration with K-12 and university in many areas," and "everyone becomes a learner." These benefits were described as long term in nature, with the learning community acquiring a sense of permanence and growth. One respondent wrote that this is an "always extending cooperative effort between the university and schools."

The mean score for success in providing an exemplary education for all PreK-12 students was 3.35, with a range of 2 to 5, indicating that respondents were somewhat to highly successful in this endeavor. Thirteen percent of responses on the open-ended question identified benefits in a closely related category, Exemplary Education. The responses fell into two subcategories, assisting students and school improvement. Respondents commented on the value of more personnel to assist students and they noted that it was beneficial to have "more helping hands and hearts" and "extra eyes and ears to help students." The comments concerning school improvement dealt with expanding diverse practices in the schools, connecting the university to school restructuring efforts, helping to expand school improvement planning strategies and efforts, and improving the climate of the school. Closely related were improvements specific to a program or curricular area. Among those reported were, "There is an increase in science teaching, [development of] physical knowledge lab" and "There is an increased level of consciousness of best practices."

Mean scores for success (3.25) in providing continuing education for professionals indicated moderate success, but the range of scores (1-5) suggests that some people are experiencing no success. When describing benefits, 14% of the responses identified a benefit placed into a category labeled Continuing Education. Benefits in this category focused on the professional development opportunities provided by the university and the aspect of self-renewal and professional growth that was occurring because of involvement in the PDS. Characteristic remarks were, "the opportunity to grow in our profession" and "many teachers are taking charge of their own professional development." One of the most positive comments was, "exciting, stimulating, exhausting, and most definitely professionally enhancing."

Conducting research and inquiry had the lowest success rate of the five PDS goals: 2.81, with a range of 1 to 5. Although this was a category of benefits, such benefits were noted less frequently than any others related to the success question (11%). There were no subcategories. The benefits noted suggested an increase in collaborative action research, the creation of a mind-set among teachers that focused on inquiry, and an expansion of opportunities to connect research with practice that had resulted in numerous publications and presentations. Comments depicting these benefits were, "having the chance to examine what we do and why it works or does not work," "more reflection on the part of teachers in examining their own practice," and "collaboration in action research in areas of mutual interest."

There were 29 individuals who chose to add remarks. All were positive and contained aspects of emotional involvement. Many dealt with the pride they felt in the very existence of the PDS. Examples were, "It has become the glue that binds us together. We are united in our efforts to become the teacher educators of tomorrow not just today," "We are gradually moving into becoming whole," and "We are creating schools of hope."

Discussion and Implications

It appears that those involved in PDS endeavors view them as having a positive impact on restructuring the education of preservice teachers and preparing them to be successful teachers. Although benefits outweighed problems in numbers, the significance of these problems should not be underestimated. There are difficulties in gaining widespread support and the efforts seem largely peripheral. There is a lack of in-depth planning and few structural transformations to support the efforts. PDS endeavors appear to be a model rather than a way of operating and functioning. This is a finding previously cited and verified in this study (Robinson & Darling-Hammond, 1994).

The barriers to change may in part be a consequence of the overarching goal of a PDS that involves "becoming" rather than "doing" (Kochan, 1996), blending of cultures (Darling-Hammond, 1994), and reinventing the organization (Holmes Group, 1990). Some organizational change researchers stress that such endeavors require sustained efforts over time (Fullan, 1993) and a systemic approach that must include all aspects of the organization (Senge, 1990). This systemic, organizational approach does not seem to be driving these efforts. There appears to be a lack of structural and institutional support for them. They are being created and maintained through the work of individuals rather than as part of an overall well developed organizational plan.

An alternative view of the organizational change process, which differs from the belief that they must be "systematically and organizationally

driven" is suggested by Hearn (1996). He comments that in higher education, the "loose coupling" of the organization, which makes it difficult to
organize and systematize change, is also a strength that has enabled
individuals who persevere to create major change through individual
effort. The data in this study indicate that people are persevering and
attending to the tasks to be accomplished. They are also engaging in
strategies to overcome the lack of institutional support by focusing on
developing strong collaborative relationships, being persistent, and gaining personal commitments. These strategies are having a positive effect on
the change process and on the extent of the benefits that have ensued. It is
not yet possible to determine if this individual effort will be strong enough
or last long enough to create the type of long-term change Hearn suggests
has occurred in the past.

Emotional Involvement as an Avenue for Change

It is encouraging to note that although the slow pace of change is the
biggest frustration of those involved in the PDS process, it is also something they understand and acknowledge as unavoidable. Although there
are problems in instituting and maintaining the PDS, there were more
benefits than problems identified and individuals appear to be garnering
personal and professional satisfaction and growth from these activities.
Perhaps the most significant finding in this study was that with all the
problems described and with an obvious lack of institutional support,
these individuals ranked their efforts as quite successful and expressed
emotions of hope, excitement, and exuberance.

Research on change stresses that the fundamental core of successful
change is not the systems we use but the people who are engaged in the
process. Thus, it is in people and their relationships that we find our
greatest potential for positive and successful change (Fullan, 1993). Responses to this survey indicated a hopefulness and excitement that seems
to supersede the frustrations and lack of structural and political support
such efforts would appear to require. Individual commitment has obviously enabled people to overcome many obstacles and reinforced their
determination to persevere.

The aspects of collaborative relationships, professional community,
and hope, which were abundantly present in the data, are strong factors
in developing greater organizational capacity to change. It is in the creation

of a culture where people are interrelating that the greatest potential for success in endeavors such as the PDS may lie (Newman & Wehlage, 1995). Fullan (1996) writes, "It is easy to be hopeful when things are rosy" (p. 230). It is essential to be hopeful when they are not. "Holding onto hope in difficult situations is a necessary (although not sufficient condition for longer term survival)" (p. 230). Fullan suggests that those engaged in reforming educational structures can maintain this hope if they seek to confront differences and bring others into the fold; work on creating structural conditions that will foster the ability to maintain hopefulness; and demand new policies, incentives, and structures to support reform.

Conclusion

This results of this study indicate that many people are making valiant efforts to support PDSs and that many benefits have resulted from their dedication. There are also indications that the effort is time intensive and requires long-term individual commitment. Likewise, it appears that for the most part these efforts are the result of individual rather than organizational commitment. Although positive comments and numerous benefits are being reported, the hoped-for "reinvented institutions" do not seem to be forming. Although the findings point to some meaningful benefits, they also lead to three perplexing questions:

1. Will the individual efforts of persistent people who are emotionally involved in PDS initiatives be sufficient to create a fundamental change in teacher education?
2. If fundamental structural and organizational change do not result from PDS efforts, are the benefits accrued sufficient to accept them as alternative models to the way teacher education and schools currently operate? What are the advantages and disadvantages of such an approach?
3. Are there any cautions to be given, or disadvantages that might result from creating a totally blended community between and among schools and universities? If so, what are they?

The answers to these questions have not yet been formulated. More time is needed to determine whether the benefits of these endeavors are greater than the time and energy required to develop and sustain them. Research studies that include information from a wide group of settings, such as this one, will be needed so that we can gain an understanding of the total impact of these activities on the field and profession. It is also vital that each PDS site engage in intensive evaluation and dissemination to determine the positive and negative impact of this approach and whether it is feasible to continue such efforts. Without this knowledge, it will be difficult, if not impossible, to make appropriate decisions related to the above questions or to gain the political and financial support needed to create the structures required to make PDSs something "organizations become" instead of something "people do."

This study documented the problems of 50 institutions attempting to establish PDS relationships, solutions used to solve them, and the benefits of these endeavors. Results suggest that the commitment of those involved is reaping many benefits. But the endeavor is requiring extraordinary dedication on the part of these individuals, which may be difficult to sustain over time. The issues of whether individual effort can overcome institutional inertia and whether these individuals can and should continue to struggle to "keep hope alive" are yet to be determined.

References

American Association of Colleges for Teacher Education. (1994). *Business meeting agenda and table of contents*. Washington, DC: Author.

Berg, M., & Murphy, D. (1992). Can we mass produce a college/school partnership for professional practice? *Action in Teacher Education, 14*(1), 57-61.

Bolman, L., & Deal, T. (1991). *Reframing organization*. San Francisco: Jossey-Bass.

Button, K., Ponticell, J., & Johnson, M. (1996). Enabling school-university collaborative research: Lessons learned in professional development schools. *Journal of Teacher Education, 42*(1), 16-20.

Carnegie Forum on Education and the Economy. (1986). *A nation prepared: Teachers for the 21st century*. New York: Carnegie Foundation: Author.

Colburn, A. (1993). *Creating professional development schools* (Phi Delta Kappa Educational Foundation Fastback No. 352). Bloomington, IN: Phi Delta Kappa Educational Foundation.

Combs, A. W. (1988). New assumptions for educational reform. *Educational Leadership, 14*(5), 38-40.

Darling-Hammond, L. (Ed.). (1994). *Professional development schools: Schools for developing a profession*. New York: Teachers College Press.

Devaney, K. (1990). Holmes's hallmark: The education core. *Theory Into Practice,* 29(1), 6-12.

Fullan, M. (1993). *Change forces.* New York: Falmer.

Fullan, M. (1996). Emotion and hope: Constructive concepts for complex times. In A. Hargreaves (Ed.), *Rethinking educational change with heart and mind* (pp. 216-233). Alexandria, VA: Association for Supervision and Curriculum Development.

Fullan, M., Galluzzo, G., Morris, P., & Watson, N. (1996). *The rise and stall of reform in teacher education.* East Lansing, MI: Holmes Group.

Glickman, C. D. (1993). *Renewing America's schools.* San Francisco: Jossey-Bass.

Goodlad, J. (1990). *Teachers for our nation's schools.* San Francisco: Jossey-Bass.

Hardin, A., & Kunkel, R. C. (1994). Professional development schools: An emerging national debate. *National Association of Laboratory Schools, 14*(1), 4-8.

Hearn, J. (1996). Transforming U.S. higher education: An organizational perspective. *Innovative Higher Education, 21*(2), 141-154.

Holmes Group. (1986). *Tomorrow's teachers.* East Lansing, MI: Author.

Holmes Group. (1990). *Tomorrow's schools.* East Lansing, MI: Author.

Holmes Group. (1995). *Tomorrow's schools of education.* East Lansing, MI: Author.

Ishler, R., & Edens, K. (1994). *Professional development schools: What are the issues and challenges? How are they funded? How should they be evaluated?* University of South Carolina, Association of Colleges and Schools of Education in State Universities and Land Grant Colleges and Affiliated Private Universities.

Kochan, F. (1996, November). *Professional development schools: Problems, solutions and benefits from university faculty perspectives.* Paper presented at the annual conference of the Mid-South Educational Research Association Meeting, Tuscaloosa, AL.

Labaree, D., & Pallas, A. (1996). A disabling vision: Rhetoric and reality in tomorrow's schools of education. *Teacher's College Record, 97*(2), 166-206.

Lanier, J. (1994). Forward. In L. Darling-Hammond (Ed.), *Professional Development Schools: Schools for developing a profession* (pp. ix-xii). New York: Teachers College Press.

Murray, F. B. (1996). The narrow and broad readings of tomorrow's schools of education. *Educational Researcher, 25*(5), 28-31.

Murray, F. B., & Fallon, D. (1989). *The reform of teacher education for the 21st century: Project 30 year one report.* Newark, DE: Project 30, College of Education, University of Delaware.

Newman, F., & Wehlage, G. (1995). *Successful school restructuring.* Madison, WI: Center on Organization and Restructuring Schools.

Nystrand, R. (1991). *Professional development: Toward a new relationship for schools and universities.* Washington, DC: ERIC Clearinghouse on Teacher Education American Association of Colleges for Teacher Education.

Restine, N. L. (1996). Partnerships between schools and institutions of higher education. In R. Ackerman (Ed.-in-Chief) & P. Cordiero (Vol. Ed.), *New directions in school leadership: Vol. 2. Boundary crossings* (pp. 31-39). San Francisco: Jossey-Bass.

Robinson, S., & Darling-Hammond, L. (1994). Change for collaboration and collaboration for change: Transforming teaching through school-university partnerships. In L. Darling-Hammond (Ed.), *Professional development schools* (pp. 203-220). New York: Teachers College Press.

Senge, P. (1990). *The fifth discipline.* New York: Currency/Doubleday.

Sizer, T. (1992). *Horace's school: Redesigning the American high school.* New York: Houghton Mifflin.

Stallings, J., & Kowalski, T. (1990). Research on professional development schools. In W. Robert Houston (Ed.), *Handbook on research on teacher education* (pp. 251-256). New York: Macmillan.

Yinger, R., & Hendricks, M. (1990). An overview of reform in Holmes Group institutions. *Journal of Teacher Education, 41*(2), 21-26.

Zimpher, N. (1990). Creating professional development school sites. *Theory Into Practice, 29*(1), 4-49.

WHAT CAN WE LEARN FROM THESE MEASURES? REFLECTIONS

Gerald M. Mager

The three studies presented in this division of the yearbook look at the professional development school (PDS) in concept and practice. They provide tentative answers to many questions we have asked of ourselves about PDSs. They give us the opportunity to consider the matter of leadership in that enterprise. Below, I first review each of the studies, pointing out issues of the research and results as I see them. Then, I suggest how the three chapters together provide grounds on which we can build an understanding of emerging leadership in the PDS.

What of These Measures Themselves?

In Chapter 7, the study by Nihlen, Williams, and Sweet is situated in a school that has been designed with core PDS principles in mind.

191

Furthermore, this PDS has been 9 years in the making. The study is not about an effort just begun from which great outcomes could not be expected; rather, this "seasoned" PDS has had time to evolve and produce. Studying it now makes great sense.

Though the present study is not a longitudinal study, it takes in the development of this PDS through an ongoing oral history project at the school. Nihlen, Williams, and Sweet argue that oral histories are particularly good vehicles for giving a stage to those not always heard in professional dialogue and research. Other vehicles exist as well. And all stakeholders need to be heard. Understanding voice and knowing how to honor it may be a key trait in the emerging dynamic of leadership.

Nihlen, Williams, and Sweet describe some of the history of how leadership, particularly teacher leadership, has been enacted over the years of this PDS. These collective memories, somewhat factual and somewhat impressionistic, seem like the histories of so many institutions: interpretive, incomplete, and situated so clearly in the experience of the teller. Yet, they are crucial to the institution. They tell us where we have come from and how we came to be as we are. As is evident even among the subjects of this study, newcomers join the school and have access to this history only if it is shared by those who were there before. And even within the limits of this form of history, this knowledge is of great worth.

Knowledge of the initiation, growth, and change in a PDS is a foundation that is often undervalued and easily overlooked in the face of daily activity. But it may be essential to long-term growth. Present policies and practices have a basis in the history of the organization. If leadership in the emerging PDS is to function effectively, efficiently, and with sensitivity, then having a grasp of the institutional history may be necessary among those who engage in leadership activity.

From this case, we also learn other matters about a PDS. Although the PDS may start off as a "project" or an "initiative" with its own design, it gets connected. In this particular PDS, the oral history project and the decision to make the Title I program a schoolwide effort are two other projects that are now thought of in conjunction with the PDS. Indeed, leadership in one project may overlap with or prompt leadership in the next. It seems inevitable that if the PDS does promote the redesign of a school, all the parts of the enterprise become considered, if not integrated, in the new design. The edges of the PDS as a distinctive effort blur. It may not be possible to determine which drives which.

It is evident that in this PDS individuals and the institution are changing and growing. Development takes on both institutional and individual dimensions. When the school changes, so do the work lives of the educators involved. And the changing lives of these educators are changing the institution.

In this case, the changes and growth revolve around the matter of leadership. The data are replete with the respondents' personal and role-related insights about issues of leadership and their struggles in coming to exercise leadership. Respondents in the interviews raise the very hard, attendant concepts of trust, power, and authority as they speak about leadership. In the uncertainties of creating a new organization, these concepts may be important in the exercise of leadership as well.

In Chapter 8, Reinhartz and Stetson offer a study that contrasts the performances of novice teachers who were prepared in different programmatic and field contexts: PDS and non-PDS sites. The two groups, each small in number, provided responses to a survey instrument through which they described themselves on a series of items related to what the authors infer as "effective teaching." These quantitative results are complemented with the commentary of their building principals who have worked with both types of beginning teachers. These data sets are displayed together to suggest what the effects of being prepared in a PDS environment might be.

Reinhartz and Stetson link "effectiveness" and areas of practice, including leadership skills and abilities. In another paper, I built on the work of Soar, Medley, and Coker (1983) to distinguish between "competence," "performance," and "effectiveness" in the work of beginning teachers (Mager, 1992). It seems that the data provided in the present study are actually descriptions and assessments of teacher performance, a forerunner of effectiveness but not effectiveness itself. Distinctions between these three concepts are useful as we consider the work of novice teachers, particularly those who learned in PDS sites and then used their learning in different contexts in their first year, reportedly with relatively greater success.

And the differences between the two groups of beginning teachers are notable. Given the small numbers in the two groups, tests for significance on the quantitative data are probably not warranted. But the pattern of responses between the two groups is undeniable and consistently favors the PDS-prepared novice teachers.

What was it about the PDS sites and the experience the teacher candidates had there that led, one year later, to this positive profile, particularly in regard to leadership? What practices were these teacher candidates exposed to and what competencies were they expected to develop during their days engaged in the PDS sites that might explain their apparent success in performing now?

In the study by Nihlen, Williams, and Sweet, we learned that even after years of development, teachers and other educators in a PDS can still find themselves struggling with the nature and exercise of leadership in that context. What is the history of the PDS sites in the present study? Are they established sites that have somehow resolved the struggle to exercise teacher leadership? Has their struggle made them choice sites for preparing the next generation of teachers and teacher leaders?

Consider that another clear difference in the preparation of the two groups of onetime teacher candidates was the length of their engagement in field experience. Sustained engagement in the field, however, might alone not result in the profile evident. Research has already made it clear that increased field experience does not always lead to desired outcomes. Perhaps, it was the opportunity to observe and emulate models of leadership among the practicing teachers that gave rise to the more positive profile of the PDS-prepared novice teachers. Or perhaps, the use of both "internship" and "residency" experiences—where candidates might model themselves after other slightly more sophisticated peers—is essential to achieving these results. It seems that we need to deconstruct their experience if we are to understand and recreate that experience for others.

Even given the clearly more positive profile of the PDS-prepared novice teachers, I could not help but wonder whether the differences between the two groups are as great as they ought to be. What can and should we expect from the investment of resources in a PDS that engages in teacher preparation? Can we create "new schools" in such a way that we can achieve clearly better results for all participants: children, preservice and practicing educators, and the community at large?

In Chapter 9, the study presented by Kochan takes a broader view of PDS work. As noted in the literature, and as exemplified by the first two studies reported in this division of the yearbook, the study of single cases to document and represent the PDS has been more common than studies that cut across PDS sites and designs. The present study does just that.

Kochan tapped into representatives from 50 institutions. Importantly, she garnered the responses of individuals representing elementary and secondary schools, both teachers and administrators, as well as representatives from higher education. The results represent better the spirit of the PDS as a new institution that accounts for all players as partners whose views have weight. Although we cannot tell whether the various constituencies of PDSs are represented in true proportion to their participation, the fact that the data include substantial responses from several role groups is itself noteworthy. Again, attending to voice may be a key trait in the emerging leadership dynamic.

The interpretation of the survey data led the author to the overall conclusion that, generally, PDSs are more successful at achieving the ends they seek than unsuccessful. In the details of this generalization other important understandings are found.

For example, although the PDS is clearly intended in concept to create new school institutions, the most frequent successes reported by the respondents are in the arena of preservice teacher preparation. Clearly, PDSs have the capacity to reshape this element of the education enterprise. This does not negate the importance of the influences PDSs seem to have on the work lives of teachers and the educational opportunities of children and youth. The creation of community among educators, the enhancement of professional development, the initiation of action research, and the support for alternative instructional approaches—all are benefits documented in the data. Evidently, accomplishments in some aspects of PDS work come more quickly, if not also more easily, than in other aspects.

Furthermore, Kochan notes a tension between individual and institutional levels of the PDS experience. Individuals' commitments and visions may not be matched by their institutions. She suggests that the PDS is sometimes seen as "individuals overcoming institutions." Is this a trait of leadership?

The first two studies seemed to view leadership as a quality of teachers and the exercise of leadership as problematic because it is emergent. By contrast, in this study leadership seems to be conceived of more traditionally by the survey respondents. They seem to see leadership as a function of persons in designated roles at either the public school or university level. The contrast between this study and the first two is particularly useful because it evidences just how unclear the notion of leadership in PDSs remains.

What Do These Measures Suggest About Our Work in the PDS and Particularly About the Matter of Leadership?

I offer the following themes as organizers of the knowledge we might extract.

Time and Effort and Commitment

Clearly the lofty ends we pursue in initiating a PDS cannot be achieved quickly and without struggle. Even after years of work on the PDS, some matters—including the matter of leadership—may remain unresolved. Individuals who are not able or willing to make a commitment for the long haul might better not engage at all. Institutions—schools, districts, schools of education, and universities—must also make commitments. And they, too, must commit themselves for the long haul.

Interfacing two or more institutions to invent yet another requires great shift in cultures. Indeed, the enormity of this shift is anticipated in *Tomorrow's Schools* (Holmes Group, 1990), although perhaps even there the task was underestimated. Even those strongly committed to the endeavor can grow weary when progress seems halting or evasive. But with time, effort, and commitment, there is evidence that shifts do occur. And leadership surely plays a role in securing these resources and focusing them on productive ends.

Focusing on Results

Positive results are a source of sustenance. In all three of the studies, the positive effects a PDS has had on individuals and institutions are documented. Beyond the data, there is the virtue of hope. Hopefulness is a characteristic of those who would create a future. It may be particularly important for those who would lead the enterprise. It may be all the more important as a trait of the enterprise itself.

Perspective

Seeing things in perspective in this complex and long-term work is also important. The perspective offered by cases contrasts with that of cross-site reports and interpretations of the PDS experience. Together, they remind us to "stand up close to see," but also to "step back and look again" to understand more fully.

Perspective can also be gained from the understanding that this work has institutional and individual dimensions. Individuals and institutions can be influenced by PDS involvement in important ways. We should not forget that both of these dimensions are important to a complete understanding of the work and impact of a PDS.

Yet another perspective is provided by seeing our work in the context of its history. Oral histories are an approach to this end that allows all to contribute; they are accessible to newcomers. Other histories would add yet again to a body of data that would help us understand how far we have come and where we might be headed.

All three of these sources of perspective allow leadership, no matter how it emerges, to act in ways that make sense for the benefit of the whole.

The Need to Document Our Work

All three studies also remind us of the importance of fully describing our work in PDSs. Accounts in great detail are needed if we are to understand each others' work and learn from it. The effort here is to illuminate the PDS in its many reasonable forms.

Leadership for and in the PDS

The concept and practices of teacher leadership are evident in these studies, but more traditional notions of school leadership are also present. Whether PDS leadership resides in a person, in a role, or in the new institution as a whole seems yet to be sorted out.

Elsewhere, I have explored how the same patterns of leadership might need to be developed on each scale of the school organization if the patterns are to be effective and sustained. Thus, between and among individuals, in the classroom, in the school, and in the community, the concepts and practices of leadership may need to be parallel if the system as a whole is to have integrity. Accordingly, leadership is more a quality of institutional character than of the behavior of individuals (Mager, 1996). Leadership in PDSs might be thought of similarly—that is, the patterns of leadership that emerge are patterns that would be fostered on all scales of the institution if they are to work and endure.

All three studies extend our thinking about the matter of leadership. They introduce ideas like voice, hopefulness, and perspective into how we might think about the emerging leadership in PDSs. And they have re-called to us issues of power, authority, and trust that may be attendant to leadership as well. Each of these threads might become a part of the matter of leadership that is woven into the PDS. But whether and just how they will add texture to that fabric is yet unclear.

Just as we are inventing this new institution, so too leadership for and in the PDS needs to be invented. Sorting out the matter of leadership is part of the task of invention, and like so much of our work, it ought be informed by inquiry. The next measures we take to inform our practice might well be taken with this in mind.

References

Holmes Group. (1990). *Tomorrow's schools*. East Lansing, MI: Author.

Mager, G. M. (1992). The place of induction in becoming a teacher. In G. DeBolt (Ed.), *Teacher induction and mentoring: School-based collaborative programs* (pp. 3-33). Albany: State University of New York Press.

Mager, G. M. (1996). The leadership of teaching. *Impact on Instructional Improvement, 25*(2), 32-37.

Soar, R. S., Medley, D. M., & Coker, H. (1983). Teacher evaluation: A critique of currently used methods. *Phi Delta Kappan 65*(4), 239-246.

DIVISION IV

INQUIRY IN PROFESSIONAL DEVELOPMENT SCHOOL CONTEXTS: OVERVIEW AND FRAMEWORK

Edward Pajak

Edward Pajak is Professor in the Department of Educational Leadership at the University of Georgia and directs the Northeast Georgia PreK-16 Initiative, a regional, systemic educational restructuring effort. He has published numerous articles and several books, most recently coediting the *Handbook of Research on School Supervision*, published by Macmillan.

During the past 10 years, or so, the artificial and counterproductive gulf between preservice and in-service education has finally begun to be bridged. After decades of scrupulous boundary management, characterized by very limited and only occasional interaction between PreK-12 schools and universities, opportunities for dialogue and collaboration are now commonly sought out and encouraged in an effort to simultaneously improve classroom practice and the academic programs that prepare teachers. A very prominent example of this attempt to deliberately link preservice and in-service education, with the intention of benefiting both, is the establishment of professional development schools (PDSs).

According to Goodlad (1994b), the idea for PDSs originated in the recommendations of two separate national reports published almost simultaneously by the Holmes Group (1986) and the Carnegie Forum on Education and the Economy (1986). In a subsequent publication several years later, *Tomorrow's Schools* (1990), the Holmes Group elaborated on the values underlying the PDS concept and provided principles for designing these collaborative partnerships. The group also formally defined a PDS as "a school for the development of novice professionals and *for the research and development of the teaching profession*" (p. 1, italics in original). As a result of efforts by educators across the country who immediately saw the advantages inherent in such collaborations, PDSs have proven to be one of this decade's most popular and widely embraced innovations in teacher education.

Typically, a PDS is an existing elementary, middle, or high school that partners with a college or university in the related tasks of innovative educator preparation and public school reform. The number of PDSs and PDS networks has expanded in recent years to the point that the National Council for Accreditation of Teacher Education (NCATE) has seen a need to develop formal PDS standards. A comprehensive volume of readings published several years ago (Osguthorpe, Harris, Harris, & Black, 1995) addressed four goals of partnerships between schools and universities, with chapters devoted to improving student learning, strengthening teacher education, promoting professional development, and supporting collaborative inquiry. A thorough and more recent review of research (Valli, Cooper, & Frankes, 1997) expands this list, identifying seven basic themes or targets for improvement evidenced in the PDS literature:

- Teacher education
- Teaching and learning
- School organization
- Equity goals

- Professional development
- Inquiry
- Collaborative alliances

Although related both conceptually and in their implementation, as Valli et al.'s (1997) review makes clear, each of these seven themes can also be recognized and understood as a discrete element of what the PDS movement has become and is striving to attain. Inevitably, certain themes are emphasized more than others at different times in any given PDS, and varied patterns of themes are evident among different PDSs, depending on their contexts and the particular interests of those involved in constructing their respective realities. Similarly, researchers are likely to define their investigations according to themes that are relevant to the data and that are meaningful to them professionally.

Although other excellent and comprehensive conceptual treatments of PDSs exist and deserve further attention (e.g., Goodlad, 1990; 1994a; Darling-Hammond, 1993: Osguthorpe et al., 1995; Hoffman, Reed, & Rosenbluth, 1997), the seven themes identified by Valli et al. (1997) provide an ideal framework for considering the chapters in this division of the yearbook. Although all three chapters represent examples of *inquiry* in PDS settings, Chapter 10 combines the themes of *school organization* with *equity goals*, Chapter 11 focuses on issues related to *teacher education* and *collaborative alliances*, and Chapter 12 addresses *teaching and learning* along with *professional development*. These chapters also exemplify the variety of innovative practices that PDSs are capable of manifesting. Together, they demonstrate the inherent versatility and value of PDSs, which will secure a place for collaborative educational partnerships well into the next century.

In Chapter 10, "Understanding Teacher Risk-Taking in a West Texas Professional Development School," Ponticell focuses on an experimental school-within-a-school that was introduced in a PDS context. Equity, and especially equity as related to student outcomes, has been almost completely ignored in the PDS literature despite an early and explicit commitment to this principle by the Holmes Group (Valli et al., 1997). Here, Ponticell describes an effort to improve success for *all* students by restructuring one segment of the school organization. The unanticipated consequences and resistances engendered by these changes in the school offer an excellent lesson to would-be reformers about the complexity of the relationships between variables in school organizations and the difficulties likely to be faced when pursuing any type of change, but especially change that is linked to equity outcomes. All of this is conveyed through the lens of a combination of factors that are believed to encourage and inhibit risk taking among teachers.

In Chapter 11, "Building the Layers of a Learning Community in a School-Based Teacher Education Program," Higgins examines the dynamics of a community of learners that emerged in conjunction with a school-based teacher education program built around a collaborative alliance of public school teachers and their students, university faculty, and preservice teachers. Higgins calls our attention to the multiple layers of learning made possible as members of these participating groups gained insight into their roles and developed new knowledge and skill. Although teacher education and collaborative alliances are two of the more commonly studied themes in the PDS literature (Valli et al., 1997), Higgins offers a valuable perspective on the elements contributing to the formation of a learning community in one PDS—trust, shared ownership, learning together, and reciprocal support. The chapter also draws attention to pitfalls that may be encountered unless unspoken assumptions and expectations are made explicit from the very beginning to everyone involved.

In Chapter 12, "Communities of Reflection, Communities of Support," Rodgers, with Tiffany, explores how the thinking of a group of mentor teachers was influenced by their participation in a long-standing series of seminars conducted in conjunction with a PDS network of foreign language specialists. This study demonstrates how the professional development of experienced teachers can be successfully centered around practical problems of teaching and learning that are confronted in classrooms every day. Examples of how processes and outcomes of teacher thinking were influenced by regularly scheduled, semistructured discussions in a closely knit group of professional colleagues are described in detail, along with elements believed to contribute to the success of the seminars and an open and honest appraisal, at the end of the chapter, of remaining questions, difficulties, and necessary next steps.

As mentioned earlier, the three chapters in this division all represent examples of *inquiry* conducted in a PDS context. They also represent varying degrees of collaborative inquiry applied to the study of teaching, a process and a focus that are fundamental to the integrity of the PDS concept. Consistent with the hallmarks of both collaborative and qualitative inquiry (Lincoln & Guba, 1985), data considered in these chapters include interviews, journals, and artifacts, which are analyzed according to the constant comparative method. The result in each instance is a coherent narrative account of events over a period of time, along with themes and categories that define and illuminate the particular group and phenomena being investigated. These themes and categories are then related to broader conceptual or theoretical constructs.

Goodlad (1994a) postulates that programs for preparing teachers should provide opportunities for students to actively inquire into knowledge and the practice of teaching. To accomplish this end, he proposes that partnering schools become "centers of inquiry" as well as forums where educational ideas and new understandings are discussed and related to what the PDS is striving to achieve and why. In this way, schools can gradually accumulate the wisdom needed to improve and renew themselves "by addressing self-consciously the total array of circumstances constituting their business—and in this way become good" (p. 271). Eventually, such collaborative inquiry is intended to drive learning for both students and teachers in PreK-12 schools, and the schools themselves will become transformed into centers of inquiry (Osguthorpe et al., 1995).

The chapters in this division of the yearbook document the experiences of three groups of professional educators who locally redefined the relationships among their roles by agreeing to collaborate around shared interests in a PDS environment. Whenever such groups are formed, boundaries are inevitably established that delineate who members are and what they are about. These boundaries should never be allowed to inhibit the connection of findings and conclusions back to the PDS context and its mission or to the wider community of interested scholars and practitioners. Rich linkages are essential if our understanding is to accrue with respect to how classrooms, schools, and teacher preparation programs can improve together. The chapters in this division provide an array of vantage points from which such understanding may be obtained.

References

Carnegie Foundation on Education and the Economy. (1986). *A nation prepared: Teachers for the 21st century.* Washington, DC: Author.

Darling-Hammond, L. (1993). *Professional development schools.* New York: Teachers College Press.

Goodlad, J. I. (1990). *Teachers for our nation's schools.* San Francisco: Jossey-Bass.

Goodlad, J. I. (1994a). *Educational renewal: Better teachers, better schools.* San Francisco: Jossey-Bass.

Goodlad, J. I. (1994b). Retrospect and prospect. In J. I. Goodlad & P. Keating (Eds.), *Access to knowledge* (pp. 329-344). New York: College Entrance Exam Board.

Hoffman, N. E., Reed, W. M., & Rosenbluth, G. S. (1997). *Lessons from restructuring experiences: Stories of change in professional development schools.* Albany: State University of New York Press.

Holmes Group. (1986). *Tomorrow's teachers: A report of the Holmes Group.* East Lansing, MI: Author.

Holmes Group. (1990). *Tomorrow's schools: Principles for the design of professional development schools.* East Lansing, MI: Author.

Lincoln, Y. S., & Guba, E. (1985). *Naturalistic inquiry.* Newbury Park, CA: Sage.

Osguthorpe, R. T., Harris, R. C., Harris, M. F., & Black, S. (Eds.). (1995). *Partner schools: Centers for educational renewal.* San Francisco: Jossey-Bass.

Valli, L., Cooper, D., & Frankes, L. (1997). Professional development schools and equity: A critical analysis of rhetoric and research. *Review of Research in Education, 22,* 251-304.

10 Understanding Teacher Risk-Taking in a West Texas Professional Development School

Judith A. Ponticell

Judith Ponticell is Associate Professor in Educational Psychology and Leadership at Texas Tech University. Her research focuses on personal, interpersonal, and organizational influences on individual and organizational learning and change in PreK-12 school and business settings. She has received the ATE Distinguished Research in Teacher Education award.

ABSTRACT

Risk taking and change are common themes in effective schools and professional development schools (PDS) research. Although the terms *risk taking* and *change* are often juxtaposed in literature on school reform, only two studies have directly focused on understanding teacher risk-taking. This study explores teacher risk-taking in the context of a specific innovation and through the lens of the psychology of risk-taking behavior. Data collection and analysis were guided by and interpreted through three essential elements of risk-taking behavior: loss, significance of loss, and uncertainty. Risk taking appeared to be most affected by negative emotional load; fear of failure; and mixed messages, unclear expectations, and unstable support. The psychology of risk-taking behavior may be a useful lens for understanding teacher risk-taking in school innovations.

Risk taking and change are common themes in effective schools and professional development schools research (e.g., Darling-Hammond, 1994; Levine, 1991; Rosenholtz, 1985). Research on schools as workplaces has found, however, that schools are intellectually stifling, controlling environments highly resistant to risk taking and change (McNeil, 1986). And in these environments, teachers and administrators are asked (or mandated) to risk changing classroom and school practices.

The terms *risk taking* and *change* are often juxtaposed in literature on school reform, but what do we know about risk-taking behavior? Only two studies have focused directly on understanding teacher risk-taking. The purpose of this study was to explore teacher risk-taking further in the context of a specific innovation and through the lens of the psychology of risk-taking behavior.

This chapter provides an overview of perspectives on risk taking, followed by a description of the context in which the study took place. Data collection and analysis methods are described, and findings are presented and interpreted in relation to three essential elements of risk-taking behavior: loss, significance of loss, and uncertainty. Finally, findings and insights are discussed regarding what was learned about teacher risk-taking through the lens of the psychology of risk-taking behavior.

Perspectives on Risk-Taking Behavior

Research conducted in the field of the psychology of risk-taking behavior has identified three essential elements of risk: (a) loss, (b) significance of the loss, and (c) uncertainty (Yates & Stone, 1992). For an action or situation to be considered a risk, the individual considering that action or situation must believe that it harbors potential for loss (Yates & Stone, 1992). A loss concerns whatever a person believes he or she already has. Common losses may be financial or performance related or physical, psychological, social, status, or aspiration related.

Losses carry different significance for different individuals. The greater the perceived significance of the losses, the greater the risk (Yates & Stone, 1992). If we perceive that certain actions or situations will carry certain losses that we believe are of value to us, we respond with caution or resistance, whether the losses we anticipate have been proven to be likely to occur or not (Trimpop, 1993).

In the construct of significance of loss, emotion is important. Positive emotions facilitate risk taking (Isen & Patrick, 1983). Frijda (1986) explained that people in general have a desire to maximize emotional benefit (e.g., self-esteem) and minimize emotional load (e.g., frustration and fear of failure). Even highly confident, performance-oriented individuals avoid situations with high emotional load, particularly those that arouse fear of failure (Elliott & Dweck, 1988). Fear of failure contributes to more cautious behavior (Trimpop, 1993).

If the outcomes of an action and the potential losses associated with those outcomes are assured, there is no risk. Risk requires uncertainty. Uncertainty resides both in the probability of outcomes and losses occurring and in the perception of their value (Trimpop, 1993). The greater the chance of a loss happening and the greater the significance that one attaches to the possible consequences of a loss, the greater the risk.

Perceptions of the level of uncertainty have been shown to affect people's behavior (e.g., Yates & Zukowski, 1976). Even if an individual recognizes that particular losses can occur, uncertainty still resides in whether those losses will occur. Uncertainty is further increased if individuals are blindsided, that is, if they are surprised by losses the possibility of which had never even occurred to them. "The very surprisingness of these losses makes them all the more devastating" (Yates & Stone, 1992, p. 13).

To what degree has risk taking been studied in relation to education? Literature on the role of innovation in school change recognizes that innovation requires risk taking (e.g., Leithwood & Montgomery, 1982; Lightfoot, 1986; Little, 1982; Mink, Rogers, & Watkins, 1989). Only two studies have directly examined risk taking as a separate construct, however. In 1975, Spitzer examined "risky shift"—an increase in positive attitudes toward risk taking occurring through group discussion of risk taking. In Spitzer's study, 92 participants engaged in discussion of questionnaire items related to risk taking as part of a teacher training workshop. From results obtained in this highly artificial setting, Spitzer proposed that "group discussion has a profound effect upon attitudes toward educational risk taking" (p. 373).

More recently, Short, Miller-Wood, and Johnson (1991) examined the relationship of teachers' perceptions of their involvement in decision making to their perceptions of support for risk taking. They found that teachers perceived a more change-oriented environment and were more willing to take risks when they worked collaboratively with administrators and had authority to make final decisions. Simply soliciting teachers' opinions or contacting them to gather information without involving them in final decisions undermined teachers' perceptions of support for risk taking.

Research outside the field of education has explored the construct of risk taking and identified three important elements (i.e., loss, significance of loss, and uncertainty). Although research on innovation and school change has indicated that teachers are more likely to try out new ideas and practices in a climate of experimentation and risk taking, little research has been done to examine risk-taking behavior or its essential elements in school settings.

Context of the Study:
A School-Within-a-School

This study looked at a specific innovation in a professional development school (PDS) in West Texas. The school, a high school serving a diverse student population of 1700 students in the central city, was a primary site for field experiences, research and collaborative inquiry, and school improvement efforts. This study looked at the school-within-a-school (SWS) that was one of the school's improvement efforts and a focus for collaborative inquiry.

The SWS was developed by four teachers and three administrators. An experienced history teacher and coach interested in teaming; a well-received and experienced English teacher willing to do something new; and two energetic, less experienced teachers, in Chemistry and Mathematics, who were willing to experiment with alternative delivery systems, were the foundation of the program. The assistant principal for instruction and a counselor provided administrative support, and the principal targeted the SWS as a school improvement priority. I served as a liaison between the college of education and the school, providing staff development, program evaluation, and program development resources.

The SWS served 90 sophomores identified in their freshman year by their junior high school counselors, teachers, and administrators as at risk for dropping out of school. Some of the students had behavior and academic problems; some had previous experience in academic teaming;

some had participated in a freshman year dropout support program; and some were average students who needed additional academic support. The SWS had four goals: (a) to initiate home visits and frequent phone contact with students; (b) to develop a caring, concerned classroom climate; (c) to enhance students' self-esteem; and (d) to provide an interdisciplinary approach to curriculum focusing on real-life problems. The students were placed in cohorts of 22 to 24. Each of the four teachers provided primary support to a cohort. The students were scheduled in a block schedule for the first four class periods and took two elective courses in the afternoon.

Teachers had two conference periods a day to make phone contacts and meet with students, parents, and each other and to engage in collaborative planning and problem solving. Conferences, together with phone contacts and home visits, kept SWS teachers in regular touch with the students and their parents or guardians. SWS teachers were sometimes excused from schoolwide staff development to focus on program-specific staff development and problem solving.

The assistant principal and counselor shuffled students to adjust the cohorts to avoid problems in group social dynamics. The assistant principal arranged staff development for teachers and field trips, gathered materials and resources for planning, and provided motivational support when problems arose. The counselor provided materials and resources for self-esteem and team building and personal counseling for individual and small groups of students. The principal provided encouragement, monitored program outcomes, and responded to the central office.

Data Collection and Analysis

Data were collected over 2 years as part of program evaluation through artifact review, critical event reconstruction, teacher and student interviews, and small focus group discussions. Common artifacts were notes from SWS planning meetings, lesson and unit plans, resources used, and student products. Critical events in SWS classrooms and in planning meetings or student project meetings were reconstructed. Semistructured interviews were conducted at the end of each year with program teachers, a random selection of 35% of the SWS students, and a random selection of 25% of non-SWS teachers. As program evaluator, I also kept a research journal recording my own observations, questions, and insights.

The constant comparative method of data analysis (e.g., Glaser & Strauss, 1987) was used, allowing for the combination of data collection with analysis. Both program objectives and the three essential elements of risk taking guided data collection and analysis. Data were examined, coded, categorized, and recategorized throughout data collection. Notes were made in my research journal exploring, describing, and attempting to account for all key issues, recurring events, and activities. Results of data analysis were compared across data sources and verified with study participants.

Findings

Findings are presented and interpreted in relation to the three essential elements of risk taking: loss, significance of loss, and uncertainty.

Loss

What did the SWS teachers lose in this innovation? First, they felt they lost congenial relationships with teachers outside the SWS program. SWS teachers perceived "some jealousy and disapproval" that they had an "additional free period." This in part was due to the isolation of the SWS from the rest of the school. Rumors spread in the school-as-a-whole, which knew little of the day-to-day workings of the school-within-a-school. Thus, there were misconceptions and misinformation among non-SWS teachers about the program, and this bred we-they battle lines. For example, non-SWS teachers did not understand what SWS teachers did during their two conference periods; they only knew that they had two conference periods—an "unwarranted perk" and "an obvious favoritism."

SWS teachers also felt they lost the "comfort of distance" between them and their at-risk students. They left the security of conventional teaching (i.e., lecture, recitation, seatwork, and specific-answer assessment) for the openness of increased classroom dialogue, interdisciplinary and problem-based approaches to curriculum, cooperative learning, and alternative assessments. Increased contact with students through smaller numbers, the cohort structure, home visits, frequent phone calls, and general availability to students made for closer, more personal relationships.

Sometimes the day-to-day realities of dealing with "highly needy, at-risk students" eroded teachers' energy and commitment. They greatly valued the work they were doing. They believed the program was helping to change students' attitudes toward school, but students' interest levels, desire to come to school, and behavior fluctuated daily. One teacher explained,

> I think of it this way. When I only thought about students in terms of the grades they made in my classes, I was safe, in a way. I didn't have to take much into account. I didn't have to spend too much time digging for explanations. I can't do that now. I know these students in an intimate way, a deeper human connection. I can't settle for an oh, well, so he or she was a miserable student today and he or she failed. I'm more in tune with the fact that it is our interaction as human beings in the classroom that very much affects students' success.

Significance of Loss

What value did the SWS teachers place on these losses? What emotions were significant? SWS teachers' congenial relationships with non-SWS teachers had changed, but their relationships with each other had also changed. SWS teachers valued the time they spent together during their conference periods, in after-school planning, and in home visits. These contacts facilitated collegial and collaborative activity and problem solving. The more time SWS teachers spent talking and working together to develop the basic structure of the program, the more confidence they felt and the more supported they felt in risk taking. They gained, as one teacher observed, "a new confidence in each other's professional abilities." That new confidence enabled them to "work together to develop special thematic projects, focus on test objectives rather than finishing the textbook, increase group discussion and group work, provide students with increased time to complete assignments, allow students to work at their own pace, and focus on the completion of work at school."

SWS teachers' relationships with administrators also changed. Teachers appreciated the facilitative support they received from the counselor, assistant principal, and principal. The SWS teachers believed the two conference periods scheduled for teacher planning and problem solving sent strong organizational messages that their work in the program was valued: "We were trusted to figure the program out and were provided in-school time to do it."

The autonomy that SWS teachers enjoyed in the collaborative development of the program was important to their investment in it. In the process of experimentation and collaboration, the SWS teachers increasingly took leadership in the program. Two important tensions emerged. First, SWS teachers were aware of their increased say in the program over time; they were "the ones doing it," and determining what happened in the program was a motivation. Sometimes, however, it was difficult to step into decision making roles and responsibilities. One teacher commented, "At times it would be easier to just say, 'So what do you want us to do?' or to be able to say, 'They [administrators] made us do it.'" On the administrators' part, it was sometimes an unsettling experience to deal with a group of teachers "telling us what they want us to do."

SWS teachers were surprised by the degree to which their new approaches to teaching and learning were noticed by students. Students were aware of the struggle the SWS teachers were having in trying to "relax with us" and "bring fun back" to the classroom. Students recognized that they were "getting good at basic skills" but also "demonstrating knowledge and thinking" in their class discussions and projects. They could "for once in school make ideas and be heard."

Personal contacts with students and their families, increased flexibility in the classroom, openness of discussion, provision of opportunity for student choice, and "a new belief in students" changed teachers' relationships with students. SWS teachers expressed feelings of "bonding" with students, building relationships where they were able to talk with students and help with problems in a different way. One of the teachers noted, "I have always thought I had good personal relationships with students, but I'm beginning to rethink what 'personal' means. It's scary. There's a vulnerability in letting your guard down with students—but I think I'm seeing a new potential in students."

Fear of failure was the most significant emotion felt by SWS teachers. This was a high-stakes program. The entire focus of the program was to keep these high-risk sophomores in school and improve their performance on state-mandated achievement tests. What if the program didn't work? Although the SWS teachers expressed gratitude for support from building administrators, a constant nagging fear was that if the program failed, central office would direct retaliation at the teachers. The teachers perceived that "the principal is getting strong messages from central office that the bottom line is test scores."

Uncertainty

Uncertainty is required for risk taking to occur. What was the primary source of uncertainty for the SWS teachers? It was the ambiguity of building a program as you go. Both the SWS teachers and the administrators realized that there were no easy answers, no quick fixes, and no existing policies or procedures to draw from. This was "aggravating."

Ambiguity also led to differences between teachers' and administrators' perceptions of readiness to move forward. During their busy day-to-day tasks, the teachers easily lost sight of results and outcomes. In group discussions, they expressed feelings of success but were hesitant to "say for sure" that anything important was happening. Thus, they wanted to move slowly and cautiously. Administrators' comments often contained the rhetoric of support for "small steps," but pressure from the central office for improved test scores sometimes led to pushing teachers where they were not, as yet, ready to go. When perceptions differed of who was ready to do what and when, the silence on the teachers' part was noticeable, together with considerable resistance to suggested next steps.

Discussion

Certainly, findings from a single case study cannot be generalized to all settings. Insights can be gained from what was learned, however. Loss may be a useful construct for understanding teacher risk-taking in an innovation. Teachers have been conservative as a group, tending to rely on traditional teaching methods and "reflexively resist" innovation (Glickman, Gordon, & Ross-Gordon, 1995, p. 25). Many adults who currently work in schools are in middle to late adulthood with 10 or more years of teaching experience (Plisko & Stern, 1985). At this point in career development, teaching is often viewed as routine. There is a great sense of taken-for-granted competence, greater nostalgia for the past, and a preoccupation with holding on to what one has (e.g., Huberman, 1989).

Risk taking required for innovation pushes teachers to test the boundaries of their conservatism. This enhances the potential for loss (Yates & Stone, 1992). For example, moving to a four-period block schedule, thematic and interdisciplinary teaching, and flexible time sharing for both individual and group projects changed the ways teachers worked with students. Students had freedom to move from subject to subject in the four-period block for additional practice when assigned tasks were completed. SWS teachers lost control over tasks and students' movements, but they hoped these practices would change students' attitudes and behavior in school.

Changes the SWS teachers made and organizational supports put into place to facilitate these changes were perceived by teachers outside the program as unwarranted perks or favoritism. So, SWS teachers also lost congenial relationships with other teachers. In the cohort and academic teaming structure, interdisciplinary and problem-based approaches to curriculum, cooperative learning experiences with students, and alternative assessments, SWS teachers also lost the traditional isolation of their content areas and classrooms.

The construct of significance of loss may also be useful for understanding teacher risk-taking. Short and Greer (1997) observed that a school's culture "conditions the degrees of freedom for administrators and teachers alike." An individual "in harmony with the school's culture can expect to always be welcome in the organization. One who chooses to ignore or clash with the culture can expect a lonely and sometimes difficult future" (p. 27). It is reasonable that teachers would fear rebuke or retaliation from their teaching colleagues if experimentation with new ideas or practices runs counter to the acceptable practices that have come to characterize the culture of a school.

SWS teachers experienced negative emotions when their non-SWS colleagues were envious and sometimes spiteful in their comments regarding the amount of "free time" that SWS teachers were provided for planning, collaboration, and conferencing with students and parents. Negative emotions were also expressed when administrators took back authority over the program in response to central office pressures.

SWS teachers' relationship with each other, however, provided them with emotional benefits (Frijda, 1986)—confirmation, support, and enhancement of their self-esteem. When emotions are positive, risk taking is enhanced (Isen & Patrick, 1983). For the SWS teachers, their new closeness with at-risk students and the students' awareness of and appreciation for their teachers' efforts to change provided the greatest emotional benefit. The teachers' self-esteem and emotional, as well as academic, investment in students' success were highly influenced by their new relationships with their students.

But fear of failure contributed to more cautious behavior (Trimpop, 1993). Schools are bureaucratic organizations. "Bureaucracies cannot tolerate change . . . a characteristic directly in conflict with experimentation and risk taking" (Short & Greer, 1997, p. 70). Bureaucracies also rarely allow for mistakes, and teachers may be fearful of potential rebuke or retaliation from the school bureaucracy for mistakes made while experimenting with new ideas. The inconsistencies that SWS teachers perceived between school-based support and assurances and central office expectations only enhanced their fear of failure.

Finally, educational change requires a "venture into uncertainty" (Fullan & Miles, 1992, p. 749). But rules, regulations, policies, and procedures— common components of schools as bureaucratic workplaces—are, in essence, designed to prevent uncertainty. The ambiguity associated with the development of the SWS program was a source of aggravation for both teachers and administrators. Teachers felt most able to weather ambiguity when administrators relaxed policies and procedures to provide the time, resources, and autonomy needed for innovation. Administrators changed students' schedules, requisitioned materials and resources, changed teachers' schedules to provide them with two conference periods a day, and excused SWS teachers from schoolwide staff development to enable program-specific staff development and planning. All of these behaviors were perceived as visible, public signs of administrators' value for experimentation and innovation. But on-again, off-again central office support and a bottom-line focus on improved test scores increased SWS teachers' uncertainty. Thus, teachers and administrators were often at odds regarding readiness to move forward with a highly ambiguous program in a context of unstable support from the central office.

Program evaluation was important in reducing uncertainty. The teachers began program evaluation with some trepidation; they ended with strong feelings about its value. Integral parts of program evaluation were artifact review, critical event reconstruction, teacher and student interviews, and small focus group discussions of emerging findings. One teacher noted,

Evaluating the program provided both confirmation and redirection. I wish we took more time [in school] to look at all the effects of what we're doing, not just test scores. We learned a lot from students that we were able to use to adjust the day-to-day operation of the program. We also gained insights into students' perceptions and experiences with school, and they surprised us. The regular recognition of small gains was a powerful motivator.

Confirmation of small gains increased the teachers' confidence, and the more confident the teachers felt, the more risks they took.

Summary

The psychology of risk-taking behavior may provide a useful lens for understanding teacher risk-taking in school innovation. Conservative teacher and school cultures make changing classroom and school practices risky; losses will be experienced. The significance that teachers attach to these losses and the degree of negative emotions associated with them can greatly affect teacher risk-taking. Changes that reduce emotional benefits to teachers, especially in relation to self-esteem, are likely to result in more cautious behavior. Changes that produce fear of failure are likely to meet with avoidance and resistance from even the most change-and performance-oriented individuals. Ambiguity and uncertainty are generally expected to be associated with change. Administrators who would provide a context for risk taking must guard against mixed messages, unclear expectations, and unstable support. Such organizational and interpersonal contexts can diminish risk taking in a moment.

References

Darling-Hammond, L. (Ed.). (1994). *Professional development schools: Schools for developing a profession.* New York: Teachers College Press.
Elliott, E. S., & Dweck, C. S. (1988). Goals: An approach to motivation and achievement. *Journal of Personality and Social Psychology, 54,* 5-12.
Frijda, N. H. (1986). *The emotions.* New York: Cambridge University Press.
Fullan, M. G., & Miles, M. B. (1992). Getting reform right: What works and what doesn't. *Phi Delta Kappan, 73,* 745-752.

Glaser, B. G., & Strauss, A. L. (1987). *The discovery of grounded theory: Strategies for qualitative research.* New York: Aldine.

Glickman, C. D., Gordon, S. P., & Ross-Gordon, J. M. (1995). *Supervision of instruction: A developmental approach.* Boston: Allyn & Bacon.

Huberman, M. (1989). The professional life cycle of teachers. *Teachers College Record, 91*(1), 31-57.

Isen, A. M., & Patrick, R. (1983). The effect of positive feelings on risk-taking: When the chips are down. *Organizational Behavior and Human Performance, 31,* 194-202.

Leithwood, K. A., & Montgomery, D. J. (1982). The role of the elementary school principal in program improvement. *Review of Educational Research, 52,* 309-339.

Levine, D. V. (1991). Creating effective schools: Findings and implications from research and practice. *Phi Delta Kappan, 72,* 389-393.

Lightfoot, S.L. (1986). On the goodness of schools: Themes of empowerment. *Peabody Journal of Education, 69*(3), 9-28.

Little, J. W. (1982). Norms of collegiality and experimentation: Workplace conditions of school success. *American Educational Research Journal, 19,* 325-340.

McNeil, L.M. (1986). *Contradictions of control: School structure and knowledge.* New York: Methuen/Routledge & Kegan Paul.

Mink, O., Rogers, R., & Watkins, K. (1989). Creative leadership: Discovering paradoxes of innovation and risk taking. *Contemporary Educational Psychology, 14,* 228-240.

Plisko, V., & Stern, J. (Eds.). (1985). *The condition of education. 1985 edition. A statistical report.* Washington, DC: National Center for Educational Statistics.

Rosenholtz, S. J. (1985). Effective schools: Interpreting the evidence. *American Journal of Education, 93,* 352-388.

Short, P. M., & Greer, J. T. (1997). *Leadership in empowered schools: Themes from innovative efforts.* Upper Saddle River, NJ: Merrill-Prentice Hall.

Short, P. M., Miller-Wood, D. J., & Johnson, P. E. (1991). Risk taking and teacher involvement in decision making. *Education, 112*(1), 84-89.

Spitzer, D. R. (1975). Effect of group discussion on teacher attitudes toward risk taking in educational situations. *Journal of Educational Research, 68,* 371-374.

Trimpop, R. M. (1993). *The psychology of risk-taking behavior.* Amsterdam: North-Holland.

Yates, J. F., & Stone, E. R. (1992). The risk construct. In J. F. Yates, (Ed.), *Risk-taking behavior* (pp. 1-25). Chichester, UK: John Wiley.

Yates, J. F., & Zukowski, L. G. (1976). Characterization of ambiguity in decision making. *Behavioral Science, 21,* 19-25.

11 Building the Layers of a Learning Community in a School-Based Teacher Education Program

Karen M. Higgins

Karen M. Higgins is Assistant Professor in the School of Education at Oregon State University. Her current research interests include school-university partnerships, mathematics education, and educational assessment. Her most recent publications appear in the following journals: *Journal of Experimental Education*, *Educational Action Research*, and the *Middle School Journal*.

ABSTRACT

This study is an examination of the evolution of a learning community that was the result of an experimental school-based teacher education program involving public school teachers and children, university faculty, and preservice teachers. It also highlights the multiple layers of learning that occurred among the participants.

Data were collected from a variety of sources: journals, debriefing sessions, and interviews. Triangulation was made possible through the collection of data from the perspectives of most of the participants. An inductive analysis was the main tactic used for establishing meaning and analyzing these data.

Four conditions contributed to the emergence of the learning community's identity: trust, shared ownership, learning together, and reciprocal support. Potential power differentials seemed to break down in this community as all participants recognized the unique contributions they were able to make to the collaboration.

Those of us who care about creating a professional development community realize that we need to move beyond structures that are hierarchical and status driven. As educators are increasingly striving to make meaning together rather than in isolation, we need to engage in a joint venture in which all participants reach parity. University and public school educators need to construct knowledge together—both thoughtfully and passionately. To do this means breaking down the ivory tower image often held by public school personnel toward university faculty. It also means that university faculty must no longer perceive public school teachers as intellectually second-class citizens.

This study describes a collaboration of public school teachers and university teacher educators attempting to do just that—to break down university-public school power structures by implementing a shared vision of merged theory and practice in preservice teacher education. Over the past 3 years, Oregon State University's (OSU) School of Education (SOE) has been engaged in creating professional development school (PDS) collaboratives (see Holmes Group, 1995) with elementary and middle schools. (For a discussion of these collaboratives, see Higgins & Merickel, 1997.) These partnerships evolved into an experimental teacher education program that brought together eight interns (preservice teachers), two university faculty, and five mentor teachers. These teachers modeled strategies for the interns directly in the classroom, so that the interns would experience the merging of theory with practice. The hour-long debriefings following each session allowed opportunities for all participants to engage in rich discussions and reflections about teaching and learning.

The following questions often surface about PDSs: "Whose knowledge counts?" and "What is our knowledge?" (Darling-Hammond, 1994, p. 3). This study argues that in a PDS *everyone's* knowledge counts and we can all learn from and with each other. According to Miller (1997), the theories and research preservice teachers are taught about schools represent the knowledge base of the university and rarely acknowledge the craft knowledge and practical wisdom of classroom teachers. We challenged that assumption and what resulted was a powerful community of learners involving preservice teachers, classroom teachers, university faculty, and schoolchildren.

This study hopes to shed light on factors that need to be present as others try to build learning communities and collaboratives with public school partners. Certain social conditions need to be in place for teachers to be willing and secure enough to put their teaching and students under the eye of the university and be cast into a very public and interpersonal arena (Powell & McGowan, 1995). This level of trust does not happen overnight. What conditions need to exist to allow this baring of teaching so that a community of learners can grow through observations and discussions of common teaching episodes? Although this study is described from the perspective of a university faculty member, I trust that one will be able to hear the voices of all the teachers—public school teachers, intern teachers, and children.

Establishing the Experimental Program

OSU's Elementary Education Masters of Arts in Teaching Program is a one-year postbaccalaureate program that leads to a master's degree and K-9 teaching license. The experimental teacher education program described in this study was designed for a small cohort of eight students who lived approximately 40 miles from the OSU campus. These students were a subgroup of the 35-member campus-based cohort and did not return to campus fall term.

The original ideas for the experimental program came out of a grant planning meeting with teachers and principals from one middle and two elementary Chapter I schools. The goal of the grant was to move teacher education off the university campus and into the public schools where teachers could actually teach the interns under the guidance of university faculty. It was hoped that this collaboration would positively impact the students and teachers in the schools, the interns, and the university faculty.

In the end, the grant was not funded. But because there was enough support and interest by the teachers and principals who would be involved in the experimental program to see it brought to fruition, the university faculty approached the appropriate personnel at the university to see if it could still happen. Since the program involved an off-campus delivery, it was decided that the interns could register for courses through the Division of Continuing Education. Since a percentage of this money is "kicked back" to the SOE, there were funds available to pay for the substitutes that would be needed to replace the teachers when they worked with the interns, as well as a $200 stipend for planning time. Although the original grant extended the model for the entire year, constraints in the university culture and funding only allowed the program to happen fall term. But because all interns were on campus only 4 of the 10 weeks winter term and in the field for all of spring term, this was not viewed as a major drawback for the participants.

Methods

Participants

The two university faculty members who participated in this program (Karen—myself—and Nora) worked in the teacher education program at OSU. I taught an Integration of the Disciplines course and was the instructor of record for the mathematics methods course and the university supervisor of two of the interns. I also taught one course on campus and maintained ties to the campus-based cohort. Nora was the overall coordinator and was assigned full-time to the experimental program. She was the instructor of record for the language arts methods and classroom management courses and the university supervisor for six of the interns.

Two of the three schools (one elementary and one middle) involved in the grant planning actually participated in the experimental program once it was implemented. The five female teachers who participated in this program came from these schools. Table 11.1 indicates the university courses taught by these teachers and whether they were from the elementary or middle school. All of the teachers except Kathi had been mentor teachers for OSU prior to their participation in the experimental program and were recognized by OSU's education faculty to have strengths in the areas in which they would be teaching.

TABLE 11.1. Information Regarding Teachers in the Experimental Program

Teacher	School	University Course	Teaching Experience (years)
Carol	Elementary	Language Arts	15
Mari	Elementary	Mathematics	12
Kim	Elementary	Management	9
Kathi	Middle	Language Arts	20
Mary Ann	Middle	Mathematics	5

The eight interns who participated in this study were all older than average students. This population consisted of three males (John, Neal, and Roger) and five females (Rina, Cat, Debbie, Tiffany, and Sherrene).

School Settings

The elementary school of approximately 300 students is located in a rural school district outside a city in Oregon with a population of about 120,000. The middle school of approximately 560 students is located in a lower-to-middle-class suburb of this same city.

Description of the Experimental Program

During fall term, course work was on Mondays, and the interns spent Tuesday through Thursday in the field with their mentor teachers. No course work was scheduled for Fridays. Course work for the first 4 weeks was held at the elementary school. During the second 4 weeks, the interns repeated the process with teachers at the middle school. All the interns, the two university faculty, several mentor teachers, and a few other teachers working on master's degrees, came together on Thursdays after school for an action research course. This was conducted by a teacher-researcher from the middle school.

A typical Monday at the elementary school looked like this:

8:00-9:45 a.m. Carol taught a language arts lesson to her students while the 10 of us (8 interns and 2 university faculty) observed and then interacted with students.

9:50-10:40 a.m. Lesson discussion.

10:45 a.m.-1:00 p.m. Classroom management techniques/discussion with Kim. Kim would often discuss a particular strategy she was going to implement, such as a class meeting, and have us observe or participate in the strategy. (Some days this time period was spent on the Integration of the Disciplines course.)

1:00-2:00 p.m. Mari taught a mathematics lesson or we observed a mathematics lesson from another teacher. We observed and interacted with students during the lesson.

2:15-3:30 p.m. Lesson discussion.

At the middle school, the classroom management time was open for Integration of the Disciplines or further discussions on classroom management. Course work was wrapped up during the final 2 weeks of the term.

Data Sources and Analysis

This study used methods of qualitative inquiry for its primary sources of data. The university faculty were participant observers who kept extensive journals and field notes during all school-based classes and debriefing sessions. Journals were also kept by one of the mentor teachers (Carol) and all of the interns. All discussions following each class were audiotaped. Formal and informal full-group debriefings and interviews with mentor teachers, principals, and interns were held throughout the term. These sessions were audiotaped and later transcribed verbatim.

For this study, inductive analysis was the main tactic used for establishing meaning and analyzing the content from the data. I purposefully did not initially search the literature looking for themes that would become "the container into which the data must be poured" (Lather, 1986, p. 267). After reviewing all the data, I realized that "learning community" continuously emerged as an indigenous concept (see Patton, 1990). My goal for this study was to make sense of this concept and to discover what aspects of the collaboration facilitated its development and evolution throughout the term.

I began the analysis by highlighting the statements related to learning and learning community. I coded the context in which each statement was made and organized the information into major categories by clustering and inductively clumping similar responses (see Miles & Huberman, 1994). A conceptual framework emerged out of this clustering that was further refined as categories were subsumed under each other. These categories were interpreted as the "layers" of the learning community.

Building the Layers of
Our Learning Community

Based on the analysis of the data, it can be seen that a strong learning community evolved out of the collaboration. Community is defined through the words of Sergiovanni (1994):

> Communities are collections of individuals who are bonded together by natural will and who are together binded to a set of shared ideas and ideals. This bonding and binding is tight enough to transform them from a collection of "I's" into a collection of "we." As a "we," members are part of a tightly knit web of meaningful relationships. (p. xvi)

There also was evidence of the existence of multiple layers of learning from and with each other. Four conditions contributed to the emergence of our identity as a learning community: trust, shared ownership, learning together, and reciprocal support.

Layer 1: Trust

The faculty from the public schools that were originally approached about the ideas for the experimental program were ones in which there was a prior history of working together. The middle school was already a PDS for OSU. I had been assigned to the building for 2 years prior to this study. Because of my work with faculty and students in the school, trust was already established with the teachers who would be working in the experimental program.

Intern teachers had been placed in the elementary school for 4 years prior to this study. The mentor teachers had worked closely with university faculty on a shared supervision model during the student teaching experience. These mentor teachers believed they were highly trusted by university faculty in their roles as mentors to the university interns (Winograd, Higgins, McEwan, & Haddon, 1995). Because of this history, the trust level was strong enough to ensure at least some level of collaboration.

This trust level was also heightened through the many social activities, always accompanied by food, that were hosted by the university faculty—times that allowed personal dialogue to strengthen our relationships. Wasser and Bresler (1996) note the importance of these "rituals" as demonstrations of caring, commitment, and trust building.

Layer 2: Shared Ownership

According to Wheatley (1994), the best way to build ownership is to give over the creation process to those who will be charged with its implementation. Because this was a collaborative effort, there was a shared commitment to the success of the program and the flexibility that was necessary to make it happen.

"Growing" the Vision Together.

We really understood that this was a developing program and that we were designers. It wasn't all laid out for us, but we had to be confident enough in ourselves and what we were doing with the training we have had—and what they were doing, Nora and Karen—that we felt that our motives were good and beneficial to the interns. (Debriefing after experience, Carol)

Senge (1990) believes that people truly want to be part of something larger than themselves and contribute toward building something important. Although there certainly were not many answers to our questions related to the design of the program, there was this conviction that we could do it together. Senge claims that building shared vision leads people to acknowledge their own larger dreams and to hear each other's dreams, and it also begins to establish a sense of trust that comes naturally with self-disclosure and people honestly sharing their highest aspirations. In the initial stages, it was the process of growing this vision together that facilitated the support, trust, and understandings that would provide the tolerance for the ambiguity and challenges each person was to face.

Implementing the Vision: Attempts at Reaching Parity. Sergiovanni (1994) asserts that, in communities, the emphasis shifts from "power over" to "power to" accomplish shared visions and goals. Also, in communities, the obligations to lead are shared by everyone. As university faculty, we saw our roles as quite different in this program compared to the roles we held in campus courses. We did not want to be "in charge." One way we believed we could accomplish this was through minimal involvement in the development of the courses—including the syllabi.

Unfortunately, we did not think about the difficulty the teachers would have with this task. We gave copies of previous campus-based syllabi to the teachers and assumed they would feel comfortable working within those frameworks to create a class that was "theirs." Carol claimed that the most negative aspect of the program was "the 'professor side' kind of stuff," such as creating her syllabus.

Although our intentions were to empower the teachers and step back from their courses, what we did not realize was that the teachers needed our guidance and often had feelings of self-doubt. Even though we completely trusted the teachers' abilities and valued their contributions to the classes, the reality was that the teachers often questioned their own abilities. When Mari was asked about the concerns she had when she began teaching the interns, she said the following:

> Self-doubt. . . . Could I do an adequate job? Did I have the background and content? . . . You know, correcting materials, getting appropriate articles. . . . So, the concerns I had, had a lot to do with lack of time, but also a little bit of concern about could I really do it.

Over the course of the term, though, the teachers did seem to be able to move beyond their feelings of self-doubt. Perhaps the reason for this was the trust that continued to mature in the community and the respect each person had for the unique contributions each could make to the program. According to Wheatley and Kellner-Rogers (1996), "Our seemingly separate lives become meaningful as we discover how necessary we are to each other" (p. 88). The appreciation for these contributions and perspectives may have been another way to equalize potential power differentials between faculties in that they acknowledged that any one person's contribution was no greater than any other person's.

Layer 3: Learning Together

The observations of classroom teaching provided authentic opportunities to observe teacher-student dynamics and view teaching episodes that later became a focus of discussion in our learning community. Through these discussions, we grew in our knowledge and understandings about different facets of ourselves as a direct result of our talking, challenging, and thinking together.

Learning Through Observations of Classroom Teaching. Before the transition to the middle school, the elementary school teachers met with us to debrief their experiences. In the program's initial stages, the teachers felt we were involved in their classes to "watch over them." Kim said, "The interns are in there to learn. You've been through all of this—it's that idea that you're here to watch and to make sure it's going to be OK." I informed the teachers that "there's this wonderful, rich opportunity to learn from. I'll be damned if I'm not going to be a part of that, and that's the bottom line!" After a moment of laughter among us, the teachers admitted that they and the students had grown used to our presence in the classes. The teachers came to view our role as learners—learning from both the teachers and their students. This learning was expressed in Nora's journal reflection:

> I feel much more like we are learning together as equals, but at different phases. . . . I am learning so much. And how presumptuous it is as university faculty, to think we have the answers. . . . We can learn a lot from interns too! . . . I learn so much because there's always new layers, new possibilities . . . we never stop learning. It's really telling me this is how we should be a community of learners together.

The teachers talked about the importance of our interactions with their students—that they engaged more in the lesson when we were all in the classroom. Our journal entries talked about learning from the students: "I learned a hundred times more about children's mathematical thinking when I was sitting there interacting with them rather than doing a formal intern observation." When the children were asked how they felt about all the adults in the room, they said, "We love it. We think it's great because they can help us and we can talk to them and learn from them" (Grade 1-2 students, field notes).

Similarly, the interns learned from the mentor teachers, university faculty, and students in the teachers' classes. After the first day, Rina reflected in her journal:

> I feel like I have learned so much in a short period of time that could never have been covered from a distance in a university classroom. In fact, my head feels a little bit like it's stuffed to the brim with the things I want to remember just from this first day. There is no substitute for actually seeing things in action.

In the final debriefing, the elementary school teachers were questioned as to why the experimental program appeared to have such a profound effect on them—after all, they all had been mentor teachers in our program for over 3 years. Mari explained it this way:

> To me, it's like you're an artist. You have been practicing your craft for a long time and then all of a sudden you get an apprentice. But you're still the "expert," see, you could still strut around, you can say anything you like, you can explain anything away . . . and you know they can accept you or reject you. But it's only that one person. As soon as you've opened it up for the team and outside experts and you've gone public, to me that's the difference between that and having an artist's public showing. Where, all of a sudden you have to have yourself together as you want to share in public and I think that's the difference.

Sometimes the teachers made special arrangements for us to observe other teachers in their buildings. During the final debriefing, they talked about how wonderful it was to actually go and observe the different teaching styles of their colleagues. This additional learning opportunity was an unanticipated benefit of the program.

The collective learning that emerged among all the participants could be viewed as a product of "connected teaching" as described by Belenky, Clinchy, Goldberger, and Tarule (1985): "Connected teaching is personal" (p. 42), and in a sense all participants in the experimental program, from university faculty to first-grade children, were all "connected teachers" who presented themselves as "genuine, flawed human beings" who "allowed students to observe the imperfect processes of their thinking" (p. 42).

Learning Through Community Dialogue and Reflection. According to Senge (1990), the purpose of dialogue is to go beyond one's individual understanding and to explore complex issues from many points of view. "Dialogue can occur only when a group of people see each other as colleagues in mutual quest for deeper insight and clarity" (p. 245).

Some of the most powerful learning happened during and as a result of the debriefings that followed each classroom observation. As a teacher in the program, Kim expressed the value of this dialogue:

> When you have a discussion with a group, the dialogue that is going on brings up other issues that may have been overlooked by just one person. . . . It grows 10-fold when you have other people to discuss it with you rather than one person just going to watch on her own. (Interview, end of term.)

During the final debriefing, I asked the interns what stood out most in their minds as they thought back over the term. Debbie said:

> Being in the classroom, doing everything firsthand, then coming back and talking to a teacher while it's still hot in our mind and you were able to debrief. "Why did you do this?" "Why did you do that?" and "Why didn't you get a reaction from this student and that student?" "What were you thinking of when you did this?" That, to me, was learning.

According to Senge (1990), people explore many different points of view in dialogue. This free exploration brings to the surface the full depth of people's experience and thought, moving them beyond their individual views. The collective thinking and learning that is the result of dialogue is vital to realize the potentials of human intelligence.

Layer 4: Reciprocal Support

Over the course of the term, there were many opportunities to support one another through our expressions of confidence in and appreciation for the unique contributions each person was making to the program. This support often seemed to manifest itself through our emergent sense of caring and advocacy toward each other. During the final interview, Carol expressed the following:

> [The university faculty] have been a great support to me and I think that our relationship is more than a professional one. . . . There is a certain caring about how I feel and about how comfortable I am and I care about how they feel and how comfortable they are.

As we spent time together, a new identity seemed to emerge—an identity that provided a sense of oneness in our collaboration. Sergiovanni (1994) claims that "communities are defined by their centers of values, sentiments, and beliefs that provide the needed conditions for creating a sense of 'we' from 'I'" (p. 4). Even early on, there seemed to be an acknowledgment of our "collaborative identity" (Higgins & Goodhue-Pierce, 1996) and a willingness to support each other without judgment. During one of the debriefing sessions, Kim talked about how the teachers and interns supported each other in the elementary school:

> We check in with each other every day we have classes. . . . How'd you do? Do you feel okay? It's like a support group. We include the interns too. It doesn't seem like we're separate. . . . We get feedback from everybody. They're very supportive.

This supportive feedback seemed to be highly valued by all the participants and a necessary layer, or capstone, to our symbiotic learning community.

Summary and Discussion

According to Sergiovanni (1994), although theories of communities do exist, "There is no recipe for community building" (p. 5). Therefore, to build community, we must invent our own practice of community, making the job harder but better. Sergiovanni stresses the importance of a transformation from an "organized collection of individuals to a community of the mind" (1994, p. 7) and emphasizes additional characteristics such as commitment to purpose and each other, unconditional acceptance and belonging, shared responsibilities, and trust (1996). Others discuss the importance of dialogue, discourse, and conversation as well as relationships and respect (Johnston, 1994; Olson, 1997; Tarule, 1996). Yes, all learning communities are unique, but shared goals and a strong commitment lead to success and a community that is real and meaningful to its participants.

Although this study has described the characteristics that formed the layers of our learning community, it is important to keep in mind that there was tremendous interplay between the many aspects inherent in each layer. Our growth as a learning community was a dynamic process and was built through trust, shared ownership, learning together, and reciprocal support. I believe that most important of all was the trust that had to be ever present throughout the process. This trust did not happen overnight but grew out of several years' worth of opportunities to work together and develop relationships. Watson and Fullan (1992) warn against attempts to force premature coordination between universities and schools.

The second layer, shared ownership, transpired through our desires to create the program together, as equals, recognizing that facilitating the professional growth of the preservice teachers could be more powerful and dynamic if we could do it together rather than separately. Our sense of parity was not grounded in a belief that everyone could do everything but rather an understanding that we all needed the skills and talents each of us could bring to the collaboration.

Through our learning together and our community dialogue, I believe we were able to begin breaking down the power differentials between us. In a sense, it was a marriage between theory and practice—with both partners attempting to enter into the relationship on equal ground. A vital condition for our growth as a learning community seemed to be reciprocal support, our fourth layer. This support took many forms—advocacy, challenge, feedback, care, trust—and all helped facilitate the emergence of our collaborative identity. This support often took the form of a silent friend, one that was always present and felt, but one with whom there was not always a need for expression.

So, where are we now? Unfortunately, there was one glitch. The principal was new to the middle school that year, and although we felt a commitment from the teachers who worked with us, there was a feeling of uneasiness around the new principal. She showed little interest in what was happening and, as a result, we experienced the "death" of a PDS after the culmination of the experimental program. In spite of this, relationships have continued to grow with teachers at the middle school, and the teachers at the elementary school are ready and willing to continue with the model. Our director claims the model is too costly, but our discussions give us hope that it will happen again. It certainly was one of the most rewarding times of our personal and professional lives.

References

Belenky, M., Clinchy, B., Goldberger, N., & Tarule, J. (1985). Connected education for women. *Journal of Education, 167*(3), 28-45.

Darling-Hammond, L. (1994). Developing professional development schools: Early lessons, challenge, and promise. In L. Darling-Hammond (Ed.), *Professional development schools: Schools for developing a profession* (pp. 1-27). New York: Teachers College Press.

Higgins, K. M., & Merickel, M. L. (1997). The promise and the promises: Partnerships from a university perspective. *The Teacher Educator, 22*(3), 165-184.

Higgins, K. M., & Goodhue-Pierce, L. (1996). The role of stories in the formation of a university/public school collaborative identity. *Educational Action Research, 4*(3), 297-306.

Holmes Group. (1995). *Tomorrow's schools of education.* East Lansing, MI: Author.

Johnston, S. (1994). Experience is the best teacher; or is it? An analysis of the role of experience in learning to teach. *Teacher Education, 45*(3), 199-208.

Lather, P. (1986). Research as praxis. *Harvard Educational Review, 56*(3), 257-277.

Miles, M. B., & Huberman, A. M. (1994). *An expanded sourcebook: Qualitative data analysis* (2nd ed.). Thousand Oaks, CA: Sage.

Miller, L. (1997). The struggle to define professional knowledge. *From the Inside, 1,* 8,11.

Olson, M. (1997). Collaboration: An epistemological shift. In H. Christiansen, L. Goulet, C. Krentz, & M. Maeers (Eds.), *Recreating relationships: Collabora-*

tion and educational reform (pp. 13-25). Albany: State University of New York Press.

Patton, M. Q. (1990). *Qualitative evaluation and research methods* (2nd ed.). Newbury Park, CA: Sage.

Powell J., & McGowan, T., (1995). Adjusting the focus: Teachers' roles and responsibilities in a school/university collaborative. *The Teacher Educator, 31*(1), 1-22.

Senge, P. M. (1990). *The fifth discipline: The art and practice of the learning organization.* New York: Doubleday.

Sergiovanni, T. J. (1994). *Building community in schools.* San Francisco: Jossey-Bass.

Sergiovanni, T. J. (1996). *Leadership for the schoolhouse.* San Francisco: Jossey-Bass.

Tarule, J. M. (1996). Voices in dialogue: Collaborative ways of knowing. In N. Goldberger, J. Tarule, B. Clinchy, & M. Belenky (Eds.), *Knowledge, difference, and power: Essays inspired by women's ways of knowing* (pp. 274-304). New York: Basic Books.

Wasser, J. D., & Bresler, L. (1996). Working in the interpretive zone: Conceptualizing collaboration in qualitative research teams. *Educational Researcher, 25*(5), 5-15.

Watson, N., & Fullan, M. (1992). Beyond school district-university partnerships. In M. Fullan & A. Hargreaves (Eds.), *Teacher development and educational change* (pp. 213-242). Washington, DC: Falmer.

Wheatley, M. J. (1994). *Leadership and the new science: Learning about organization from an orderly universe.* San Francisco: Berrett-Koehler.

Wheatley, M. J., & Kellner-Rogers, M. (1996). *A simpler way.* San Francisco: Berrett-Koehler.

Winograd, K., Higgins, K., McEwan, B., & Haddon, L. (1995, April). *Relinquishing field supervision to the mentors: University teacher educators rethink their practice.* Paper presented at the meeting of the American Educational Research Association, San Francisco.

12 Communities of Reflection, Communities of Support

How the Windham Partnership Mentor
Seminars Affected and Supported
the Thinking of Mentor Teachers

Carol Rodgers

with Peggy Tiffany

Carol Rodgers is Associate Professor at the School for International Training in Brattleboro, Vermont. She has coordinated the Windham Partnership Mentor Seminars for the past 6 years. She recently was awarded an Eisenhower Grant to continue similar work with local teachers.

Peggy Tiffany teaches all subject areas in the seventh and eighth grades at Marlboro Elementary School, Marlboro, Vermont. In her 22 years of teaching, she has taught at inner-city as well as rural schools and served as principal as well as teacher. She has been a mentor in the Windham Partnership for the past 6 years and currently co-teaches the seminar for the Windham Partnership interns with Carol Rodgers.

ABSTRACT

This study probes the ways in which teachers' thinking has been affected by their work in the two reflective seminars in the

Windham Partnership for Teacher Education and identifies supports to that process. The findings presented here indicate that a disciplined reflective process in a supportive community leads to shifts in how teachers frame their experience. These shifts represent a more complex view of themselves, their students, their colleagues, and their workplace. Such shifts in turn hint that a change in practice may follow.

This study describes the Windham Partnership for Teacher Education and its Mentor Seminars and investigates how the thinking of the mentor teachers was affected and supported by those seminars.

The Windham Partnership is a modified professional development school (PDS) project dedicated to the improvement of foreign language instruction and to the advancement of multicultural education in rural Vermont. It provides students from the School for International Training's (SIT) Master of Arts in Teaching (MAT) program the opportunity to participate in a collaborative enterprise that integrates their graduate course work with actual classroom teaching in public elementary and high schools. The partnership also enables participating elementary schools to offer a foreign language program to children who otherwise would not study a foreign language until high school. Finally, it provides participating teachers the opportunity to expand their work as veteran teachers to include the mentoring of new teachers.

A major component of the partnership is support for mentors. All mentors must participate in the Reflective Teaching and Mentoring Seminar, even if they are experienced mentors. They also have the option of enrolling in the Special Topics seminar for graduate credit. In the Reflective Teaching and Mentoring Seminar, mentor teachers receive training in mentoring and are also given the chance to raise and examine issues related to their mentoring experience. In addition, they are given space to reflect on their own teaching, their students' learning, and their out-of-classroom work in their schools. The content of the second seminar, Special Topics, is determined by the teachers in collaboration with the facilitator from year to year. In its first iteration, teachers focused on teacher-initiated research. In the second year of the Special Topics seminar we explored the nature of the wisdom these teachers have gained in their many years of teaching. Motivated by their role as mentors and the awareness that there will soon be a large cohort of new, young teachers entering the workforce (the average age of teachers in Vermont is 45), teachers felt compelled to ask, "What do we pass on? What really matters about what we do?"

Both seminars provide, in the words of one mentor teacher, "a window for gathering strength" in the face of the relentless complexity of their work as teachers and mentors. The work that goes on in these seminars and the effect it has on teachers' thinking about their practice is the focus of this study. To enable readers to understand this work fully, however, some background information on the partnership itself is necessary.

Factors in the Success of the Partnership

Origins

The Windham Partnership was started in 1991 as a collaboration among three different groups: parents from the greater Brattleboro, Vermont, community; the faculty of the School for International Training's Master of Arts in Teaching program; and teachers from three local schools— the faculty of the foreign language department of the local high school, and three teachers from two Brattleboro area elementary schools. The goals of the partnership were and remain to give Brattleboro children an in-depth and varied exposure to foreign languages and cultures, to introduce student teachers to the full complexity of public elementary and secondary schools, and to give mentor teachers the opportunity to expand their work to include teacher education and supervision.

Since 1991, the partnership has included as many as 10 schools and 17 mentor teachers from eight surrounding towns and four separate districts. The 10 schools include two regional high schools and eight elementary schools. The mentors are all veteran teachers with 8 to 40 years of teaching experience. Most are in their mid- to late 40s; they have an average of 22 years of experience. There is almost no turnover among mentors. If they leave, it has been from lack of interns rather than lack of interest. (The number of interns fluctuates from year to year due to fluctuations in enrollment in the MAT program itself.)

As a result of the teachers being integral to the project and having equal power within it, they have experienced an empowerment not always characteristic of the experience of cooperating teachers. Mentor teachers in the partnership feel empowered in two significant ways: first, they were included from the start in the planning of the partnership and assumed equal powers of decision making; second, they were listened to and deferred to as authorities on their own teaching and their own teaching contexts.

Susan Johnson (1990), in *Teachers at Work,* writes that teachers' "commitment to participate [in school initiatives] is closely related to the ability to have a real influence—being deprived of any genuine chance to influence policy [is] for teachers the root cause of withdrawal and cynicism" (p. 189). To illustrate, one teacher in the partnership recalls:

> I understood exactly what the objectives of the program were and felt that for some reason we were empowered to do this program. It wasn't something that was imposed upon us. We took the direction. I wouldn't say we took the total initiative; certainly SIT was very clearly involved in this. But being involved in the structuring of the program . . . empowered us to structure it the way we felt it would work best for our students and for ourselves as teachers. (JA, 3/30/93)

The structure of the program, described below, was developed by mentors in conjunction with the MAT faculty.

The Structure of the Partnership

The partnership exists in the larger context of the MAT program. This program educates not only foreign language (Spanish and French) teachers but also teachers of English as a second (ESL) or foreign language (EFL). The program lasts for one year with an extensive portfolio for certification capping the year of course work.

The year is divided into three sections:

The Fall. Early in the fall, MAT foreign language interns are matched with a school and a mentor. The matching is a collaborative effort between mentors and MAT faculty. The fall consists of course work and weekly, daylong visits to their schools. The interns observe and teach classes and sit in on department and school faculty meetings when possible. They also may be involved with parent-teacher meetings. Course work includes the Intern Seminar, a three-credit course taught by a mentor with a MAT faculty member.

The Winter. Starting in early January, the interns begin their intensive internships. They are at school all day, every day and become fully involved in school life and culture: They teach, attend faculty meetings and parent-teacher conferences, and write student evaluations. Many get involved with extracurricular events. By the end of the winter internship, interns in the high schools will have taken over most if not all of their mentor's classes. Interns in the elementary schools, as the only foreign language teachers in the school, start teaching full-time to students in Grades K to 8 as soon as they arrive in January. All interns continue course work in the Intern Seminar.

The Spring. Interns return to a full-time schedule as MAT students. Many choose to teach once a week to maintain contact with the school, however. Due to the relationships that now exist between the intern and the school, they are able to continue to link practice to theory in a much deeper way. But this continued relationship is currently optional.

The mentors, meanwhile, are involved in their own program that runs parallel to the interns' program. Through the fall, winter, and spring, they participate in the Reflective Teaching and Mentoring Seminar and may choose to be a part of the credit-bearing Special Topics Seminar. The fact that the seminars exist in the larger context of the partnership gives them a legitimacy that other, isolated teacher study groups must struggle harder to establish.

The Mentor Seminars

There are two mentor seminars. The first, the Reflective Teaching and Mentoring Seminar, bears continuing education credit, and the second, the Special Topics Seminar, graduate credit.

The Reflective Teaching and Mentoring Seminar is obligatory for all mentors. Case studies generated by the mentors' work with their interns form the core of these seminars. The rest of the 2 hours is dedicated to announcements, to checking in with the mentors about their interns, and to an up-date on the Intern Seminar. The check-in time is critical and often raises important issues that become on-the-spot mini-cases.

The Special Topics Seminar is an optional, one-credit course. About two thirds of the mentors choose to enroll. Topics are codetermined by the mentors and Carol Rodgers, as the MAT faculty member facilitating the course. We meet for 3 hours every 5 weeks or so, for a total of 15 hours. We meet in one teacher's home where there is ample food, tea and coffee, sometimes wine, and sufficient time to dive deeply into the topics at hand. Special Topics have included teacher research and veteran teachers' sources of wisdom.

This study focuses on both of these seminars. Because of the preliminary nature of the study, we have not made an attempt to separate out the kind of thinking that emerges from one seminar in contrast to the other.

The Study

Methodology

The data for this chapter come from Rodgers's field notes and from interviews conducted in February 1996 and March 1997 with six teachers who have been with the partnership for 4 to 6 years. We verified conclusions using member checks (Patton, 1990) with other mentors in the group. Analysis was conducted by coding the notes and transcripts and looking for emerging themes. The coding and initial analysis were carried out by Peggy Tiffany (mentor from the Marlboro Elementary School) and Rodgers, with follow-up analysis by the mentors in the Special Topics Seminar, which focused, at the time, on teacher research.

Theoretical Frame

There exist many conceptions of reflection. For the purposes of this study, we return to John Dewey. Dewey (1916) defines reflection as a disciplined way of thinking that involves the "reconstruction and reorganization of experience which adds to the meaning of experience, and which increases [one's] ability to direct the course of subsequent experience" (p. 76).

Teacher education at its best, be it in-service or preservice, educates the whole person into a way of perceiving and proceeding in the world, rather than training the teacher to solve particular problems in particular ways. Teaching is too complex, too varied, and too uncertain for formulae or fixes. Wisdom comes from experience, but it must be experience from which meaning has been extracted—that is, it must be experience that has been reflected on.

The function of reflection is making meaning: formulating the "relationships and continuities" between the elements of an experience, between that experience and others, and between that experience and the knowledge that one carries.

> In discovery of the detailed connections of our activities and what happens in consequence, the thought implied in cut and try [*sic*] experience is made explicit. . . . Hence the quality of the experience changes; the change is so significant that we may call this type of experience reflective—that is, reflective par excellence. (Dewey, 1916, p. 170)

An experience in and of itself has no meaning, argues Dewey. It has meaning only when the individual perceives the relationships that that experience has to others. Below are descriptions of the relationships and connections that mentor teachers perceived as a result of their work in the seminars.

The Findings

The study seeks to understand how the seminars have affected the way teachers conceptualize their teaching, their students' learning, and their work in schools. Initial findings indicate that this conceptualization is affected in two broad ways: First, the teachers' actual thinking *process* has evolved into a more rigorous, more reflective, more complex way of thinking. The teachers are less likely to jump to conclusions and more likely to explore the various dimensions of a problem. Second, their thinking has resulted in their reframing their experience. As one of the participating teachers put it, "[The seminar] liberates me to step back and to look at my teaching in a different way" (MDB, interview, 2/97). This has all been facilitated by two important contextual factors: (a) a supportive community consisting of experienced teachers and an experienced facilitator, and (b) a program to which they are all accountable.

Process: How We (in the Seminar Discipline Ourselves to) Think

The allusion in the heading to Dewey's seminal work, *How We Think* (1933), is no accident. As Dewey suggests, we begin the process with a problem or question that perplexes us. In the seminar, this happens during the check-in time, when we check in with each mentor about her work with her intern, or when a teacher presents a case to the rest of the group. The problem always arises from a teacher's practice. It has never been specified that the teachers must present a problem rather than a success that they want to understand better. The teachers simply find problems more compelling.

The process of attacking the problem is a reflective one. It begins with the presentation of the problem. It is, in fact, the very act of trying to present the problem clearly to others that begins the act of reflection. As one teacher said,

> If we as a department [of high school language teachers] want to talk about our own small micro-politics [in the seminar] we have to explain it to others. We couldn't just say "those turkeys up there [in administration]"—we have to label it accurately. (MC, interview, 2/97)

This need to articulate a problem accurately is compounded by the fact that this teacher is a high school teacher talking to elementary school teachers who do not necessarily share her assumptions about the high school's administration.

Having to articulate the problem also forces the teacher beyond a mere emotional interpretation and begins the process of what Dewey (1933) refers to as "intellectualization." Intellectualization slows things down, as it were, and stands in contrast to a more rapid, spontaneous, and often emotional interpretation of experience. Dewey advocates not leaving emotion behind but objectifying feelings along with other data from the experience: "In every case where reflective activity ensues, there is a process of intellectualizing what at first is merely an emotional quality of the whole situation. This conversion is effected by noting more definitely the conditions that constitute the trouble" (p. 109).

This process of intellectualization also enables a teacher to begin to face the assumptions she is making and to ask herself if they are valid. And if she doesn't ask, her colleagues will. As a group, we probe with the teacher, trying to uncover the assumptions underlying her interpretations. As one teacher put it, "People are there doing a reality check." For example, one seventh/eighth grade teacher in the Special Topics Seminar wanted to know how she could "make" her students be more reflective about their writing process. The group and facilitator consistently questioned her assumption that she could "make" that happen. Finally, that assumption hit home. Rather than "making" her students learn, she began to talk about "helping" them. This change of language indicated a change of mind and, ultimately, a change in the way she worked with students. She says,

> Even defining the problem forced me to confront my issues—my issue of control. "How can I make my students" versus "How can I help my students," which casts me as more of a facilitator. It forced me to ask where else in my life I am doing that [trying to exert control]. Once I changed my questions from "make" to "help," then it helped me to put the onus on the students instead of all on me. (PT, interview, 2/97)

The next phase in the process engages teachers in digging for alternative explanations for the causes of the problem. "Why do you think this is happening?" we ask. Once a range of explanations is on the table, the teacher has the opportunity to reflect on which ones make sense and, again, to explain why.

As we generate various explanations, compare experiences, and find relationships between experiences, themes begin to emerge. As themes repeat themselves, we begin to generate our own theories about teaching, learning, and schools.

But we also work with larger frameworks and theories (for example, constructivist theories of learning) from outside authorities. The most familiar framework that we utilize is from David Hawkins's essay "I-Thou-It" (1974). Hawkins's framework (where "I" represents the teacher, "Thou" the student, and "It" the subject matter) has helped us to organize our thinking. Other frameworks include Dewey's process of reflection (1933), Howard Gardner's multiple intelligences (1983), and Robert Kegan's orders of consciousness (1994).

Once a problem has been named and causes and theories that might explain the problem have been generated, the next step in the reflective process is to propose some strategies that would address the source of the problem. The process usually involves a mixture of questioning the teacher, "Have you tried . . . ?" and offering ideas from one's own experience, as a way of asking, "Would this work in your situation . . . ?" It is important to note that this is a process of inquiry rather than giving advice.

The final step in the process is experimentation. The teacher has the opportunity to try out these strategies and report back to the group the next time. Thus, teachers begin to take "intelligent action." It is at this phase that theory and practice, reflection and action, begin to integrate.

New Frames

The most significant aspect of the seminars is the ways in which they have allowed teachers to reframe their experience. According to the data, teachers reframed their experience in four ways: by seeing events in terms of the process of human development, by seeing curriculum as continuous, by applying theoretical frameworks from thinkers in the field of education, and by seeing themselves as part of a larger community of professionals.

First, teachers talk about things in developmental terms. This is an outgrowth of the mixed nature of our group of high school teachers and elementary school teachers. The teachers get a sense of where students come from (elementary school), where they are going (high school), and the developmental changes that happen along the way. One high school teacher comments,

> I get kids right out of eighth grade. It's very helpful to see them as part of a continuum. It makes me willing to extend myself. They haven't come to me fully formed. They come from different stages [of development]. (MC, interview, 2/97)

Another teacher adds, "It's a forum for thinking long term about kids' education." Teachers indicate that understanding that people change over time extends beyond students to one's colleagues, one's interns, and one's self. In the words of one teacher,

> It's thinking about things in a developmental way that's helped me with my teaching partner. Developmental issues have become more and more core. (PT, interview, 2/97)

And another:

> Developmental issues come up everywhere. There's a [way] of looking at things that [implies a] span and fluidity. There is a sense that everyone is in process. This encourages patience with myself, with colleagues, and with students. It's made me more tolerant of everyone. (MDB, interview, 2/97)

Second, they have begun to see curriculum as something continuous—with their own piece as part of a larger continuum. One teacher talks about how that knowledge has given her not only perspective but the freedom to be more directive with her intern:

> It affects how I think about my kids' French lessons [with the intern]. It affects how I interact with my intern around the curriculum, knowing what will be expected in high school, knowing the format of the high school program. I can say to my interns, "You can push my students more." Knowing what they've had and will have. I have felt a freedom—especially knowing that kids can test out of novice level language—that I could take some decisions about the curriculum. (MDB, interview, 2/97)

This teacher feels connected to the high school, its language teachers, and its language curriculum in a way that is unusual among elementary school teachers. The same can be said about high school teachers relative to the elementary school curriculum.

A third frame that teachers use is a theoretical one. One teacher refers to articles she has read in the seminar and makes specific mention of Hawkins's "I-Thou-It":

I really like the articles. They gave me something more to think about—they took me above it all—provided a new dimension. Maybe there is not a direct impact [on my teaching], but, for example, the I-Thou-It becomes a filter. It's one of those things I can back up to make sense of what I do. (PT, interview, 2/97)

Theories like Hawkins's serve to filter, name, and organize experience. They connect one experience to others, lending continuity and meaning to what otherwise might remain isolated and insignificant.

Finally, and perhaps most important, the teachers say that they no longer see themselves as isolated individuals but as part of a larger whole, causing them to feel fortified, and "bigger than [themselves]:" "You start carrying around a group perspective—your perspective isn't just an individual perspective anymore." Besides cutting through the isolation, this group perspective empowers the teachers to act differently. One high school teacher with 25 years experience explains how the shared perspective of the group has given her the strength to hold on to her principles:

Individually I can now hold on to my principles, knowing that they are also others'. By this time [in my career], without the support of the group, I may have given it up. I know when I speak from my principles that there are people I speak for other than myself. (MC, interview, 2/97)

The next section describes the context in which the process of reflective thinking and the resulting new ways of framing experience have been nurtured.

Support and Accountability

The growth described above does not happen in a void. It happens in a strong community of experienced professionals that offers support to its members and demands accountability of them.

Support

Support is evident in a variety of forms, none of them surprising. Primary among them are respect and trust. The respect is in large part due to the number of years of experience each teacher brings. This was expressed in a number of different ways in the interviews:

"People here respect you."

"I don't feel judged."

"When you know it's your turn to present, you know people will really listen."

"Your turn is always honored."

"[From] the very first year I felt valued and supported."

"It's important that we're all veterans." (Interview, 2/97)

This kind of respect and nonjudgment engenders trust and the courage to risk. In addition, over the years this trust has not been violated and has therefore grown. This stands in contrast to the climate found in many schools, where exposing one's questions or doubts and asking for advice is often seen as a weakness. One of the teachers expressed it as being able to "shed the shawl of shame" associated with asking for help. As Rosenholtz and Kyle note in a 1984 article discussing barriers to professionalism:

There is the sense in isolated settings [schools] that to seek advice from other teachers is to admit, at least to some degree, a lack of teaching competence. The offering of unsolicited advice is equally poor etiquette, because it implies that the advisor possesses greater teaching competence. In other words, teachers do not generally approach each other with requests for, and offers of assistance because those actions convey, undeservedly, an aura of superiority or inferiority. (p. 12)

In addition, there are no turf issues to contend with, since teachers come from different schools. Unlike faculty meetings, where, as one teacher puts it, "There are always politics of some kind, always doubt about where people are coming from, and whether they're pushing their own agenda," the seminar offers a politically neutral environment. (LB, interview, 2/97)

Another characteristic of the seminar is that it nourishes the teachers rather than draining energy from them. And the more energy there is, the more there is to give to each other, further strengthening the community.

A high school teacher describes how she feels coming into the seminar and leaving it 2 hours later:

> The seminar feeds me. I get energy so I can give my energy to others, instead of [having to] conserve it for my own place. At 4:00 [when teachers arrive at the seminar] I'm just a hollow shell. I look terrible—sunken cheeks, pale, awful—we all do. But I leave with energy and new ideas. (MC, interview, 2/97)

Support also comes in the person of the facilitator, who takes responsibility for "holding the whole." At its most elemental, this means keeping time, keeping people on track, and facilitating the rigorous work of reflection. But it also includes weaving in theory.

> [The facilitator] serves as an anchor. I don't drift. [She] is a source (though not *the* source) of knowledge and expertise. [She's] willing to share and include [that knowledge and expertise]—willing to put things into an intellectual perspective. There isn't any other place that happens in my work. (PT & LB, interview, 2/97)

Another aspect of holding the whole means remembering what happens during a session and from week to week. Weaving seemingly unconnected threads into a somewhat coherent piece of material (albeit with ragged edges) helps to create meaning.

> [The facilitator] says, "Remember that X said . . . "—tying things together and bringing in the intellectual thread. . . . She pulls the pieces together. (LB, interview, 2/97)

The teachers also indicate that "the stories of [the facilitator's] own teaching and supervision are very helpful" (LH, interview, 2/97). The facilitator helps to make the unimportant important. That is, those "little things" that come up in teaching—like students' not paying attention—become important aspects of the story of teaching and learning, worth spending our time looking at. Although having a representative of the university there to affirm teachers' stories is not the only way to legitimize them, it does provide the perspective of someone from outside.

Accountability

A critical factor in the sustainability of these seminars has been the teachers' accountability to the partnership, without which the seminars would not exist. The Windham Partnership provides the teachers with a raison d'être. Their work is a service to the profession rather than something that might otherwise feel like an indulgence or an extra. It is integral to their work lives. Not insignificantly, the mentors are also paid for their work by the partnership ($750). The money for this has come from a combination of SIT funds and a major grant from the National Endowment for the Humanities.

Not only are the teachers accountable to the partnership and the interns whose professional education depends on the investment of their mentors, they are also accountable to one another. They have built a community of like-minded professionals, and they do not want to let each other down.

Finally, because the teachers are not accountable to something that they *have* to be a part of, but rather something they *choose* to be a part of, commitment is high. These teachers have agency, responsibility, and control over their own participation and the course of their own professional development.

Summary

The purpose of the study was to begin to probe the ways in which teachers' thinking has been affected by work in the seminars and identify supports to that process.

The findings presented here indicate that a disciplined reflective process in a supportive community leads to shifts in how teachers frame their experience. These shifts represent a more complex view of themselves, their students, their colleagues, and their workplace. Such shifts in turn hint that a change in practice may follow. In addition, teachers leave the seminar with energy, with new insights into teaching and learning and with new ideas to apply in their classroom the next day. Finally, and perhaps most significant, the teachers are part of an ongoing community of reflection and practice that is sustained by the commitment of its members to each other and to the partnership in which it is contained.

We are always learning in the seminars. As one sixth-grade teacher remarked, "[In the seminars] you are reminded that you are always beginning at something. The seminars keep me at a beginning." How to keep all teachers at this edge of learning is the final goal of studies like this one.

References

Dewey, J. (1916). *Democracy and education.* New York: Macmillan.

Dewey, J. (1933). *How we think.* Boston: D. C. Heath.

Gardner, H. (1983) *Frames of mind: The theory of multiple intelligences.* New York: Basic Books.

Hawkins, D. (1974) *The informed vision and other essays.* New York: Agathon.

Johnson, S. M. (1990). *Teachers at work: Achieving success in our schools.* New York: Basic Books.

Kegan, R. (1994). *In over our heads: The mental demands of modern life.* Cambridge, MA: Harvard University Press.

Patton, M. Q. (1990). *Qualitative evaluation and research methods* (2nd ed.). Newbury Park, CA: Sage.

Rosenholtz, S. J., & Kyle, S. J. (1984). Teacher isolation: Barrier to professionalism. *American Educator, 8*(4), 10-15.

THEMES FOR PROFESSIONAL DEVELOPMENT SCHOOLS: REFLECTIONS

Edward Pajak

The chapters in this division of the yearbook nicely illustrate how the basic themes or targets evident in the professional development school (PDS) literature are linked in their implementation by processes that facilitate their accomplishment. *Risk taking* is obviously crucial if school organizations are to pursue equity goals. Likewise, collaborative alliances that seek to improve teacher preparation must develop into *learning communities.* Also, *reflective thinking* is needed to meaningfully focus professional development around issues of teaching and learning. Together, the chapters suggest that reflective thinking and risk taking within a community of learners are essential for substantive change to occur. In the following pages, some alternative perspectives on the issues raised by the various authors are suggested, as well as another direction that collaborative inquiry might take.

Chapter 10: "Understanding Teacher Risk-Taking in a West Texas Professional Development School"

We educators are accustomed to thinking about risk almost exclusively in relation to students and typically as something that must be overcome or circumvented because it poses a threat to their academic success. Our literature frequently refers to "at-risk behaviors," for example, or to students who are "put at risk" by circumstances governing their lives over which they have little or no control (Richardson & Colfer, 1994). Ponticell refocuses our attention in Chapter 10 with her observation that although teachers' willingness to take risks is commonly associated with successful change in the literature surrounding both effective schools and exemplary PDSs, *teacher risk-taking* itself has almost never been studied. This insight could conceivably open an important line of research with potential for significantly improving our understanding of change in classrooms and schools.

In an interesting twist, Ponticell's study of teacher risk-taking occurred in a school-within-a-school (SWS) that served high school sophomores who had been identified as being at high risk for academic failure. An unstated and underlying premise behind this study, therefore, is the intriguingly simple yet powerful premise that teachers and schools must be willing to *take risks* if they expect to be successful when teaching students who are academically *at risk*.

Ponticell isolates three "essential elements of risk" from the literature. These include: "loss," "significance of the loss," and "uncertainty." The resulting schema predicts that a teacher is *more* likely to engage in risky behavior (i.e., risk loss associated with changing) if the significance of the loss for that teacher is low and if the perceived probability of the loss is also low. Conversely, a teacher is less likely to risk loss if the significance of the loss is high and if the perceived probability of loss is also high.

But by adopting a priori this construct that focuses risk taking entirely around the avoidance of loss, Ponticell overlooks the importance of *gain* as a factor in determining teachers' willingness to take risks on behalf of students. Consequently, important advantages that the interdisciplinary team received in a tacit exchange for their participation in the SWS project receive little consideration. The fact that special accommodations for the team (i.e., two planning periods, exemption from mandatory staff development, more administrative support, and access to additional resources) were viewed as unfair perks that provoked jealousies among other teachers and generated expectations of measurable student gains among district administrators underscores the real value of the incentives that the SWS teachers received.

Ponticell hints at the importance of gain when she elaborates on how an increase of collegiality among team members compensated for the loss of congenial relations with other teachers. Also, the loss of distance from students can easily be reinterpreted as a *gain* in closeness to them. In fact, the notion of gain is more consistent with Ponticell's ensuing discussion, in which feelings associated with student relationships are described as uniformly positive. SWS teachers and students are described as more relaxed and having more fun, and the teachers are said to have experienced feelings of "bonding" as a result of more frequent and in-depth contact with students and their parents outside the classroom. Positive emotions associated with administrators who facilitated the teachers' efforts are also discussed as highly valued, as well as the high degree of program autonomy that SWS teachers enjoyed.

Ponticell begins to get at what I think is the central issue of loss in this chapter when she notes that innovations introduced by the SWS teachers themselves, such as flexible block scheduling and problem-based, thematic, instructional units designed to encourage independent thinking, led to *loss of control* over students and the tasks they performed. The teachers experienced further loss of individual control, according to Ponticell, because interdisciplinary planning required group decisions and interdisciplinary teaching opened instruction to external scrutiny.

This raises a number of important questions for future research: What do teachers stand to gain by *not* changing their practice? Can resources be redistributed in schools to ensure success for all students without creating dissension? Can losses and gains be balanced so that teachers are motivated to take the risks associated with improving instruction? Further study is needed, as well, comparing teachers who tend to be risk takers with those who are not. Attention should be given to both intrinsic and extrinsic rewards and costs that are associated with change for teachers, in terms of psychological, social, and organizational dynamics, as well as in relation to teachers' personal lives.

Chapter 11: "Building the Layers of a Learning Community in a School-Based Teacher Education Program"

The idea that schools can become more community-like (Sergiovanni, 1993) and that organizations can become learning communities (Senge, 1990) is popular in the literature on PDSs (Murphy, 1995; Osguthorpe, Harris, Harris, & Black, 1995). The school as a learning community has been linked conceptually to the idea of the school as a center of inquiry and an arena of democratic discourse (Darling-Hammond, 1993; Pajak, 1993; Goodlad, 1994) and is sometimes proposed as an alternative to bureaucratic organization.

In Chapter 11, Higgins describes an experimental master of arts program specifically designed for a group of eight postbaccalaureate preservice teachers who lived approximately 40 miles from campus and were placed at three schools near their homes. Despite the considerable physical distance between the university and the PDS sites, Higgins reports that a "learning community" emerged among interns, mentors, and university faculty, as evidenced in comments made by individuals, in field notes, and in transcripts. She identifies and elaborates on four "layers of learning," or "conditions," that contributed to the formation of this community: *trust, shared ownership, learning together,* and *reciprocal support.*

Higgins presents findings that very capably document the harmony and successes achieved by this group. An important counterpoint to the theme of community in this chapter, however, deserves closer consideration. Throughout her account, Higgins alludes to subtle issues of power associated with existing structures and status differences that at times seem to hinder the formation of community. It is worth examining this subtext more closely, if only to avoid pitfalls that may be encountered in seeking to replicate learning communities like the one that Higgins and her colleagues attained.

In addressing the theme of *shared ownership,* Higgins rightly stresses the importance of school-university collaboration in developing commitment to a shared vision. But the discussion that follows illustrates how tricky this process can be. The university faculty initially viewed their role as simply relinquishing power to teachers and, specifically, *not* being in charge of the collective endeavor. What this meant for some of the elementary and middle school mentors is that they were suddenly and unexpectedly delegated responsibility for teaching courses to postbaccalaureate students. It quickly became apparent, as Higgins makes clear, that the teachers lacked confidence in their ability to carry out this assignment and, especially, had difficulty developing syllabi for the courses they were expected to teach.

Higgins suggests that this lack of confidence might be due to the fact that the teachers were female and that women are socialized in a way that makes them reluctant to accept responsibility. Although perhaps plausible on its surface, this interpretation conveniently neglects the reality that all the professors involved were also women, suggesting that differences in power between professors and teachers is really at stake here. What professors represented as relinquishing power was apparently experienced by teachers as something closer to abandonment, which may have had the unanticipated effect of accentuating differences and reinforcing the power relation between the two roles.

In describing the theme of *learning together,* Higgins discloses a related stumbling block to collaborative work. The teachers assumed that classroom observations conducted by university faculty were supervisory in nature. Higgins tells us that this matter was clarified during a debriefing session when university faculty explained that they were participating as learners, just like everyone else. That this explanation fully convinced the mentor teachers and interns so easily is truly remarkable. Traditional roles in existing structures are usually much more difficult to alter, despite our protestations and best intentions. Issues of accountability, especially, must ultimately be addressed.

Chapter 12: "Communities of Reflection, Communities of Support"

Encouraging teachers and prospective teachers to consciously *reflect* on their actions, knowledge, beliefs, and assumptions has been one of the most prominent themes in teacher education and professional development during the past 10 or 15 years. Schon's pioneering work (1983, 1987) drew heavily on the seminal thinking of John Dewey and was quickly extended into teacher education (Grimmett & Erickson, 1988; Zeichner & Liston, 1987; Zeichner, 1990). Influencing cognitive processes and presumably the practice of teachers by encouraging reflective thought has become central to educators' recent efforts to change schooling and improve teacher preparation (Alley, Furtwengler, & Potthoff, 1997).

Rodgers and Tiffany present an account of how foreign language teachers' thinking was affected by a series of "reflective teaching seminars" conducted in a network of PDSs known as the Windham Partnership. The process guiding the reflective teaching seminars is explicitly based on Dewey's concept of reflection. As with the earlier chapters, it may be worth examining more closely two partially developed subthemes that suggest slightly different perspectives on certain elements of the account provided.

The mentor teachers think of themselves, we are told, as "a self-selecting group." All 17 are female and their 400 years of collective experience averages out to almost 24 years each, suggesting that most if not all are seasoned veterans who are much more alike than they are different from one another. Also, although the partnership is said to be dedicated to the dual purposes of improving foreign language instruction *and* advancing multicultural education, it is interesting that only foreign language interns and mentors are represented. English as Second Language students are part of the larger MAT program, Rodgers and Tiffany inform us; yet, they inexplicably do not participate in the partnership. Rationalizations can no doubt be generated, but the meanings and implications of homogeneous exclusivity in this tightly knit community might be profitably raised at some future meeting of the seminar group.

Rodgers and Tiffany also strongly privilege objectivity and intellect in the construction of meaning. We are told that the process of reflection is effective in forcing teachers "beyond a mere emotional interpretation" and at getting them outside their own dramas. One example provided by the authors is that the seminar teachers reconceptualized their role upon recognizing that they cannot "make" students do anything. The insight that students are responsible for their own learning, and that teachers can facilitate but not force learning, is said to have reduced feelings of guilt and inadequacy among members of the group. Although arguably true, one would hope that in objectifying their students in this way, the teachers continued to recognize that they, themselves, remain the single most important influence on student learning in their classrooms.

My purpose is not to criticize the valuable work of the authors or the teachers who participated in the reflective seminars, but rather to suggest less comforting images of community and reflective thinking. Any time that we establish a community, we simultaneously define the nature of the *other* and eliminate other ways of being. Similarly, by collectively seeking only rational solutions to practical problems, we may become technically more proficient but limit the possibility of other kinds of growth. Questions of practical application are certainly important and represent one very obvious direction that collaborative inquiry may take, but it might also be appropriate to ask, "Where *else* can we go?"

Where Else Can We Go?

A very promising direction for inquiry is recently offered by Britzman (1998), who suggests a method that draws on psychoanalytic concepts to extend and deepen the interpretation of data. She proposes that we explore "three dimensions of time: the ethnographic (or the place of detail), the reflective (or the consideration of the significance of anxiety), and the uncanny (or the force of secrets)" (p. 13) in describing and attempting to comprehend educational phenomena. The first two dimensions already fall within the repertoire of many educators and are well represented in the chapters under discussion. According to Britzman, however, "the story of education must pass through" all three to fully transcend the trappings of technical rationality and policy considerations. The uncanny, she proposes, requires a much deeper exploration of self and other, love and hate, projection and introjection, and the unconscious as well as the conscious.

Britzman challenges educators' overreliance on cognitive content and processes, noting that "reflective practice has been reduced to the utility of correcting practices and devotes itself to propping up the practitioners' control and mastery" (1998, p. 32). She reminds us that teaching and learning are both psychic events and that learning inevitably provokes a troubling crisis in the self, along with flights of fancy and bursts of creative insight that can never be rationally settled or contained. Education should properly be understood as an unsettling encounter between the internal and the external, the psychical and the social, and as a crossing of the boundary between self and other.

The task of restructuring educational institutions through collaboration and redefining the roles of learners, teachers, and university faculties is very much about redefining professional identities. Britzman's work posits identity formation as the central task of education and offers original insights into many of the themes appearing in these chapters—risk; loss; community; privilege; power; jealousy; control; and, of course, teaching and learning. Psychoanalysis has potential to illuminate unconscious processes that influence education (Pitt, Todd, & Robertson, 1998), but it requires brutal honesty and an especially formidable kind of risk taking, "the capacity to risk love and work" (Britzman, 1998). The alternative is to allow what we do not acknowledge to undermine our best efforts.

References

Alley, R., Furtwengler, C. B., & Potthoff, D. (1997). Process for implementing change in teacher education. In D. M. Byrd & D. J. McIntyre (Eds.), *Research on the education of our nation's teachers* (Teacher Education Yearbook V, pp. 65-73). Thousand Oaks, CA: Corwin.

Britzman, D. P. (1998). *Lost subjects, contested objects: Toward a psychoanalytic inquiry of learning.* Albany: State University of New York Press.

Darling-Hammond, L. (1993). Reforming the school reform agenda. *Phi Delta Kappan, 74,* 761.

Goodlad, J. I. (1994). *Educational renewal: Better teachers, better schools.* San Francisco: Jossey-Bass.

Grimmett, P., & Erickson, G. (Eds.). (1988). *Reflection in teacher education.* New York: Teachers College Press.

Murphy, J. (1995). Changing role of the teacher. In M. J. O'Hair & S. J. Odell (Eds.), *Educating teachers for leadership and change* (Teacher Education Yearbook III, pp. 311-323). Thousand Oaks, CA: Corwin.

Osguthorpe, R. T., Harris, R. C. Harris, M. F., & Black, S. (Eds.). (1995). *Partner schools: Centers for educational renewal.* San Francisco: Jossey-Bass.

Pajak, E. (1993). Change and continuity in supervision and leadership. In G. Cawelti (Ed.), *Challenges and achievements of American education* (ASCD Annual Yearbook, pp. 158-186). Alexandria, VA: Association for Supervision and Curriculum Development.

Pitt, A., Todd, S., & Robertson, J. (Eds.). (1998, Summer). *Journal of Curriculum Theorizing on Psychoanalysis and Education, 14*(2).

Richardson, V., & Colfer, C. (1994). Being at risk in school. In J. I. Goodlad & P. Keating (Eds.), *Access to knowledge: The continuing agenda for our nation's schools* (pp. 107-124). New York: College Entrance Examination Board.

Schon, D. A. (1983). *The reflective practitioner: How practitioners think in action.* New York: Basic Books.

Schon, D. A. (1987). *Educating the reflective practitioner.* San Francisco: Jossey-Bass.

Senge, P. M. (1990). *The fifth discipline: The art and practice of the learning organization.* New York: Doubleday/Currency.

Sergiovanni, T. J. (1993, April). *Organizations or communities? Changing the metaphor changes the theory.* Invited address at the annual meeting of the American Educational Research Association, Atlanta.

Zeichner, K. (1990). Changing directions in the practicum: Looking ahead to the 1990s. *Journal of Education for Teaching, 16*(2), 105-132.

Zeichner, K., & Liston D. (1987). *Teaching student teachers to reflect.* Harvard Educational Review, 57(1), 1-22.

Index

Telecommunications, 8, 15. *See also* Communication
  learning and, 22 (*see also* Learning)
  teacher education program and, 7 (*see also* Teacher education program)
Tests, 7
  achievement, 10
  administration and, xi
  collaborative settings and, x
  ExcCet, 23
  Houston Consortium and, 24-25
  school-within-a-school and, 212, 215-216, 252
  scores and, xi, 27
  standards for, 4, 9, 74-75 (*see also* Standards)
  state-mandated, 22, 27, 212
  states skills, 74-75
  teachers and, 27
  Texas Academic Skills Program and, 162
  Texas Assessment of Academic Skills and, 23
  Texas schools and, 23
Texas:
  Concern-Based Approach Model and, 117, 118 (*see also* Concern-Based Approach Model [CBAM])
  understanding teacher risk-taking and, 201-202, 208 (*see also* Risk taking)
Texas Academic Skills Program, 162
Texas Assessment of Academic Skills (TAAS), 23
Tiffany, P., 202, 234, 239, 256
Traditionally trained teachers, 56, 157
  critical incident and, 37 (*see also* Critical incident)
  information lacking for, 166
  leadership roles and, 169-170 (*see also* Leadership)
  leadership skills and abilities survey and, 168-169

  needs greater of, 169
  preparedness of, 166 (*see also* Preservice teachers)
  rethinking roles of, 81-82
  students who chose to be, 161
  teachers rely on methods of, 213
Training. *See* Mentor(s); Preservice teachers
Tutoring, 15, 25, 26. *See also* Mentor(s)

Universities. *See also* schools
  administrators and teachers critical of, 56-57
  bridges built between PreK-12 and, 40-41
  culture and, 4, 174-175, 179-180 (*see also* Culture[s])
  democracy and, 66
  educators work to improve learning in, 31
  faculties and, x, 73
  historic role of, 65-66, 132
  Houston Consortium and, 26-27 (*see also* Houston Consortium [HC])
  knowledge and, 65, 66, 192
  lack of commitment in, 176
  partnerships and, 1-2, 80, 81-82 (*see also* Partnerships)
  PDSs not in, 65 (*see also* Professional development schools [PDSs])
  PreK-12 and, 1-4, 183-184 (*see also* PreK-12)
  Praxis in, 3
  reform and, 31-32
  risk taking and (*see* Risk taking)
  teachers and, 82 (*see also* Teacher[s])
  workshops and, 19, 20, 115
University of New Mexico, 144
University of Texas, 117
University researchers. *See* Researchers
Urban teacher education program. *See* teacher education program
U.S. Department of Education, 11, 65

CORWIN
PRESS

The **Corwin Press logo**—a raven striding across an open book—represents the happy union of courage and learning. We are a professional-level publisher of books and journals for K–12 educators, and we are committed to creating and providing resources that embody these qualities. Corwin's motto is "Success for All Learners."